Praise f

"*About Natalie* is a candid, eye-opening look at wha.... to be the parent of an addict. A courageous memoir that will tug at your heart, make you grin, and fill you with hope."

—**Jack Canfield,** international bestselling author of *The Success Principles* and co-creator of the Chicken Soup for the Soul series

"Bold, brave, courageous, and captivating, *About Natalie* is Christine Naman's masterfully written memoir of what it is like to wake up one day to find out your beautiful, beloved fifteen-year-old little girl is a heroin addict.

"Naman's book takes the reader into the mind, heart, and soul of how to love unconditionally when faced with addiction, a cunning and baffling disease based on denial. She shows how her family experienced ups and downs in this uncharted territory, remained loving while living with an addict, and never gave up hope.

"*About Natalie* is groundbreaking. It doesn't preach or pretend to offer a panacea. Instead, it offers a refreshing, authentic look at one family's struggle with addiction, easily the most powerful book published on the subject in the twenty-first century."

—**Dr. Maryel McKinley, PhD, CADCII,** syndicated reviewer, addictions expert, former co-host/co-producer "All Talk Recovery Radio" CBS 97.1 FM KLSX Los Angeles Arbitron rated #1 in Southern California

"*About Natalie* is a testimony of motherhood. Sometimes heartbreaking and raw. Sometimes insightful and brave. But always hopeful. *About Natalie* spreads the message that you are not alone."

—**Patty Aubery,** #1 *New York Times* bestselling author of *Chicken Soup for the Christian Soul*

about Natalie

A Daughter's Addiction.
A Mother's Love.
Finding Their Way Back to Each Other.

Christine Pisera Naman
with Natalie Anna Naman

Health Communications, Inc.
Boca Raton, Florida

www.hcibooks.com

Library of Congress Cataloging-in-Publication Data
is available through the Library of Congress

© 2021 Christine Pisera Naman

ISBN-13: 978-0-7573-2385-0 (Paperback)
ISBN-10: 07573-2385-5 (Paperback)
ISBN-13: 978-0-7573-2386-7 (ePub)
ISBN-10: 07573-2386-3 (ePub)

Publisher: Health Communications, Inc.
        1700 NW 2nd Avenue
        Boca Raton, FL 33432-1653

Cover and interior design by Larissa Hise Henoch
Formatting by Lawna Patterson Oldfield

This book is dedicated to my beautiful,
fearless, funny, quirky, talented, brilliant, best
thing that ever happened to me daughter,
Natalie. Thank you for making me better and
more than I ever thought I could be.
Being able to call myself
Natalie's mom is when I am proudest.
It is the best title I will ever have.
Forever and always, Mom

This book is for everyone suffering
from addiction of any kind. We hear you.
We feel your pain and acknowledge your
struggle. And while we may not have perfected
our methods of helping you just yet,
we are trying our best and are hurrying
to your rescue. We promise.

This book is also dedicated to
all of the parents who suffer, struggle,
and fight right along with their children.
We are in this together.
You are not alone.

Contents

Acknowledgments

**There are so many people to
whom I am grateful . . .**

*T*hanks to everyone who is traveling the journey of Natalie's life with me.

First and foremost, as always, thanks to my husband, Peter, my one true love, who said, "Yes! Let's!" When I said, "Want to have a girl?"

Thank you to the doctors, nurses, and staff of Highmark Health, Allegheny Health Network, East Suburban Obstetrical and Gynecological Associates, who cared for me during my pregnancy, and for helping the miracle that I know as my daughter into the world.

First you said, "Yes, you are pregnant!" introducing me to Natalie when she was only a wink on an ultrasound screen and a *swish* on a Doppler. Then, when she was born, saying, "Look! It's a girl." "She looks like a winner!" "She's beautiful!" You were right every time. None of us had any idea just how beautiful she would be.

By name they are:

Dr. Mark Rubino

Dr. Michael Pelekanos

Dr. Bernie Petticca

Dr. Elizabeth Knepp

Dr. Leonard Selednik

Dr. James Duggan

Dr. Traci Wojcik

Thank you to Dr. Elizabeth Knepp and Dr. Diem Nguyen from Highmark Health, Allegheny Health Network East Suburban Obstetrical and Gynecological Associates for helping Natalie through some difficult times.

Thanks go to the doctors, nurses, and staff of Premier Pediatrics who cared for Natalie as she grew.

By name they are:

Dr. Jeffrey Ubinger

Dr. Stephen Greene

Dr. Christine Patti

Thanks for saying, "She's a spirited one!" Little did we know just how much spunk Natalie would have and how well it would serve her.

Thanks go to the people who helped Natalie grow, providing her with safe places to learn. We still speak fondly of all of you and look back on the memories created there during more innocent times.

The Rainbow Connection School, especially, Miss Tami, Miss Dana, Miss Libby, and Miss Loraine.

North American Martyrs Church and School, especially, Mr. John Marino.

St. Bernadette Church and School, especially, Sister Carol Arch.

The administration and staff of Gateway High School.

The Community College of Allegheny County, especially, R.J.

Thanks to all of you for allowing Natalie a soft place to land while embracing her with kindness and understanding.

Thanks go to the Monroeville Police Department and the Monroeville paramedics who helped keep Natalie safe and rescued her.

Thank you to the doctors, nurses, and staff of Highmark Health, Allegheny Health Network, Forbes Regional Hospital Emergency Department who told Natalie that she had value, saved her life, and cared for her when she needed it.

Thank you to the many rehabilitation centers and clinics that have treated Natalie. Thank you to all of the therapists, counselors, psychiatrists, and psychologists who have offered their care. You have all made a positive impact. I assure you of this.

Thanks go to Highmark Health, Allegheny Health Network Behavioral Health Team who continuously help Natalie through her journey.

Thank you also to Christian Blonshine and Christine Belleris (the other Christine) and everyone at HCI Books for taking a chance on me when I probably didn't deserve it. I will always be grateful to you all for allowing my words to be read.

Thank you to Janet Switzer for your knowledge and guidance.

Thank you to Patty Aubery for starting me off all those years ago.

Thank you to the staff of Kings Family Restaurant, First Watch, and Panera who poured me cups and cups and cups of tea as I wrote this book.

Thank you to all of my friends at FedEx Office in Monroeville for always polishing things up for me.

I am also just as grateful to those whose names I have regretfully forgotten: the people who did not look at Natalie judgmentally or with disgust but instead offered her a genuine smile, touch, or hug. I thank those who offered understanding and heartfelt kindness. This was not unnoticed and was greatly appreciated. May the kindness that all of you offered come back twofold.

They say if you have just a couple of true friends, then you are lucky. Natalie is lucky.

Thank you . . .

To Logan.

To Yuzu, her first preschool friend, who came to the US and never spoke a word of English, but somehow it never seemed to matter.

To Justin, whose love always spoke for him.

To Manda, who is never more than a phone call away.

To Sam, who was loyal and understanding always.

To Trinity (most of all), who has loved and always been there through thick and thin.

Peter and I are lucky and blessed with many understanding, loyal friends who listened and offered heartfelt advice and tried to help. And when there was nothing else to do, caught our tears as they fell.

Not just thanks but love and love and love go to Natalie's family, who have stood by her and have loved her forever.

Especially, Natalie's brothers Jason and Trevor—who defend her fiercely and love her unconditionally.

And who, just by being Natalie's brothers, makes them the bravest boys on the planet.

Thank you to my mother, who listens to every word and loves unconditionally.

To Nunnie, Pap, Teta, Jedo, Uncle Rocco, Uncle Dan, Aunt Lisa, Aunt Myrna, Aunt Carole, Aunt Suzanne, Uncle Ronnie, Natasha,

Alexander, Tatiana, Frederic, Christine, Matthew, Diana, John, Nina, Marissa.

And, last but not least, thanks and belly rubs go to Obie, the most dysfunctional, unconditionally loving, spectacular dog, who has really, really helped a lot.

Part of the proceeds earned from this book will be donated to Highmark Health, Allegheny Health Network.

✻ There are days when I imagine myself
standing up in the middle of this mess that I call
my life, demanding to see a manager just like
you do in a restaurant when you have received
unacceptable food or poor service.
I will raise my face toward the sky and say,
"I want to see a supervisor!" And when I do,
instead of a man in a sloppy shirt and a
ketchup-stained tie, God arrives.
He listens attentively to my complaints,
agrees with me, orders someone
to get me a free dessert, and gives
me a coupon for a new life.

Prologue

August 1996

They say it's not over until the fat lady sings. Well, in pregnancy it isn't really beginning until the obstetrician says, "Congratulations!"

I am in the parking lot of the doctor's office and I am a nervous wreck. I am pregnant. It's not official, but I know that I am pregnant. I am experiencing all of the symptoms that satisfy everyone else. I haven't had a period in two months, I am nauseous, and my breasts are aching.

I also cried during a sentimental Hallmark commercial. I ate eleven of a one dozen box of cookies, and I didn't speak to Peter for two hours after he inconsiderately ate the twelfth. (He did show up an hour later with another dozen. I told him I loved him—and cried.)

And I have a pee stick with two blue lines. So, I know that I am pregnant. I just need to convince my doctor of this for it to all become completely official, even though it has been completely real for me for weeks. I am anxious, though, because we have all seen those movies where some girl thinks that she is pregnant and goes to her doctors only to have them say that there is some other bizarre or heartbreaking explanation for her symptoms.

I check my face in the rearview mirror and decide I need a little color. I pinch my cheeks, trying to plump and pinken them up, then I apply a fresh coat of watermelon-colored lipstick onto my lips. I try on a couple of faces. One serious and one smiling. Okay, I think these finishing touches make me ready. And these really were finishing touches because the actual getting ready for this probably-not-even-fifteen-minute appointment began early that morning when I showered and scrubbed every part of me, shaved every hair I could locate, and creamed, powdered, perfumed, and exfoliated.

I painted not only my fingernails but, for sure, my toenails as well, thinking that since the doctor does spend a little bit more time in that vicinity. Sometimes, I feel like I should apologize for this, but he had to know this is where he would spend his time when he chose this field. Right? I took extra time on my makeup and even almost put on some glittery eyeshadow before coming to my senses.

I chose my clothes carefully, trying to pick something momish but slightly hot-momish, even though he never sees me in my clothes because I am undressed when he comes into the room, and by the time I am clothed again and back out into the hallway, he is in with another patient and never actually gets to see my outfit. If you think about it, it really is a bit of an awkward, odd dynamic.

I am always tempted to linger after the appointment and say, "See this is what I look like all dressed." And even though I realize he is trying to be professional and all, just once, I wish he would acknowledge all of the work I put into getting ready for this appointment. Maybe he doesn't exactly have to tell me that I look pretty. But gosh, at least once he could say, "Well done" or "Nice effort."

He has been my doctor for years now, so I know that he is not going to say this. I redo my lips one more time with an extra layer of gloss, I fluff my hair, and attempt to make the hair I spent forty minutes on look like I somehow did not work on it at all but instead woke up that way.

Inside, I check in with the receptionist. Though she does not ask the reason for my visit—why would she?—I blurt out in a whisper, "I'm pregnant!" She offers a polite smile. She's probably heard this before many times. Apparently, it is not real to her until someone writes it in a manila folder. Still, I don't need her affirmation to feel what I know in my heart.

I take my seat in the waiting room, apply one final coat of lipstick, and pretend to read a magazine while actually scanning the room, trying to figure out what the other women are there for. Some are obviously pregnant. Some are a little too old to be pregnant. And others might be but seem a little young to be carrying children. I'm nearly done categorizing them all when I hear my name.

I pee for one nurse and am tempted to tell her to be sure not to lose it or mix it up with someone else's, but she probably won't appreciate me telling her how to do her job. Still, I know this kind of thing can happen. I watch *Dateline*.

Another nurse sees me into the exam room, takes my blood pressure, comments that it is a little high, and weighs me. I want to tell her that my blood pressure is high because her scale is a little liar and has offended me. But I know she won't listen.

She leaves, and I know the process. I undress and sit on the exam table with all of my important parts covered by the disposable cloth drape. The crinkly paper crackles underneath me. I am trying to decide if I have enough time to make it to the scale, reweigh myself, and make it back to the table and cover up before the doctor arrives. I decide that I do, and I have one leg dangling off the table and am trying to peel off the paper that is stuck to me when the doctor knocks twice and, without waiting for an answer, walks in.

I don't think I actually cover up my awkward position. I just know he politely ignores and we carry on. He sits down and opens the mysterious manila folder and scans the papers inside. What's written about me in there? I mean, other than my blood pressure, vitals, and all of that, does he put his opinions? She's a wonderful girl but seems a little neurotic. I decide I am both hoping that he does make extra notes while at the same time hoping that he doesn't. I watch his face expectantly, but he doesn't give himself away. "Let's take a look," he suggests, which really means that he is going to take a look.

I lie there and practice my least favorite subject, math, in my head and count thirteen tiles on the ceiling while he inspects the business end of my business. The soft scent of the doctor's musky aftershave makes it up to me and I am tempted to tell him that he smells good. But I reason that if I can smell the few spritzes that he put on, he certainly can smell the rose and peony scent that I practically drowned myself in. And if he's not complimenting me, I won't compliment him. After all, if you don't count his twenty-two years of schooling, I have done all of the preparation for this appointment.

Finally, it is time to sit up. I cover back up while he looks at the chart again. He looks up at me, smiles, and says, "Congratulations! See you in a month." Then he adds, "Tell your husband congratulations, too!"

I let out the breath I have been holding and smile back. He leaves the room. I re-dress with a huge smile on my face and exit the room. I go out into the hall and decide that if I run into him, I will ask him if he likes my dress. I check out and minutes later, I am back in my car. I replay the entire fourteen minutes in my head. I want to remember these moments forever. He did not say, "Great job getting ready for the appointment" or that he liked my sandals or that I was the greatest pregnant girl he had ever seen or that I was carrying an exceptionally super baby inside me, and he definitely didn't sing, but come to think of it, he did kind of drag out the word "congratulations" in a melodic kind of way, so I decide to take that and be happy with it. Maybe he did sort of sing.

Before I back out of the parking space, I glance at my reflection in the rearview mirror again and smile. When I do, I realize I have lipstick smeared all over my teeth. Apparently, it was there through-out the entire appointment. I cringe and grimace as I wipe it off. For a moment, this threatens to dampen my joy. But I don't let it. Who cares that I have watermelon-colored teeth? I am having a baby.

I am having a baby!

November 1996

I am staring off into space, thinking about absolutely nothing, when a woman sits down next to me. I wiggle a bit in my chair trying to give her some space and offer her a half-hearted smile to convey that I am tired, worn-out, and nauseous. She smiles back with a better smile that somehow tells me she is not as tired or nauseous as I am, but she is sympathetic and has been there.

As pregnant women do, I compare our bellies. She wins. She is taller, slimmer, more fit—and if that isn't enough to announce her the victor, she is also older.

"You look great!" she whispers, apparently reading my mind and saying exactly what I need to hear. I decide that she is a natural mother, and I am a seasick flop.

"You look better," I whisper back.

"Rubbish," she proclaims, dismissing my insecurity with that one word. Her lack of acknowledgment of my own words somehow has made me feel slightly more secure.

"Is this your second?" she asks. Wondering how she knows this was indeed the second baby I was carrying, I face her, deciding to be jealous of her super white teeth and naturally blond hair in addition to her better bump.

"Yes, how can you tell?" I ask.

"You are not studying," she winks, nodding toward several other women in the waiting room who are reading various pregnancy books and magazines right in front of us.

I stifle a giggle and am tempted to tell her that I abandoned my copy of *What to Expect When You Are Expecting* after the first trimester of my first pregnancy when I discovered that even a glimpse of the book's cover caused me to be nauseous. Before we began talking, I had been reading an article on the Kardashians. Am I already a bad mother for being more interested in how Kim keeps her behind so perfect instead of the new advances in electric breast pumping?

"How about you?" I ask. "What number is this?"

"This is six!" she exclaims with a wide smile. Then, she laughs at the shocked expression I don't even try to hide.

"I'd be dead," I tell her unceremoniously.

"You would not!" she laughs. "Do you know what you are having?"

"A girl," I tell her. "The first was a boy." I feel oddly efficient that I am somehow able to create both genders.

"Yay!" she celebrates. "A nice family then!" This makes me smile.

"How about you?" I ask. "Do you know?"

"This is a boy," she tells me. "He evens the score at three and three." I push the thought that she has won again out of my mind and decide to be happy for her.

"Big, nice family!" I tell her.

"It's fun," she admits. "How far along are you?"

"Halfway," I tell her. "You?" I estimate her to be about as far along.

"Oh, this one," she tells me, caressing her tummy, "is nearly thirty years old now."

Puzzled, I lean in questioningly.

"Well, maybe not thirty yet. But I have him to twenty-six or twenty-seven anyway," she insists with a playful smile. "The moment I found out I was pregnant, I began to imagine him...his face, his hair, his grin.

"Then I daydreamed him through his happy life. I started with his birth. I imagined him through babyhood, childhood, his teenage years...he was good. But a handful," she laughs. "And right now, I've dreamed him all the way through law school and he's found the right girl and is thinking about settling down."

I blink in astonishment and laugh out loud. "I thought I was the only one who did that!" I exclaim so heartily that a few of the other women look up from their reading.

"Aw, no," she assures me. "We all do it. And anyone who tells you that they don't is lying. We all have secret hopes, dreams, and futures for our babies. So, how far along are you?" she asks me again with a broad smile.

"Well, she's younger than yours!" I tell her. "But...she's already about sixteen. She was the most adorable baby. Always in pink. Then kind of a tomboy in elementary school. She's a dancer. Confident like I wasn't. And smart. On the way here in the car, I was thinking she might get accepted to an Ivy League school."

"Of course, she will!" my new friend says. "What else?"

"That's it so far," I say. "I haven't gotten to the rest."

March 1997

"Ready?" Peter asks, putting the car into reverse and beginning to back out of the driveway. "Yep...wait!" I yell. He halts suddenly, causing the car to rock. I jump out and scurry up the walkway, back into the house, up the stairs to the bedroom. I kneel by the bed and reach deep under the mattress, feeling around until I locate the pair of tiny, pink baby socks I had hidden there so many months before. I tuck them deep into my purse and hurry back down to the car.

"I can do this," I whisper as we restart our journey.

"Of course, you can!" Peter says, overhearing me.

"I'm not talking to you," I say with more of an edge than I mean to have. I was talking to myself. I'm apprehensive and need a pep talk. I am nervous and uncomfortable as I fidget with the positioning of the seatbelt over my protruding belly.

We ride in silence during the ten-minute trip from home to the hospital and I concentrate on the pink and blue morning sky. How appropriate. A pink and blue sky on the day I am going to have a baby. Another sign. I squint upwards, trying to gauge the percentage of the colors. The pink seems to be winning.

"I can do this," I say again as Peter silently puts the car into park and turns off the ignition in the hospital parking lot.

"Why aren't you answering me?" I ask him offended.

"Oh, oh yes! You can do this!" he says stuttering a bit and seeming surprised to be asked to speak.

I feel bad and say, "Sorry." And smile at him and hold his hand as we walk into the hospital.

Nine hours—and a whole lot of physical labor—later, I glance up and catch just a flash of a tiny pink body before I collapse, exhausted, back into the pillow. A moment later, my daughter is laid across my chest. The doctor who again smells like musk says, "You did great, Christine! And this baby's a winner!" Look at that, he finally said it! I look down at Natalie's perfect little face, and as I hold her in my arms, I promise to be this grateful for the blessing of her forever. I also promise to love her with my entire heart and take care of her, no matter what.

chapter *One*

Discovery

*S*ometimes, I feel neglectful that I didn't worry more about the baby inside of me when I was pregnant with Natalie. I mean, I did worry a little. I knew enough to be concerned about her physical health. Of course, I wanted her to be well and when they showed me the sonogram on the screen, I asked them if they had doubled-checked that she had the correct number of fingers and toes and that she was well in all of the ways that they knew because they were medical people and I was not.

In some ways, I think I was lucky not to be a medically knowledgeable person.

I was pregnant at the same time as a very dear friend who was a nurse, and she far out-worried me. I know that we cared the same and loved these amazing little beings inside of us the same. It was just that she knew much more about what there was to worry about than

I did. I actually felt bad for how much she worried about herself and the baby she was carrying.

I would watch curiously as she took her pulse, measured her heart rate, and felt her glands. She was not satisfied with one round of blood work, and she had insisted on so many sonograms that she had an entire baby album complete before her baby arrived.

Wanting to be a perfect mother from the start, I attempted to keep track of my vitals—even panicking once, and almost calling Peter at work to urgently tell him that I did not have a pulse before realizing that maybe I just didn't know how to take my pulse.

And I asked for a sonogram every time I went to an appointment; the doctor always said no.

So, I think I worried pretty much like a regular mom did twenty years ago, but I now feel embarrassed that I didn't know to worry about Natalie becoming an addict. They say that worry doesn't help anything, but, and I know that it is silly, I keep thinking that if I had known enough to worry, and worried hard enough, that somehow all that worrying would have fended off her addiction.

Someone once asked me if I ever thought in my wildest dreams that any of this would have ever happened. I told them no; up until then, all of my wildest dreams had been the good kind.

There were warning signs. Many of them were quiet and practically imperceptible. Like the missing five or ten dollars that you figured you just spent but hadn't remembered, or her slightly red nose. There were probably many signs, but in my own defense and to assuage at least some of my guilt, I have to say that not all of them were obvious or glaring.

If you want to know the truth, though, I will tell you that the last thought was a lie, because the fact that some of the warning signs were subtle really doesn't lessen my guilt. No one could feel guiltier than I do. No one could ever feel more regretful than the mothers of the addicts that I know. I am a mother and should have seen all of the signs. That is the truth of it all. And the long answer, too.

Realizing that Natalie was an addict did not happen overnight or suddenly.

Instead, it was like I took a long, painful slide down a steep hill before I crash-landed into the truth. I started standing so firmly on solid ground, secure with my view of the world from high above. Then my foot began to slide. I lost my balance and then my footing altogether, sliding for a while, picking up speed. Tumbling end over end, careening out of control, until finally crashing at the bottom, beaten and battered, dazed and confused, asking myself, "What now?"

When Natalie was a little girl, preschool age, we would do work-books together practicing phonics and basic math skills. One after-noon, we were working on the concept of "more."

In each section of the paper was printed a number, which was highlighted. Then beneath it, there were two other numbers in smaller print. One number was more in value than the larger, printed num-ber and the other was less in value. The objective was for the child to identify which number was greater in value than the spotlighted numeral and circle it.

Natalie, being a fast study, picked up on the concept quickly. Once she understood, Natalie exuberantly circled the number that represented "more" and, to my amusement, expressed her sympathy for the number that was unfortunately tagged "less."

"That's sad for them!" she exclaimed, feverishly circling. "Huh, Mommy?" she asked. Entertained, I agreed.

The only thing that puzzled me was that no matter how many times I stated that we were circling the number that was *more*, Natalie consistently used the word "mucher."

I corrected her several times, plugging the word "more" into her sentences, but she continued to say "mucher."

"Six is mucher than four!" she proclaimed with glee. "One is mucher than zero!" she gushed.

Any math problem that contained the number zero was always met with special intrigue and joy!

Because it was obvious that she had mastered the objective of the lesson, I let the improper, albeit entertaining, word go. I was amused that she had invented her own word and was always fascinated by the way her mind worked. I knew she would soon understand and move on to the correct term, so I enjoyed her sweet innocence.

Later that evening, we went through our nightly routine. I tucked her into bed, we said a prayer, and I straightened her comforter and kissed her forehead. I stood in the doorway as I shut off the light, I called, "I love you!" over my shoulder.

I had just stepped into the hallway when she called out, "I love you mucher!"

When the taste hit my lips
It made my stomach lurch
How can something be dangerous
If they serve it in church?

A simple bottle
Covered in grapes
Hidden, just slightly
Behind my parents' drapes

I sneak around silently
Only the clock ticks
I tiptoe as if
To hush my shoe clicks

The purple liquid
Hits my tongue
I was not prepared
For how it stung

A simple bottle
Covered in grape art
Who would've known
That, that was the start

— Natalie

The warning signs came early, but addiction was certainly not on my radar. After all, Natalie was only eight years old. This was the earliest event that I can remember that could—in retrospect—be labeled as troubling.

Natalie was just getting over a cold, and I was relieved that she seemed to be getting better. For the three previous nights, I had given her a teaspoon of cold medicine to keep her comfortable and free of symptoms, but not tonight since she was breathing easier and didn't need it. I was going through the usual tuck-in routine when she asked, "Where's my medicine?"

"No medicine tonight," I said casually. "You don't need it anymore. Your cold is gone."

Her protest started off mild enough but quickly escalated in intensity. I reasoned patiently at first, explaining why it was important to not take the medicine when you don't need it anymore. Unable to reason with her, I finally simply told her, "Enough. And stop." Then I tucked her in and turned out the light.

I remember being a little annoyed and kind of puzzled but not concerned or troubled like I wish that I would have been. I chalked her tantrum up to just being dramatic. I was wrong.

While I didn't know it at the time, the problem went much deeper. Ten years later, I would find empty bottles of NyQuil hidden under her bed.

"Where are all of the spoons!" I shriek, calling up to the second floor, where my three children are in their bedrooms.

"Sorry!" they each call back with varying degrees of volume and sincerity.

The dishwasher is empty and the silverware drawer seems complete with plenty of forks and knives. But I am trying to set the table for dinner and I find only one spoon for the five of us.

"Dinner is almost ready, and some of you are going to be eating with your feet!" I threaten.

"Don't have any up here!" Jason yells down to me.

"Of course not," I mutter to myself, adding something about him being the resident clean freak.

Trevor appears with two spoons and two dirty bowls.

"My ice cream monster," I grumble, putting the bowls in the dishwasher and beginning to wash the utensils by hand.

"Sorry," he says walking away, grinning, not sorry at all.

"I am still short at least three!" I shout again to the only kid left, my daughter.

"Okay! Okay!" she says, appearing unexpectedly beside me with three cereal bowls and a handful of spoons.

"Thank you!" I sigh, snatching the spoons from her hand.

"Put the bowls in the dishwasher. And stop eating cereal in your room," I order, tossing the cutlery into the soapy dishwater and beginning to scrub them.

"Will do," she giggles, walking out of the room.

I didn't notice that there were three more spoons than bowls. And I didn't see the circle-shaped burn marks in the center of the spoons.

I always wonder what I would have done if I had.

Down the rabbit hole I go
Anywhere is better than here
Further and further I choose to go
Even when trouble is near

Eat me, drink me
Until you can't see
Eat me, drink me
Trapping myself, to be set free

Turning left, turning right
I think I may be lost
I think I found what I'm looking for
But at what cost

Here comes oblivion
There goes my soul
The problem is, I'm not Alice
And this isn't my rabbit hole

—Natalie

"Ugh," I groan. "I know that teenage girls sometimes tend to be messy. But this is ridiculous," I mutter to myself.

It's Monday, a cleaning day. And I have promised myself to dive into cleaning Natalie's chronically untidy room. It has been far too long since I have been in this pink cave. I had no idea at the time that it had been much, much too long.

This day, I make the bed, replace hastily discarded clothes to their wayward hangers, run the vacuum, and begin to dust. I clean what I can of the night table and dresser, trying to find places for the makeup, loose jewelry, and other odds and ends.

Oh, look, tattoos in the little pouches. Or are they tiny stickers? I said to myself. *I thought she had grown out of such things. I guess not.*

"Oh well, you are only young once. Let her be young," I say, opening up the bottom drawer of the small jewel box.

I bought her this box because it was nearly identical to the one I had as a girl. When you open the lid, the tiny ballerina balancing on a spring pops up and begins dancing around and around as the tinkling of music accompanies her. I used to keep folded up photos of Donny Osmond in mine.

I put the pouches inside for safekeeping and close the lid, stopping the dancing as well as the music.

They were not tattoos, or tiny stickers, or even photos of Donny Osmond, of course.

I had just dusted packets of heroin.

All mothers snoop. Good mothers snoop often. I know now that I should have snooped more.

A gnawing feeling told me something was wrong. But it was just a feeling. Right? But don't "just feelings" sometimes mean something?

Natalie was at school, and I was putting away her clean laundry. It was only a few weeks after I first discovered the heroin in Natalie's bedroom. I gazed around the pink flowery room. Nothing much seemed amiss. What made me zero in on the Hello Kitty change purse on the bookshelf, I will never know.

I picked it up. Feeling light and empty, I almost didn't bother opening it. But I did.

The heat and nausea hit me instantly when I discovered the pills she had been stealing stashed inside. My head spun and I had to sit down, then lie down on the bed to keep from falling to the floor.

It was the beginning of a nightmare for me. I had more questions right then than I would ever have answers. I closed my eyes for a bit, trying to get control of myself, and when I opened them, her favorite stuffed toy, Kitty Cat, was looking back at me.

I stared into Kitty Cat's blue marble eyes and said out loud, "My God! Why didn't you say something? You have been here the whole time! You are her best friend! You could have helped me save her!"

Medicate me
Medicate me
Release me
Sedate me

Free me
Take me
Stop me
Make me

Lose me
Find me
See me
Hide me

Save me
Drown me
Leave me
Surround me

Push me
Shove me
Pick me
Love me

— Natalie

"Where is my Tiffany bracelet?!" I huff, exasperated.

Peter and I are getting dressed for a rare evening out with other adults. He is already dressed and looking handsome. I, on the other hand, feel like a disheveled mess, hopping on one foot and trying to jam my other foot into a high heel that I rarely wear and now hate while trying to wiggle an earring onto my earlobe.

"I do not know," Peter assures me, resisting the temptation to make some sort of joke about me wearing it last and not him.

I am glad that he does resist. I don't think I would have taken it well. I am holding an undeserved grudge against him.

Why is it that without even trying men just age better than women? While women try so hard, and we—me at least—just look older?

Peter doesn't eat when he is upset. I eat extra well when I am stressed.

We have been both upset and stressed over Natalie, lately. So, he is looking slim and fit but, well, let's just say I am not.

"It's here somewhere. Just wear another one. We're late," he tells me. I agree and wrap another piece of jewelry around my wrist.

But we are both wrong.

My Tiffany jewelry—all of it, it turns out—is not just misplaced in the bedroom somewhere. Instead, it is sitting behind glass in a case in a pawn shop somewhere in a not-so-great part of town.

And the reason that we overdrew the checking account last month was not that I visited my beloved Macy's one too many times. Instead, it was because for the past several months, while I was in the shower each morning, Natalie was taking my debit card from my purse, running down to the neighborhood gas station, withdrawing money from the ATM, and putting my debit card back into my wallet before I had turned off the water. My pin number was her birth date. Peter thought I was making the withdrawals and I thought he was.

And then there was that old laptop we could have sworn we had saved purposely in the garage. Plus, where did I put my iPad? Well, those are keeping my jewelry company downtown.

Those brand-new clothes that Natalie got for her birthday that she never seems to wear? Because they still had the tags on, they have been returned for cash.

It is a completely sickening feeling when you discover that your child is stealing from you. It makes your stomach queasy when you know that it is the undeniable truth.

It is a certain, gnawing type of hurt when you are betrayed in such a way from someone that you not only trust entirely but love completely.

It is a deeper hurt. The wound is sharper and more painful.

You will be told that they are sick and cannot help it. That they are not themselves when they are doing these things... your child is not your child when they are acting this way.

But these words don't make it hurt less. Your child is always your child. Sometimes, they just aren't the people that you hoped they would be.

People even tell you not to take it personally, but it is impossible not to.

You understand that they are sick and can't help themselves, but you will still think that if they really loved you, loved you enough or even a little, then they wouldn't do these things.

You think that after all, you let them see you cry. They saw the very real tears in your eyes. And didn't they notice the look on your face? The look that clearly announces that your heart is not just broken but shattered?

You wonder why all of this is not enough. Why these things don't make a difference.

Regardless of what you have been told, you believe that they should. But you are wrong and the people who have told you these things are right and all that has been told to you is apparently true. It doesn't matter. Because addicts don't stop stealing and lying about it.

You will start off with reason and calm. But reason and calm will morph into screaming and yelling, crying and even threatening. These ugly things will not work either. Nothing does.

So, you sleep with your wallet under your pillow, put your purse right outside of the shower, make new gifts a little old before you give them, buy a jewelry box with a lock, and change your ATM pin to a non-sentimental, random number instead of the cuddly birth date of your daughter.

These precautions very rarely solve the problem. They might lessen it a little.

Addicts are desperate people. And desperate people are ingenious and one step ahead of most of us. They see these moves as survival, as a way to lessen their pain, when they are only on the path to further destruction. It is a cruel irony.

There is, by the way, no medicine, no ointment, salve or pill for the pain you will feel over this either. That is here to stay and all yours to suffer through.

The signs were all there. I just didn't see them. Or maybe I saw them but just didn't know what I was looking at, like when you go to a foreign country and are trying to read the road signs and billboards. You can decipher most of them enough to get the gist of it. But you don't understand them as surely and as clearly as you do when they are in your native language.

I have guilt. I should have studied up. I should have known. It was my job as a mother to anticipate and I did not.

If you do take the time to study up or even casually google around, you will find that there are certain emotional, physical, and behavioral signs of addiction. Most of them were staring me right in the face while I apparently was looking away.

Emotionally, Natalie was erratic; her moods all over the place. She was picking a fight one minute then sobbing in my arms the next. There was an almost constant rotation of I love yous and I hate yous. She was declaring me her best girlfriend in one breath and her cold-hearted, non-understanding enemy in the next.

There were so many physical signs as well that had Natalie fitting right into the profile of an addict. She became unclean and disheveled. How could a child who never went a day in her childhood without a bath suddenly go a week without seeing a bar of soap and not care? I offered her twenty dollars once if she would agree to spend ten minutes in the shower. She wouldn't brush her hair, and she'd wear the same, soiled clothes for days at a time. I offered fifteen dollars if she would introduce herself to the washing machine.

She looked grey and, honestly, kind of greenish at times. Her eyes were bloodshot, and more than once, Peter commented on her dilated pupils. She sniffled and I worried that she was getting a cold. And when I noticed that she was shivering one minute and sweating minutes later, I diagnosed her with the flu.

Behaviorally, she was a flop. She was lazy and unmotivated. She missed school and the few little part-time jobs that she was expected to hold. There always ended up being problems at both places that were never her fault.

She barricaded herself in her room. She was up all night and slept all day. She was secretive and defensive.

She had two subjects that she talked incessantly about, money and drugs. She always needed money no matter how much you just gave her, and the urgency at which she would open a birthday card searching for a monetary gift was embarrassing.

She would go on and on about how dumb people overdosed because they mixed this or that, and she was always the first to suggest what I might take for my cold, headache, ache, or pain.

Stupidly, I remarked to Peter once, "Maybe she is going to be a doctor like you! She certainly has an interest and a lot of knowledge of chemistry and drugs!"

"Too much of an interest and too much knowledge," Peter had warned me.

Once when I was not feeling well and had called Peter to ask him what from the medicine cabinet I should take, Natalie rushed to my side to supervise that I didn't take the wrong thing or too much of it. She was genuinely concerned that I would take too much of something or the wrong combination. It was as if she didn't want me to fall down the same hole that she had even once.

All of Natalie's relationships were rocky and eventually broke. There always seemed to be a new friend appearing from some random, unexplained place with a sketchy, unclear background.

Her weight fluctuated. She seemed to have lost interest in everything that she used to enjoy and did the little that she did poorly. She was unreliable and selfish.

And when I confronted her, she was defensive, and either denied it all or minimized, diverted the blame, or offered an endless supply of alibis or excuses for my concerns.

She ate odd combinations of food, in huge quantities at odd hours of the day.

My girl was not my girl anymore. I didn't recognize her.

"How was your day?" I call out, wanting him to say, "Fine," so we can move on and talk about what I have been thinking about. It's not that I don't care about his day because I do. It's just that so much has been pressing on my mind. And whatever it is, it is pressing on my heart as well. Because my chest is tight, too.

Peter and I are settling in for the night. He's undressing in the bedroom, and I am talking to him from the adjoining bathroom.

"It was fine!" Peter calls back and then sighs in a way that indicates it may not have been all that fine. On a different day, I would have asked him to clarify the exhaling of the extra air. But although I pride myself on being a supportive, tuned-in wife, I am in mom overdrive right now. Momming is taking all of my energy and all of the space in my head and I can't juggle both jobs. So, I have to choose.

"Maybe she's telling the truth," I suggest, squeezing a dab of toothpaste onto my brush.

"Who?" Peter asks.

I want to snap back with, "Who do you think I mean?" But I don't. Getting testy is not going to help anything, and if I do, it will lead to a fight that will distract from the conversation I want to have and will force us into another dialogue. And second, I really need to remind myself that Peter cannot read my mind. And it is unfair to expect him to even though I wish that he could climb inside my head and sit down on a bench, taking up permanent residence there, and counsel me through all of my craziness.

"Natalie," I answer Peter, proud of my patient tone.

"Telling the truth about what?" he asks. (I can't believe he doesn't know.)

"About the drugs and holding them for a friend and everything!"
I say testily, breaking my own "Don't be testy" rule.

I estimate that I have just enough time to brush while listening to
his response and am just about to put the toothbrush into my mouth
when he appears in the doorway, readying for his shower.

Silently, he turns on the water, takes off his clothes, and grabs a
towel from the rack. I am waiting expectantly, momentarily confused
by his silence. I know he heard me. I stare at Peter's grim expression,
trying to read the meaning, wondering if he knows something more
that he's not telling me.

I realize that he does know something I don't know. It is something that I should know but am refusing to accept, and his expression
is serious because he is trying to figure out how to break my heart but
not hurt me too badly at the same time. As Peter steps into the shower,
he turns to offer me a sad look over his shoulder.

"I think that we are coming to realize that our daughter, unfortunately, lies about a lot of things," he says. "The drugs were hers,
Christine. Natalie is an addict."

I flinch like I have just been smacked across the face. Saying nothing. I'm frozen, the surety of his words sinking in. It is difficult to
argue with someone who is so decisive—especially when this immov-
able opinion is held by someone you respect as much as I respect
Peter.

Peter closes the shower door, and for a few more moments, I am
motionless, watching the splashing water drip down the frosted pane
of glass.

"See you in a little bit, Baby Girl!" I would say when I left Natalie
at preschool or with a sitter when she was very young.

"See you in bits, Mommy!" she would always call back cheerfully.

We were never apart for long. And would always find our way back to each other. We use this expression to this day and the meaning still holds true.

"No matter where you go," I tell her, "I'm not far behind. I promise."

I couldn't have known, back then, the dark and dangerous places she would go. I would be following right behind her, seeing but not comprehending, with my hand always outstretched.

They say it's better to laugh
Than to cry
But what if you can't do better
No matter how hard you try?

Using to feel good
But just end up numb
Willing to do anything to feel
No matter how dumb

Started using at first
To not want to die
But to say that it lasted
Would be a bold lie

So, what do you do
When your tolerance is so high
That even if you wanted to OD
You just cannot die

So, you use and use
Until hopefully one day
The drugs will be strong enough
To take you away

—Natalie

Once, I was sitting in the waiting room of my elderly mother's primary care doctor's office, waiting for her to get out from her appointment, when I picked up a magazine and began to leaf through it. I stumbled upon a section with questionnaires that were supposed to be predictors of various health issues.

The title of the article was "Your Family's Health." There were questionnaires that pertained to me about women's health and a few that would pertain to Peter with the heading, "Men's Health." And others that were designed to indicate children and adolescent issues.

I filled out a couple on myself, assessing my risks for breast and uterine cancer and thyroid problems. Pleased, I passed them all with "low risk" scores.

I filled out others pertaining to Peter. He did not appear to have heart disease or prostate cancer.

For my children, I filled out several: one on diabetes, one on autism, and then finally one on allergies. I scanned the results, enjoying my family's better than average scores, arrogantly taking credit for these results, complimenting myself, and deciding that they scored as they did and were all as healthy as they were due to my excellent care.

My mother was still in her appointment and I had time for one more test. Confidently, I began to answer the questions on "Substance Abuse." Halfway through the list of questions, my mother appeared.

While she was checking out with the receptionist, I hurriedly answered the remaining questions, checking the "yes" box to bloodshot eyes, slurred speech, deteriorations of grooming, and changes in appetite and sleep patterns.

As my mother headed for the door, I quickly tallied the numbers and matched it to the appropriate level of risk. It matched to "High Risk of Substance Abuse."

Out of time, I tossed the magazine back onto the waiting table, went to help my mother, and left.

Throughout the day, the questionnaire bothered me, but I was eventually able to push the thoughts out of my mind, deciding that I must have added wrong.

Two months later, things at home with Natalie are worse and I am back at the same office with my mother. As I sit in the same waiting room, I think about the last time that I was there.

I look around the room and spot the pile of magazines on the table. I locate the one from before, with all of the questionnaires, take it back to my seat, and rifle through the pages until I find the one that I had filled out on substance abuse. It feels odd to discover and recognize my own handwriting.

Methodically, I go through the questions again, reading each one more carefully than I had previously and re-marking my responses.

I change only one of my answers, to something worse, and tally again. I match my score to its indicator. I had done the math correctly.

My daughter is an addict. My head spins and I feel almost faint as I search in my purse to find a pen and scrap of paper to copy down the number of the suggested hotline.

Before my mother and I leave, I think better of this, and when no one is looking, I fold the magazine and stuff it in my purse, taking the entire thing with me.

"I think she's on drugs," I repeat, almost unable to get the words out a second time. I am sweating all over my cell phone; I pull it away from my ear for a moment to wipe it on my shirt.

"What do we do?" I am speaking, but I'm breathless. The shock of finding syringes hidden in the bathroom wastebasket has stolen my air.

"I don't know," Peter says, a rare quiver in his voice. "We will figure it out. I'll be right home."

Private time in the bathroom is sometimes difficult to find for young mothers. When I needed a moment, I would put Natalie in front of the TV and a *Barney* video and sneak away. It never worked.

Before I had a chance, Natalie would be outside of the bathroom door pounding and crying. Finally, opening the door, she would appear with tears in her eyes like I had betrayed her. She would see me sitting on the toilet, and she'd analyze the situation. And because we did everything together, she would take off her diaper, not even knowing why, and join me, climbing up on my lap. Now that's love.

Parents of addicts have a quiet understanding. We are gentle with one another. We don't make a show about it all. We look at one another with kind, sympathetic, understanding eyes. And we don't judge.

We don't pry but we don't avoid saying the child's name like it is a dirty word either. We ask how their child is.

"How's Natalie?" the husband asks.

"She could be better," I admit, which are four words that somehow tell them much more and sum up the fact that Natalie is struggling but is still alive.

Then I add, because it is what I do, "She's my girl."

I am sure to smile when I say this because I want to solidify the fact in any doubting mind that Natalie is my daughter and the best thing that ever happened to me. And that I love her more every day.

When I tell people this, I always hope that they repeat it. Of all the things that people repeat or gossip about, I want them to spread the fact that I will stand by my daughter forever, regardless.

While they are gossiping and exclaiming, "Can you believe Natalie Naman is an addict?" I want them to also be exclaiming, "And can you believe that Christine still loves her?!"

The couple nods, and the husband says, "I remember her in the talent show."

His words bring back a memory that had gotten buried underneath the sadness. I am grateful to him for reminding me of this, and an image of Natalie dancing her cute little legs off and singing her heart out on the stage of the kindergarten talent show washes over me. I actually smile and genuinely laugh for a moment.

He smiles when he says this, and I know that he truly likes my daughter, which means I love him.

"How is Melissa?" I ask with a small smile that I hope tells them that I remember their daughter in happier times, too.

At the sound of her daughter's name, the wife reaches for her husband's hand for support like she is momentarily afraid of me. I try to ignore this and continue to smile, hoping that my smile tells them I liked Melissa then and am still fond of her now.

There is a pause, then the husband says, "We lost her."

This statement clobbers me like a punch in the stomach. I know that I now look horrified, and I try to correct my expression but know that I am failing.

"I'm sorry," I say, never meaning a worn-out platitude more.

I swear my heart stops for a moment. But I recoup and say it again and nod. I look directly at the mother.

Her expression is unique to grieving mothers. It is a mask that I swear they hand to you when you lose a child, the moment your child's heart stops beating. I received a similar mask the day that my daughter was diagnosed an addict and I was declared unhappy forever.

The mother says, so softly that I am barely able to hear her, "We didn't know."

This I understand and convey this by nodding more fully, hoping that she realizes that I am sorry for this, too.

The husband squeezes his wife's hand in support.

"We just lost it in the sun." A baseball analogy to mean they just didn't see the signs.

With nothing else for any of us to say, I only offer a "me, too," wanting them to know I missed the signs, too. And that not seeing them is easier than most people would think.

"Mine, too," I say.

The lady sitting in the booth next to me turns suddenly. I have startled her. I regret my words, not because they are not true but because I now think I have scared her. I was sitting alone in Panera having a cup of tea and trying to warm up, even though it is not cold outside or cool inside and the only thing that seems to be cold is me. I am a little embarrassed; I have obviously eavesdropped on a conversation between her and her teenage daughter who has just excused herself to the bathroom. The mother looks worn-out and worried. And I can relate to her so completely that I wonder if I look like her.

The tables in Panera are very close together, and I couldn't help but hear and then be captivated by the dialogue between this mother and daughter. They could have been Natalie and me. Natalie and I could have written the script of the lunch; we could have played these parts.

The mother starts off calm, measuring her words, sliding in reason and logic. She then moves on to speaking a little more off the cuff and emotionally interjecting strong suggestions and demands until she finally lands on hysterical and exasperated, peppering her care and concern with threats and ultimatums.

No matter what adjectives you use to describe it, no matter how pretty or ugly you want to present it, no matter how you wrap it up, it was just "I love you." While the mother was playing the part of the concerned mother, the daughter was playing the part of the troubled daughter at the level of an Academy Award-winning performance. She was erratic and spontaneous. She was unreasonable and belligerent. She kept telling her mother that she understood and that she loved her mother, who she kept calling "Mommy," making my heart squeeze every time she did.

The daughter, of course, insisted that her mother and her suspicions were unfounded; her mother's opinions were wrong, and the daughter, of course, was just fine and had everything under control. Her mother had it all wrong. Her friends were really nice people, and her mother should be a little ashamed of herself for judging them on-sight, that everyone stayed out that late at night. They were all just talking and watching movies. Her mother needed to relax. She was urgent to get over with this lunch and conversation and back to her friends. Her mother needed to trust her and get off her back. She wanted out of Panera and, more urgently, she needed to get up from the table and go into the restroom. Off she went, dragging her backpack with her even though the mother said to leave it there.

That was when the mom and I found ourselves alone.

"I'm sorry," I say to the woman. "I should not have listened. But I did overhear a bit, and my daughter struggles like yours."

Waiting for her to answer, I pray that she is not angry and realizes I am just reaching out with compassion. When she looks up, I am relieved to be able to tell that she understands my true intention. "It's so hard," the woman says, anguish and pain in her voice.

"I know," I say, feeling my eyes moisten in sympathy.

"Is your daughter..." the woman starts, then trails off as she realizes the answer may not be one that she wants to hear.

"She's okay," I reply quickly, wanting to put her mind at ease. "My daughter is working through it. And yours will, too."

I can see in the distance that her daughter is making her way back from the bathroom and I know our conversation is about to end. So, I cut to the chase and say what I know she most needs to hear: "Not everyone dies." She nods her head up and down emphatically and frantically, trying to assure herself of this.

"Everything that I read online tells me that her chances of recovering are so small," she says, looking away from me, trying to act casual and waving to her girl in the distance.

"But her chances are not zero," I tell her.

"Yes," she says.

"Have hope," I say as I get up to leave, knowing that she will because one thing all mothers cling to is hope.

Peter and I are out in the backyard, surveying our property after a bad storm. Specifically, we are looking at the spot where a shutter had fallen off when we notice a ladder propped up beneath Natalie's window.

We question each other, then we blame the workmen who had been to the house, then we decide it was the window washers who were there the week before.

The only person we never think to blame is Natalie, who had been sneaking out of her bedroom at night to do all of the wrong things.

The first time I ever saw Natalie's face was when they laid her on my chest in the hospital a minute after I delivered her.

After studying her for a moment, the first thing that I noticed was her deep dark eyes. I remember thinking, *Did I give her those?* My eyes are a very deep brown. I would have never dreamed then that now, twenty years later, I would study her and ask myself, *Did I give her this? Did I give her addiction?*

I am the kind of mother who enjoys talking about her children. I try not to be obnoxious about it. I also try to be honest, as well, by telling about their accomplishments as well as their lesser moments.

And because in most ways, I believe us to be a normal family, we have plenty of both to share. Depending upon the day, I like to share them to let people know that we really are normal.

We are an average family that has been infected by this horrible disease.

While the following anecdotes are admittedly self-indulgent, with me bragging a bit in some and sadly remembering in others, I am hoping that in telling them, they will have value.

I think that it is normal to look back and wonder how the good times, as well as the not-so-great moments, affect a child. I don't know the answer to this.

And I can't help but wish that I could go back in time, reliving some of them just for the laughs, amplifying others so that Natalie could have more good times and blocking others with my mother's shield to protect my daughter from other experiences.

The two most common questions that people ask when I tell them that Natalie is an addict are "How is she?" and "When did she start?"

The answer to how she is varies. But the answer to the age that she started to experiment with things that she shouldn't have was at age twelve. Invariably, after I tell them, most people exclaim, "My goodness that is so young!"

When I first found out, I thought so, too, only adding to my shame and embarrassment. The unfortunate fact for those who begin early, including Natalie, is that the earlier young people start with substances, the more likely they are to fall into addiction.

I always thought that not only did I drop the ball on keeping after Natalie but I always believed that I dropped that ball early.

I understand now that just like she was an early talker and walker when she was a baby, Natalie may have been a little early in venturing into drug use, but not by much. With this, unfortunately, she was right on target.

Who would have ever thought that a competitive mom like me would wish that her daughter would be delayed in doing anything? And it seems that as far as dropping that ball goes, I was late to make that catch. I swear, I just didn't see it coming.

My rock bottom is not foreign
I know it well
I know what hell is
Even if it's hard to tell

When you bend and bend
But do not break
Is truly when
You know what you can take

This badge, these scars,
I do not wear honorably
When deep down here I know,
I'm so much less than I was meant to be

—Natalie

chapter Two

Something
I Don't Know

*T*rinity and I are standing at the kitchen island while Natalie showers upstairs. I share my worries with this girl who has been Natalie's one true friend.

I am asking her to promise to keep my number handy and call if she needs me. As she promises that she will, she tells me that she lost her phone and has a new one. She doesn't know if she has my number, so I am reciting it to her as she logs it into the device. I am peeking over her shoulder, wanting to make sure that she has it right.

"That's it," I confirm, watching for just another moment as she types "Natalie's Mom" in the space for the contact name.

I gulp, overcome with emotion and am transported back to when Natalie was little...a time when that was my most commonly used title and I liked it.

I remember writing notes to teachers and sitters signing them "Natalie's mom" just so they were sure to know who I was. Invariably, I would receive return correspondence addressed back to me, again labeled "Natalie's mom."

I remember one particular May, around Mother's Day, when the mothers were invited to school for a tea. We enjoyed juice and cookies together. The children sang us songs and then each of them presented their mother with a portrait that they had drawn of their mother surrounded by positive attributes that they felt their mother possessed.

The children were young, so the teacher was pretty much able to control the adjectives that the children penned on the pages, only writing positive ones on the blackboard for the kids to copy. What the teacher couldn't control, though, was the artwork. Apparently, most small children view their mothers a little bit differently than maybe their mothers would like to visualize themselves. Most of us appeared to be yelling, including me. Once we all got over our embarrassment and stopped clutching our portraits to our chests, we laughed and laughed, sharing these masterpieces.

I remember sharing a chuckle with the teacher, with her exclaiming that she tried and tried to encourage them to soften these pictures. Most of the children resisted, insisting, "But that's what she looks like!"

The only compromise the teacher could come up with was getting the children to agree to decorate the perimeters with symbols. Which explained all of the butterflies, music notes, sun rays, and turtles around the borders. While I have never sung a note or felt a particular affinity towards turtles, I found myself grateful that my screaming face was surrounded by these gentler touches.

Of course, at the bottom of the page, in Natalie's childish heart-melting scrawl, was written "MY MOTHER."

I remember the sight of those two simple words bringing every mother at the table to tears.

I stand there in the kitchen thinking that it is true that no matter how things change, certain feelings stay with us. I also stand there scolding myself for not saving that piece of artwork. I guess that as much comfort as I had taken in the additions, comically, it wasn't enough for me to put a frame around it.

I stand, feeling grateful for memories, and I comfort myself by thinking that surely the crayoned artwork would have faded by this time while the image in my mind only gets clearer.

Hollering for shampoo from the shower, Natalie wails my name then, "MOMMMMM!" I look upward toward her bellow and can't help but smile and think that her calling to me just might be my favorite sound.

"She hates me," he said evenly.

"Uh, yeah, actually she does," I admitted. Then we laughed, cleansing the tension from the room.

We were at the pediatrician's office and nine-month-old Natalie was red-faced and screaming loud enough for the three surrounding counties to hear her.

I had been nervous about the appointment for a week because she never made it easy. She tended to act up and cause a tremendous scene. And although I knew it was supposed to be about her, I couldn't help but feel like it was a reflection of me and my parenting skills.

She had become quiet and looked around suspiciously as we pulled into the parking lot, as though she recognized where we were going. Then she began to whine and fuss in the lobby, scaling the chairs and climbing the drapes while the other children sat glumly and sickly—as they should—on their parents' laps.

By the time the doctor entered the exam room, she was hysterical. I supposed "stranger danger" was not a bad thing, but this was a little extra. She writhed and fought to get off my lap while the doctor sat on a stool to face us.

He had already tried to prove himself friendly by talking to her in a soft voice, showing her his Mickey Mouse tie, and making his tiger puppet speak to her. Now he had his stethoscope poised and at the ready, but every time he wheeled himself closer to place it on her chest, she tried to bite him.

He wheeled himself toward her, then away from her, her mouth opening and closing. "How many teeth does she have?" he asked. I didn't know if he was asking for medical reasons or if he was wondering just how bad her bite was going to be if she connected. Either way, it seemed a fair question.

"A bunch," I said, holding Natalie's mouth shut so the doctor could momentarily land the instrument on her tiny, heaving chest.

"Her lungs are good," he announced. Maybe he said this because she wouldn't be able to scream the way that she was if they weren't. I was exhausted, and it was only ten o'clock in the morning.

"Well, Natalie," the doctor said as he washed his hands. "You seem just fine to me."

He placed his hand on the doorknob and then turned back to laugh and say, "Take care, Christine. Hold on for the ride. She's a wild one!"

As if I didn't already know this.

Natalie recognized the fact that the doctor was leaving and stopped screaming. She was still quivering and wiping at her watering eyes and gooey nose, though, while I fought to intercept all of the mess with a tissue.

Almost out the door, the doctor raised the tiger puppet in the air next to his face and, in an animated voice, said, "Goodbye, Natalie." He was almost gone when Natalie said one of only a handful of words she knew, enunciated more clearly than she ever had before: "Bad."

I cringed, hoping the doctor didn't hear her. But he poked his head back in the door and, in his own voice, said, "I heard that, Natalie."

When Natalie was about two years old, and her chocolatey-colored hair had begun to fall into her eyes, I knew it was time for a haircut. I took her to the local department store, forgetting, as usual, to make an appointment.

We signed in and sat among the rectangular grouping of plastic chairs, waiting to be called back to the next available stylist. I felt my neck tighten up as I mentally scolded myself.

When you didn't have an appointment, and we never seemed to have one because we were never quite that organized, you were at the mercy of luck. You would be serviced by the next available stylist. And this random system put us in the precarious position of having Delores as our stylist.

While Delores was an excellent stylist, she didn't seem to be fond of children. Well, not my children anyway, or so I thought.

When it was time to get my son Jason's first haircut, it was a big deal. Or I made it a big deal. I insisted Peter take a couple of hours off of work. We showed up armed with a still camera and a camcorder to document the event. And because I was firmly in mommy overdrive, we also showed up with a stuffed doll with retractable hair that, according to the catalogue description, was going to make this entire first haircut experience relaxed and magical. I even had a tube to collect and store the first lock cut from my precious firstborn Jason's head hidden in my purse.

When it was Jason's turn, we were led like sacrificial lambs to Delores who was waiting for us with hands on her hips, a scowl on her face. I tried to change the script by making Delores one of the family and introducing her to Jason as "our new friend" and pointing out how nice she is. "See, Delores is going to cut your hair!" Delores was having none of my niceties, ignoring both Jason and me. Was she put off by our entourage, or did she simply not like children? In any case, she didn't warm up to us. Instead, she stooped over Jason's head, leaning in with her black-rimmed eyeglasses perched on the tip of her nose. Her expression made it clear that she just wanted to get this over with.

Delores was also not appreciative of my making my movie directorial debut in the middle of her work day.

Peter, who I was directing as well, held the camcorder, dutifully capturing every moment. All was going relatively well, even though I wasn't sure Peter was getting all of it at exactly the correct angle (I was probably yelling this at him) and Delores was not as smiley as I had hoped.

We were doing okay until Jason had had enough and began to fuss and squirm in my arms. I added cooing to the endless instructions that I was giving Peter in addition to my cheerful chit chat to Delores. Peter was ignoring me and Delores was getting aggressive, chopping off Jason's locks with the loudest *snip, snip* I'd ever heard.

I was still cooing when Jason moved in exactly the wrong way, causing Delores to cut her own finger. She yelped and began alternately examining her wound and sucking on it.

Peter kept filming, continuing to follow my original instructions to "get it all" even though now I was shouting "Cut" and "Fade to black."

I was frantic and still cooing loudly now, not at Jason but instead at Delores. It was clear that no matter how hard I tried, Delores was not going to forgive me. I knew the haircut was officially over when—with her finger still in her mouth—Delores motioned to the front of the salon and said, "You can pay up front."

We apologized profusely, accepted the half-done haircut, and left an obscenely big tip. We exited the salon with Jason's first haircut and all of its horror on tape.

So, when it was time for Natalie's first haircut, I was alone. Peter had said, "Hell No!" when I asked him to come along. I was also unarmed, leaving all recording devices at home.

When Natalie's name was called, we were led directly to the back of the shop—to Delores. We had no choice but to take her. And I became intimidated at the sight of her.

Delores made a face as we approached and her eyes fell on Natalie. I tried to ignore her face. I wondered if she remembered us and whether this look was reserved for us or if this was just her generic "I'm annoyed that you are here" expression.

I plopped Natalie like a cherry on top of a sundae on the booster seat. "Just do whatever you can do," I muttered.

Motherhood had somehow taken its toll on me already. Life was winning. I was tired. I didn't care as much as I did with the first child. I didn't have the special golden tube to collect Natalie's hair but was pretty sure that I had an empty plastic bag in my purse.

Delores grabbed her scissors and a comb, and if it wasn't my imagination, was readying them more like they were weapons of defense just in case there was a familiar head-jerking gene. Yes, Delores remembered us.

She was just about to begin when at exactly this wrong moment Jason, who was now almost three and potty training, decided he needed to use the restroom and began clutching his privates and popping up and down to emphasize his need.

The bad mother in me wanted to tell him to just go in his pants. But with the scene Jason was causing, there was too much of an audience, making this impossible without all of the motherly and grandmotherly witnesses mommy-shaming me.

Not sure what to do, and cursing Peter in my head for not coming, I looked at Delores pleadingly, and she simply muttered, "Make it quick." I grabbed Jason and ran. Of course, he insisted that he needed to poop as well. He did not; he was just curious about this unexplored bathroom.

When I finally dragged him away from the hand dryer screaming (he loved all things electric) and back to Delores and Natalie, I stopped short in utter amazement at the sight before me.

Natalie was still in the chair but with a fresh new haircut, her hands raised high in the air, roller-coaster style, squealing with glee as Delores laughed and spun her around and around in the chair. Natalie hollered in delight, and Delores laughed so hard she needed to dab her tear-stained eyes. The other patrons were cheering and laughing along, too.

It would have been a fantastic scene to have on video, if only I'd brought the camera. I couldn't even locate the plastic bag that I thought that I had brought to collect Natalie's hair.

"She's spectacular!" Delores told me before we left. I thanked her. Gathered the kids. Left a tip that was even bigger than the one before and exited the shop with the entire event undocumented except in my mind.

The whole experience is typical of Natalie. She is fun. She loves people and people love her. Her kind heart and pure spirit are magnetic. She arrived in this world with these qualities that I have always admired and wish were stronger in me. Qualities that I believe will aid her greatly to get through her challenge of addiction and beyond.

When I finally could relax in the mall parking lot, after placing both kids in their car seats, I looked at Natalie in the rearview mirror. God how I loved her. And her haircut.

It is something you cannot imagine
If you have never felt it
So chilled to the bone
While the other half of you has melted

Cannot stay still
Too exhausted to move
As if your skin doesn't fit
Too tight, yet too loose

The cure is so close,
Yet so far away
What will make it cease
Is the same thing that makes it stay

—Natalie

One afternoon, when Natalie was in second grade, I went to pick her up from school. Any parent, if being honest, will tell you that picking a child up from school is not often the happy experience that movies, ads, and TV, especially on the *Brady Bunch*, portray it to be. It is not even the experience that it looks to be on the surface.

While the children may appear to be cheerfully and carefreely skipping toward their parents from the school's pickup line, they are very often covered with invisible bruises and abrasions. Some of these wounds are old and are already turning into scars. Ones that they received in past days. And others are fresh and raw, having gotten them just that day. These are the injuries they receive from going to the emotional battlegrounds of school.

I have found that most children hold their emotions together during the school day, then fall apart once in the safety of the car. My children tended to do this. And because I really needed to know what was going on with them, I would often take a pass through the McDonald's drive-thru or a loop around the block an extra time so that they could get it all out.

Natalie was always pretty happy and resilient, on the outside anyway, but she still had stuff. I would find out later she had more than her fair share of stuff.

On this day, Natalie bounced toward me, and we walked to the car hand in hand, with her sucking on a wad of gum that I had just slipped her. It was the bribe I had promised in the morning if she would agree to try to survive the perils of second grade because she had said that none of the other little girls liked her.

I opened the van door, and just before climbing in, she turned to scan the parking lot behind her. "I forget to ask Celia something. I've got to ask her!" she said and darted toward Celia and her mother, who were walking about fifty feet away toward their car. I let her go and waved to Celia's mother, a very young, fit, pretty woman. She waved back.

As Natalie galloped toward them, I studied Celia, who had lucked out in the gene lottery by winning her mother's pretty features and perfect blonde wavy hair.

I watched as Natalie reached them and apparently asked her question while bouncing excitedly on her tiny legs. I couldn't hear the question, but by the shake of Celia's head, I could tell that the answer was no.

I saw Natalie match Celia's shake with a shake in response, then turn and gallop toward me. As she did, Celia's mother smiled brightly and waved goodbye to me. She actually stopped Celia and instructed her to wave to me as well. By the daughter's body language, I could tell that she would rather have oral surgery than wave to me. But she did. So, I smiled and waved back.

Natalie reached me and jumped into the van, and I closed the door behind her. I backed out of the parking spot and began heading home. Curious, I asked in my best fake, I am not prying but simply casually interested voice: "What did you have to ask Celia?"

"I needed to ask her if she liked me," Natalie said.

My heart felt as though it plummeted into my stomach with a thud. Fearing where this was going, I adjusted the rear view mirror to inspect Natalie's face, which was unreadable. "What did she say?" I asked, pretty sure that I knew the answer and not caring if I sounded as desperate and panicked as I was. I had witnessed Celia's wagging head and was hardly betting that her response had been, "Yes, Natalie, I like you very much because you are a sweet, kindhearted little girl!"

"She said no," Natalie told me.

"What did you say?" I asked, possibly wishing that Natalie had responded that she didn't like Celia either and that she actually didn't like her so much that she was *glad* that she didn't want to be her friend. And furthermore, she would rather eat a jar of pickles—which she hated—than be Celia's friend.

"I asked her if she maybe just liked me a little bit," she told me. I drew in a sharp breath.

"She said no, not even a little," Natalie said. While I was regrouping and thinking about what to say, Natalie asked, "Do you have any more gum?" I reached behind me and handed her the entire pack.

"Want to go to McDonald's?" I asked.

"Sure," she replied.

You don't know what it is like
To be in my head
Always wishing for death
So full of dread

I have never known anything else
And I think that makes it harder
All the racing voices telling me
You're a bad friend, sister, daughter

Everything becomes loud
It becomes very hard to breathe
Try and find my bearings
As I clench my teeth

The world rushes past
As I try and catch up
All I am ever yearning to feel
Is that I'm enough

No need to pity me
Just try and understand
You may think I can do better
I am doing the best that I can

— Natalie

Natalie and I are watching the local news. A middle school child has committed suicide after being bullied by her peers who, among other unspeakable things, texted her repeatedly to kill herself, convincing her that everyone and the world in general would be better off without her.

I gasp at the horror of this. But when I look at Natalie, while she seems truly saddened for the victim, she does not seem as startled as I am. With her tone flat and emotionless, she says, "They did that to me."

"Who?" I demand, alarmed.

"Mom, relax," she tells me. "Lots of years ago. Middle school. They would get together at sleepovers and spend the entire night calling and texting me to kill myself. It was fun for them."

"You never told me," is all I can whisper. "Why?" she says quietly back.

"Because I am your mother. I am supposed to know and be there for everything," I insist, feeling hugely inadequate and wondering what else I didn't know.

"That's why I didn't tell you," she answers. "Because you are my mother. Why would I want to make you feel bad?"

Natalie's bravery and strength always astounds me. I sit there quietly with her, trying hard not to say all the wrong things that are racing around my mind. I want to know who and when. It isn't too late for me to call these awful children and their mothers! I want to tell Natalie that the children who do these things are despicable and that they should feel as much pain as they cause others.

But I remain mute and paralyzed. I want Natalie to elaborate, but she doesn't. Instead, she is squinting at the television, concentrating on the next story on the news.

"I know him," she says, pointing to the mug shot of a drug dealer that has just appeared on the screen.

My mouth goes dry. I can't think of a thing to say, but it doesn't matter because there is no way I can speak with my jaw clenched so tightly shut. I nod, waiting for Natalie to say something else, but she doesn't and instead stands up from the couch and walks up the stairs to her room.

I sit there collecting myself, realizing that at least some of the time, my daughter lives in and navigates a world that I know nothing about.

I guess it is natural to wonder how much our childhoods affect our personalities, decisions, relationships, and the overall trajectory of our adult lives. Sometimes, I think the answer is plenty if not completely. But then I hear of people overcoming adversity and this theory tips in the other direction.

I wonder how the good and the bad affect a child. I know that I personally drag the baggage of my childhood around with me. Sometimes it feels like I am lugging oversize luggage through a ten-mile-long, crowded airport. Then other times I am saddled with just a carry on.

I feel the effects of the past every day, and because I believe that I have failed Natalie in so many ways, I think I should be in a constant state of apology, walking around saying, "I'm sorry," every minute of every day for not protecting her from bullying and hurt.

When I realize that I was less than I could have or should have been and I apologize to Natalie and express to her that I hope that it is not too late to lessen the damage, she is always kind and tells me, "What do you always say ... water under the bridge."

Even though she is kind enough to say it, I am not naïve enough to believe it. I always want to tell her that this is not water under the bridge because at times I can tell by the look on her face that the ache in her heart has not passed us by, but this water instead is still swirling around us, knocking us about and threatening to take us under at any time.

I hope and pray that there is enough good to tip the scale back and even it all out somehow.

How many "I love yous" does it take to delete even one "I wish you would kill yourself"? I certainly don't know the math on this.

One last time
That's what we all say
We laugh when others believe it
But this dangerous game we still play

So, pick up your weapon of choice
Your favorite substance as well
If it's just one more time
No one will be able to tell

Little did you know,
You knowing is enough
Oh god, what have I done
I thought I was out of this stuff

—Natalie

I'm stopped at a red light when a large public bus lumbers through the intersection and the giant worried face of woman about my age glides by. Beneath her are the words, "How can I keep my child off of drugs?"

"I don't know," I tell her, "I don't. So, don't look at me." But she is looking at me.

Traffic has stopped, and the bus is now stuck in the middle of the intersection, blocking my path and leaving me unable to proceed even though my light is now green. So, the woman in the bus ad is staring right at me.

The guy in the car behind me beeps. "Jerk," I mutter at him through my rear-view mirror. I don't know what he expects me to do. I look forward again.

"Not you," I say to the face on the bus, who somehow seems to be even more concerned than she was a moment ago. The lines on her face are very pronounced. But I guess that is to be expected when your face is ten feet tall, making your creases three feet in length.

I feel bad for her and wonder if she is a model or a real person. If she is actually a suffering mom, I want to be her friend. And if she is a model, then she is good at her job. Still, I could be her friend.

I decide that we are friends and that she looks like a Mary Beth. So, she is now my friend Mary Beth. I look around. Traffic is blocked in every direction. "I will find out for you," I assure my new friend.

I pick up my phone and type "How can I keep my child off of drugs?" in the search bar; dozens of articles appear. Well, there certainly is a lot of advice out there.

"Hang on," I tell Mary Beth. It might be too late for me, but it isn't too late for her. Quickly, I begin to scan the articles, pressing on the links one at a time. Each of them contains a list. The one bit of advice

that is common to each is, "Talk to your child." Every specialist agrees
that talking to children about drugs is a very important key to deter-
ring drug use. They all agree that parents should talk to their children
from when they are young through college age. Parents should talk
clearly and often.

"So, talk," I advise Mary Beth. I definitely talked a lot to Natalie.

I am a talker. The person who really bears the brunt of my energetic mouth is Peter. Sometimes I am surprised that the guy's ears
don't fall off with all that they are subjected to.

But I talk to my children a lot—too much, according to them.
But I always seem to have something to say, something to warn them
about or counsel them through, and I am pretty good at chitchat, too.

I know that sometimes they think all of my words are overload,
and they are probably right. I still think that my words may be helpful.
And all of my talking is out of love anyway. Especially, I don't want
to ever regret leaving the good words unsaid. I just know that I will
feel better having said what I feel I need to say. What they do with it
is their decision.

Sometimes, like with all of us, what I say doesn't sink in until later.
But that is okay and normal. We all do this. We all hear things that are
not relevant to us, dismiss them, then have an "Aha!" moment later
where we rehear those words, recycle them, and are grateful to have
the knowledge or advice they contain.

When my children are patiently pretending to listen to my endless
counseling, trying not to roll their eyes, and agreeing to sit there in
the first place because Peter has issued a stern instruction to "Listen
to your mother," I always tell them, "I will say this now and you can
hear it later."

Natalie and I have always been close, and we talk a lot. The conversations that I have with her are the most intelligent, honest, insightful, heartfelt, loving, funny, volatile, angry, brutal, and disturbing that I have had—and will ever have—with anyone.

But I don't think I talked enough about drugs. I think I assumed too much. Drugs were not on my radar simply because we had never had any drug abuse in our family or in our immediate circle. I did not speak often enough, clearly enough, or emphatically enough about the perils of drugs and the horror of addiction. Talking about drugs would not have been the typical overexaggerating to make a point that mothers do. It would have all been true. I just assumed she knew drugs are bad. How wrong I was.

I think about all of this wishing for a redo that I know I am not going to get.

The guy behind me beeps his horn again. He is right this time. The intersection has cleared. The light is green. And Mary Beth glides away.

It doesn't matter where you go
It doesn't matter where you've been
There are only limited places to go
With this particular sin

Everything you always thought you couldn't
Things yours never thought you'd do
Become everyday actions
That are able to tear you into two

So, don't look at me
With a misguided look of chagrin
You don't realize I am you
Or at least once upon a time, I had been

You'll drop your pants
Throw away your pride
Steal from everyone
Forget your "cant's"

Cut your strongest ties
And horrid lies will leave your tongue

If you stop, you can still save yourself
Please tell me all the things you won't be
But after all, just keep in mind
Not once, I'd thought I'd become me

—Natalie

"You were born with superpowers," I would often tell Natalie.

I had constantly expressed this to all of my three children. And years before, when I taught young children, I had told my school children the same.

"Everyone is born with unique talents and gifts," I insisted. "And *you* have been given an extra helping. At no additional cost!" I was only half joking.

"The thing is, you must use the powers you have for good and not bad. Because there is almost nothing that we have been given that can't be used for both good and bad. Make the decision," I'd encourage, "to use what you have been blessed with for the better."

"I fucked up, huh Mom?" she once asked me during a particularly bleak time. The situation was so bad that we were sitting together and barely speaking.

I sighed. It certainly was a bluntly phrased, difficult question. I toyed with different answers in my head. I didn't want my words to be crushing, and while I could cheer up almost any situation, I didn't want to sugarcoat it all either. We were in horrible shape, and everyone needs to have it laid on the line for them sometimes.

"Yep," I said.

"I want to die," Natalie says flatly. I believe her. She does want to die. I know this because at one point in my life, I didn't really want to continue either.

When she says these horrific words in such a matter-of-fact way, I am further convinced that she means them. This is a case of "takes one to know one." And because I was one, I recognize that she is one, too.

I know and acknowledge that people express their true feelings in different ways. I know that for some people and for me, when I was at my lowest and at my personal rock bottom, I, too, spoke quietly and matter-of-factly about it. I had given up and didn't have the desire or strength to fight anymore. I felt defeated. Depression had won. And I had lost.

People always speak about the strength, determination, and hope that they can see in other people's eyes, predicting good things and success in their future. So, the problem at this moment is that in Natalie I see none of those things. In her chestnut eyes that are usually bright and beautiful, I can see nothing but hopelessness, defeat, and hurt. Her eyes are cold and lifeless. They look disturbingly darker than usual, and I am unable to detect even a glint of hope.

"I've been there," I tell her. "I've been where you are right now." These words do get her attention, and she looks up at me. While there are so many things that can be said to help a person through depression or any bad experience, I believe that the three most important things they need to hear are that, first, someone has felt this way before; second, things will change; and, third, they are not alone.

Which is why I add, "I can see that you are suffering. But you won't feel this way forever." I believe that the beginning of getting better is for someone to acknowledge their pain, to tell them that others have felt the same. People like to feel that they are unique, except in times of suffering. Then they want company.

They then need to be told that whatever they are feeling will change. One of the things that we know for sure is that everything, good or bad, changes. Nothing stays the same. Sometimes this is a relief and sometimes it is unfortunate.

Probably most importantly, they need to know that help has arrived. And that this help is in the form of you.

I then do what I remember helped me the most when suffering from my profound depression; I sit with her. There will be plenty of time for more words, but she doesn't need to hear them all now.

We sit for a long time, saying nothing. In the silence, I wonder what thoughts are going through Natalie's head as the guilty thoughts go through mine.

I feel pretty sure that all of this is my fault, that I gave her both addiction and depression. Just like I gave her dark brown eyes and hair, just by being her mother, I passed along these unfortunates as well. While I never have had a problem with addiction, I have succumbed to anxiety and depression, and maybe they are all intertwined.

"It's my head," she tells me. "I just can't get out of it." This may sound odd to some, but I understand it. I can relate to trying to run from your own thoughts. I know what it's like to be badgered by thoughts and feelings that just won't stop chasing you.

"I'm sorry," I tell her. "But there is help for that."

She turns to me with her eyes looking somehow darker and even more hopeless than before. I know that this is what people's eyes look like when they are dying.

"I don't think that I can run that fast," she tells me. All I can think to say is, "Please try."

I have handcuffs on
And no one can see them
My screams are so loud
Yet no one can hear 'em

It's like drowning
With everyone in full view
It's like losing my body
And my sanity too

How can no one see
My so obvious pain?
When I make it so clear
With every prick of a vein

But I can't expect them to know me
I don't even know my self
Every trauma I box up
Every emotion I shelf

Regardless of what happens
Especially to me
Things will turn out
Exactly how they were meant to be

—Natalie

"I once got three hundred dollars for myself," she says. We are out to breakfast. I shift uncomfortably in my seat across from her, playing mindlessly with the tea bag, bobbing it up and down. I watch as the drink steams, becoming increasingly darker with each dunk. Her words make me sick to my stomach, and I feel as if I need to run to the bathroom.

But I don't because, first, I want to hear anything else that she says. And second, I am not sure that I will make it anyway. I nod, but she is looking down and doesn't see this. So, when she looks up, I nod again.

I truly believe that children tell the worst of their behavior to their mothers and then watch their faces intently for the single purpose of seeing if any of the love their mother feels for them rises from her face, evaporates, and disappears at the confession.

I have always vowed that my children will never watch my love disappear. So, I work hard at keeping a poker face. I do not play poker and don't know if I am doing this correctly or not.

"I'm sorry," is all I can think to say. And I guess it is appropriate because I do not believe that I have ever felt sorrier in my entire life. I am profoundly sorry that my precious baby girl ever felt so desperate that she lay down and spread her legs for a man in exchange to get what she needed to feel better for a few minutes.

When she says, "It's okay, Mom," I know I have failed at the game of trying to keep an acceptable expression on my face. "I made it through it," she says in consolation to both of us, I guess. But knowing her, mostly to me.

There is not much to say, so I say the only thing I can think that might help. "It's not okay," I mutter, and then a little clearer, I add, "I love you."

I excuse myself to the restroom, leaving Natalie in the booth, playing on her phone. My legs feel wobbly and the bathroom that is twenty feet away looks like a mile in the distance.

As I stare at the ceiling
Wondering how long it'll last
I think of all that's brought me here
All of my past

I know it's not my fault
At least that's what they say
But this comes as a risk
In this dangerous game I play

He held me down
And separated my thighs
I will myself to be anywhere else
But shortly my hope dies

So, as I stare at the ceiling
I will my soul away
It is just too painful right now
In my body to stay

—Natalie

Not often, but every once in a while, Natalie will start the conversation or have a question for me. "What is your greatest fear?" "What's the worst thing you've ever done?" "What's your biggest regret?" Her conversation starters are always a little on the blunt side and often catch me off guard no matter what preemptive padding I have set up. But fair is fair.

So, I answer them truthfully and honestly. Often baring myself to her in ways that I would never expect that I would. During these conversations I have confessed that I got cold feet and almost delayed my wedding; that when I was in competition with a coworker for a promotion and did not get it, I probably deserved to be passed over; and that once upon a time, I dated the lead singer in a band and was a little bit of a groupie.

And on even more rare times than that, I control the radio for a few minutes and play a song for her. My musical choices always lean toward the sappy, sentimental, hopeful side. The songs I like always tell a story. I am a sucker for heartfelt lyrics. Unlike in Natalie's favorite songs, most of my people live in the end.

"Just listen. For a minute. Not even the whole song," I tell her, pressing the play arrow on my connected phone. We are in the car out for a drive with no particular destination, having decided to just "talk."

The piano music begins, and the chorus of voices begins singing, "Surely, the presence of the Lord is in this place..."

I tell her that when Dad and I were first married, we attended a church where this was their closing song every week. I told her that the song spoke to me. And that I try to remember when things are difficult that God is with me and present.

"It helps," I say, my voice trailing off and sounding funny as I lose my courage, worried that she will think what I am saying is stupid.

She is silent, and I cannot tell if she is listening or not. But she is because she says, "I'm really glad for you that this kind of thing helps you. I want you to have comfort." She is genuine and means this. But I am left hanging in midair, wanting more.

In my head, I phrase and rephrase my next sentence, juggling the words. "But it doesn't comfort you?" I ask, with the words coming out exactly how I had decided they wouldn't. I hold my breath, waiting for a response.

Faith is important to me. A cornerstone in my life. As my children were growing, I worked hard at making religion part of their lives. Truthfully, with the older two, I practically injected Catholicism into their eyeballs. More appropriate and less fanatical (and probably more tired), I was less urgent with the third. He got his fair dose of religion. Just in more of a relaxed way. While the book is still out, at the moment, child number three is more religious than the other two.

So, as I await a response that I am not sure is even coming, I am actually waiting for a determination if this is another area in which I tried to succeed and failed.

She answers me. "Not much," she says. Fail. "But I am glad it helps you," she repeats.

"God loves you, Nat," I remind her, thinking that this is probably the very first thing I told her about God on the day and moment I introduced her to Him. I likely pointed to a photo in a children's Bible or to a sculpture on the church altar and said, "That is God." Then I would have said, "He loves you."

"You still love Him right?" I ask, hoping a frantic tone doesn't match my urgent words.

"He kind of stopped loving me first," she tells me more matter-of-factly than I wish.

"So, you don't ever feel Him?" I ask, my last attempt.

There is silence in the car, and I think the conversation is over. She leans back in the seat and sighs.

"But I guess that isn't entirely true…" Wait! Hope? "I actually do have my moments," she admits. Tiny. But still something. "He may come by occasionally," she smirks. Not complete and total failure.

I calculate my score in my head and give myself a passing but dismal grade of C minus.

If she still has moments when she feels the presence of God in her life, then there is hope. She is not without faith. She has religion in her life in some form. God is calling her. He just needs to start shouting so that she can hear Him over the messy, loud noises in her life.

At that moment I feel grateful for what we have and say a one-word prayer, "Please," that God will stop beating around the bush and show Himself to my daughter.

"Save her," I add as I reach over to the dial to stop the song. I had promised her that she only had to listen for a minute. Before I can, she says, "No. Let it play. It's nice."

I withdraw my hand and recalculate: God and I got a solid C+.

I had seen people in movies and television shows withdrawing from drugs. Some of these depictions were better than others, as you would imagine. They are hot and cold. They sweat. They shiver. They talk obsessively. They are silent. They swear, cry, and scream.

No matter how realistic, these portrayals do not do it justice. Witnessing a person, especially a person that you love, go through withdrawal is horrific.

Because television needs to be wrapped up in an hour and movies need to be completed within two, it goes faster than in real life.

When you are watching it and trying to help—while being actually helpless—it is endless.

Natalie once came to me in the middle of the night and told me that she was sick. She asked me if I would sit with her. Of course, I told her that I would. It wasn't long, but it was probably longer than it should have been, before I realized that this was not an ordinary kind of sick.

"Is this withdrawal?" I asked her helplessly. She closed her ashen eyes and I could see the veins in her eyelids. Her hands were clenched and her body was rigid, occasionally jerking involuntarily. In anguish, she nodded yes. She couldn't see me, but I nodded in understanding and closed my eyes in anguish, too. And together, we settled in for an unsettling night.

I have lied, oh have I lied
And I wish that was the worse
The struggles I encounter
Is it karma or a curse?

I have stolen from family
Always saying it's the last time
I have stolen from strangers
For no reason or rhyme

I have sold pictures
I have even sold me
All lines eventually get crossed
No matter what they may be

You can try and continue
But just give it some time
You will go against your beliefs
Whether it's moral or crime

So, heed my warning
Or just don't
But I can promise you you'll do all the things
You swore you won't

—Natalie

"Tell me something I don't know," I tell Natalie.

When I am alone with each of my three children and want them to talk to me, I always ask them to tell me something that I don't know about them or about anything at all actually.

There are few rules to this game. The "something" can be about them or someone else. It can be funny or sad, startling or mundane. It can be huge or just a detail. It can be obvious or a secret confession.

Sometimes, I am so eager in wanting to find out something new about them that, if we are driving, I tell them that I won't stop driving until they tell me something.

When I appear in their bedroom as unwanted, drop-in company, I refuse to leave (which they desperately want me to do) until they hand me over at least a crumb.

I guess, the only rule there actually is to this game is that there is no lying. Whatever they tell me must be the truth. I think this game is good for both of us. They get something off their chest that they might not normally think to say. And knowing something, anything, else about them helps to calm my crazy. Therapeutic for all of us.

For me, it is a peek into their lives that I might not normally get. I am always careful to be okay with whatever they offer. Or more accurately, I should say, I am always careful to act okay with whatever they tell me. I know that my reaction or lack of reaction, which I guess is actually a reaction, is important to keeping the game pure.

Keeping myself from reacting too much is sometimes difficult, though. I have been guilty of laughing out loud or gasping in spite of my vow. And keeping my poker face is not easier with one kid versus another. No matter the child, I ask and then brace myself. Each one of them has surprised me happily or sadly at one point or another.

When I play with Trevor, my youngest, he often tells me about school and friends while I am secretly praying for more information about his love life and the long list of female friends rummaging around in his life. I also, being the creator of this game, have veto power and can reject an offering if I already know this droplet of information or if what they tell me is unfairly tiny. Although, when Trevor simply noted, "I knew Tom," referring to a classmate who had tragically taken his own life, it was enough. The tone in his voice and the expression on his face told me all of the words that were too troubling to speak.

During this game is also when I learned that Trevor, whose life is mostly happy, had won an award at school. But then, on the other side, he told me all of the details of a broken heart that I am sure that I would have never been privy to otherwise.

I have learned so much about my oldest child, Jason, while playing this game. Jason and I talk a lot, but this practice is still a great conversation starter, and just when I think I know everything there is to know about him, he comes up with a bit of his life that I never knew.

With Jason, I have found out the truth about situations that were previously hazy as well as that he has so many fears I never knew he had. And most notably, it was during this game, when I showed up at his apartment, flopped comfortably down on his couch, and announced that I was not leaving until I was somehow smarter than when I arrived, that he told me that he secretly suffered from severe anxiety and depression.

Actually, this was old information. Sometimes mothers just know their children better than they know themselves. I knew this about six years before that day. This would be, technically, a breach of the rules of the game, but I let it pass. He needed to say it out loud, and I wanted to hear it verbalized.

And as you would expect, because Natalie's life is a little messier than her brothers, playing this game with her tends to be riskier and, might I say, a bit more interesting than with my other children. But of course, playing any game with Natalie is more interesting than playing with anyone else.

It was during a car ride with Natalie in which I was driving at a steady clip the opposite direction of home, promising to never return to our house again, that she told me she lost her virginity way too early.

She told me that she has tried to commit suicide. I remember exactly where I was when she told me this. We were in the middle of the grocery store surrounded by canned goods and I was loading the shopping cart with creamed corn for Thanksgiving dinner. I've never held another can of corn since without thinking of that moment.

It was in the dark at three o'clock in the morning with her sitting on the edge of my bed that I learned she had an abortion at fifteen.

And it was sitting in the backyard on a sunny, hot summer day, staring into a perfectly cloudless sky, that she told me she thinks it would be better if she had not been born.

All when I simply asked her to tell me something I don't know. I always ask, because I always want to know. Even when I don't.

chapter Three

In the Middle of It All

"Thank you for coming. Nice weather, huh?" I say, hoping that I don't sound as uncomfortable as I feel.

Jeez! Listen to me! I am attempting to feign a lightness I do not feel while I put the car in reverse and begin backing out of the garage. *My God! Did I really just talk about the weather?* I do not feel light.

Actually, I feel as if I am suffocating. Things with Natalie have not been good or even okay for too long now. And while we are people who seem to have more lows than highs, we are at a particularly low, low. She is obviously using, and if I were to guess, she is using many substances and all of the time.

She had been missing for two or three days at a time, several times, over the last month. And at this moment, I am grateful to have her sitting beside me in the passenger seat.

Many times, over the past few months, I have wondered if I would see her again. So, I had promised myself that if I got her physically back, I would do everything that I could to hold her long enough to talk some sense into her. She needed help urgently and needed to see this.

But I also know my daughter, and I am not going to get anywhere by screaming and yelling at her. I feel if I can engage her in some heartfelt, meaningful conversation, I just might be able to break the glass surrounding her and get through.

She stumbled through the door early this morning, my heart skipping a beat when I heard the key in the lock and the jangling of the metal tag on the dog's collar as he joyfully, at three o'clock in the morning, rushed to meet her.

That is one of the ways I knew it was her and not an intruder. His happy trot was music to my ears. I was sure that her condition wasn't great, but alive and home were more than I had before.

For the first time in weeks, I rolled over in bed and actually slept. Before I did, I whispered into the darkened room and possibly to Peter, "She's home." I am pretty sure Peter had not been roused and hadn't heard me, but maybe my words seeped into him anyway so he could sleep more peacefully.

The next morning, Natalie was in the kitchen when I went downstairs. With a hug and a kiss, I kept my greeting pleasant, hoping to convey that I was glad she was back. I suggested a ride, holding my breath for her answer.

She doesn't always accept. Her anxieties and fears make her a little reclusive. I was desperate. I needed to have her alone for a bit in order to reach her. I was relieved when she volleyed my offer pleasantly back to me and headed off to get shoes.

Taking rides together is something that we have often done. We are both comfortable in the car. I think she feels safe, and I have her trapped. There must be something about the motion that soothes both of us.

Our route is always the same. We start out at our home and drive through our town and the next two towns, make a U-turn, circle back, and do it all in reverse. I drive and Natalie controls the music. She selects the playlist from her phone.

They say that you can tell a lot about a person by the art they like. The art, music, and movies that speak to them can help you understand them. I believe this to be true.

Often Natalie's song choices disturb me. Mostly, she plays country songs from a mix of artists. They are all always sad. They speak of heartbreak, betrayal, addiction, and suicide. We don't even pretend that the reason she chooses these particular songs is for any other reason than that they resonate with her and that she feels them.

I went out on a limb and asked her once, praying in the moments that I waited for her answer that she would say anything but this. She did not and confirmed my guess by telling me, "They are me."

We start our drive and I always promise to ease into the difficult subjects, the topics she doesn't want to discuss, the hard things, the hurtful things. I always fail at this. I know my time is limited, and with the digital numbers on the dashboard teasing me and counting down before me, I feel urgent.

When we begin our journey, someone in the song has just lost the love of their life and is thinking that life is not worth living.

"Thanks for riding with me," I tell her, reaching over and caressing her arm. "And thanks for coming home." I always start off good this way. Then the song changes, someone is drunk and doing things that they plan on regretting in the morning. And I blow my easy entrance by going full-on into a lecture on how "we" (I include all of us) are struggling and follow it up by spouting off the virtues of rehab. She becomes angry, and I ask her not to.

"I'm really trying to help. Really!"

With an eye roll, she tells me that I must have been reading again. This is an insult. Because, according to her, I don't know what I am talking about. Because the books and the people who write them are stupid, cliché, lame, and useless. With my sensitivities exposed, what I hear her say, even though she hasn't said this at all, is that I am all of these things.

My voice gets a little louder as I point out that maybe all of the people who write these books are truly trying to help. And defending a bunch of people that I don't even know, I ask her if she thinks all of us should run out, buy heroin, and stick needles in our arms so that we truly, truly understand?

We both retreat, both cracking our separate windows a couple of inches to cool off.

In silence, we listen to a girl who has apparently died young, expected it all of the time, and wants everyone to wear pearls to her funeral.

Natalie knows that I am dying with every lyric and compromises her vow of silence by saying, "I love this song," while turning up the volume. Four simple, unfair words. Four simple words that hurt as they were designed to, and I resist the urge to beg and plead with her to not die young like the girl in the song. *Don't make me wear pearls!* Nobody ever promised that they would fight nice.

"What are you doing?" Natalie asks as I pull off the highway.

"McDonald's," I say, motioning toward the golden arches and easing into the drive-thru lane.

"I don't want anything!" she insists.

"I do," I say, blunt and snide. "Maybe everything isn't about you."

I have found that Natalie and people her age are masters at hiding whether they actually receive subtle messages, so I have no idea if she got my message or not.

I order a Diet Coke and a large order of french fries. "Not even fries?" I ask.

"Nope."

When I was pregnant with each of my children, I craved one food while I carried each of them. With Jason, I ate chicken with onions. With Trevor, I ate almost nothing but burgers. And with Natalie, it was McDonald's french fries. She consumed a million in utero. And I actually have a photo of her at about nine months old eating her first fry with only two teeth and a mouth full of gums. We share this love affair with french fries together.

I will be able to gauge just how angry she is with me by her response to my offer. "Nothing," she insists.

"Wait!" she blurts out quickly. "Water."

I always think it funny that water is the drink of the disgruntled. It is the drink that people choose when they are being uncooperative, belligerent, and want to send the message that they are angry. Water is also a great I-want-a-divorce or Grandma-has-died beverage. Apparently, when people choose to drink water, they demand respect and should be taken more seriously. Drinking water is the equivalent of holding a picket sign and marching around in a defiant circle.

"Are you sure?" I ask one last time as I am paying the young man in the window.

"Completely," she tells me.

Okay, she's not mad. She's furious. I take my change and pull up a few feet to put the coins in my purse and open the straw.

"Wait!" Natalie says, suddenly turning to see if there is anyone behind us. "Back up!" she orders. "Fries." I am not sure if it is the amazing aroma of the potatoes or if she just isn't that mad. But I will take it either way.

Armed with our comfort food, we continue our journey. The young girl in the last song has been put to rest, and in the new song, someone has a gun to their head. Sad, but to me, not as devastating as the last.

We continue our ride. I listen to the dismal lyrics and wonder if Natalie is listening as closely as I am. I glance over at her but still can't tell. Her eyes are closed and her face is tilted up toward the light.

"The sun feels good, huh?" I ask. *Jeez, I'm back on the weather again!* She agrees with a small sound and a nod. Then I say the only thing I can think to say. I decide this is okay, because it's the only thing that matters. It's the only thing I really care if she remembers. "I love you," I tell her. "And I don't want to lose you. You are the best thing that ever happened to me."

"And you are the best thing that ever happened to me," she says, her eyes still shut, reaching for my hand.

I take her hand and squeeze it. Mother, daughter, forever connected. It feels good to agree on something. Maybe our love for each other is the only thing that we agree on. But maybe this is all that we need to agree on to get through this nightmare. Maybe this is enough.

The song changes and I listen closely to the words of pain and despair. And without meaning to, I sigh, feeling a little tired from the driving and defeated by the song.

"Wait for it," Natalie tells me, yawning loudly, with her eyes still closed.

I lean in, turn the volume up, and listen more closely. At the last moment, when there is nothing but despair, hope is found because the woman in the song, who is compared to a broken-winged bird, learns to fly anyway.

In my head I am explaining passionately to Natalie: *"You see! We are those injured birds! But injured birds can learn to fly again!"* But I know this would be overdoing it. So, I settle for exclaiming, "Oh!" while turning it up even louder. "I like this one!"

Natalie laughs, shakes her head, and opens her eyes just long enough to roll them at me.

"You make it hard for me to kill myself." She sighs in frustration. Her words make me flinch.

"Good" is my sighed retort.

Natalie and I are driving home from a miserable lunch together. I am not in the best of moods, and she is struggling even a little more than usual. She has a lot of nervous habits, and while I try to be sympathetic and patient, I do not always succeed. On this day, I am failing.

She is nervous and jittery, which is making me nervous and jittery. I am displeased at the way she is dressed, and we have been arguing over the stupidest things the entire time we have been together. She told me something horrid, and I said something critical in response. Then she told me to leave her alone and I told her I loved her. I'm not even sure why I said it, it just seemed to fit. Because as awful as it all is, I still think we can try to rebuild. Because I love her anyway.

Actually, what she said is that most people hate her. So, I said, "I don't hate you." That's when she said I make it hard for her to kill

herself and I said "good" more bitterly than I wished to, kind of spitting it out of my mouth.

"If you do, I will never have another happy day," I remind her. I am
glad I am looking directly at her because I am able to detect the slightest, most imperceptible nod of her head, signaling her understanding.

I don't say anything else for the rest of the ride home. I am too
busy juggling all of the thoughts of the ways I am going to love her
so much that she will never want to leave me even if she wants to
leave herself.

What an awful thing it is
Being betrayed by your head
It leaves you feeling hopeless
And just filled with dread

Searching everywhere
For a cure that exists
Looking and looking
For some kind of fix

Always looking for
A release in this life
Something away from the pain
And away from the strife

So, I search and search
Until I'm tired and alone
There's only so many mistakes
For that I can atone

But I still continue and try
In hopes for a better day
In hopes of comfort
And a reason to stay

—Natalie

Will in a lil'

Natalie! This is ridiculous! You have been saying that for three days!

There is no response for four minutes. I am staring at my phone, begging for that little conversation bubble with the dots to pop up that tells me that she is typing a reply. I wait and watch. There is nothing.

"Natalie," I whine out loud. *Natalie?!* I type.

Then thinking that I am kind of yelling at her via text and that the double punctuation, especially the question mark followed by the exclamation point, is overdoing it, I soften it and type: *Nat?*

Still nothing for another five minutes. *Natalie?* I try again.

Then finally there is life from the other end and the dots dance. They tease me and rotate in a circle for an awfully long time, making me think that this is going to be a long message and not the measly few words it ends up being.

I'll come soon. Promise

Where are you? I ask, knowing I will likely get either a meager reply of just a word or two or a possibly lengthy flat-out lie. Natalie rewards me with the latter.

The text is quite long for her, but she is lying. *I am really fine. Have just been with a friend. Having a good time. Watching movies and eating. Just chillin. You would like him.*

Somehow, I doubt all of that, I text.

And I know, in fact, she is not fine. This person is no friend. I will concede that she might be having what her definition of a good time is. And I doubt that they are simply watching television and eating. And I know for sure that I would definitely not like him, whoever he is.

You need to get help. Let me help you honey please. Come home. I know with this text I am being emotionally suffocating and a load. No one likes this. But I am desperate.

The last four days have been pure hell. I was really thinking this was it. This was finally the time that I was not going to hear from her again. This was going to be the moment when the nightmare turned into a tragedy. The tragedy that was going to assure that I would never have another happy day in my life.

She walked out the door on a Tuesday around dinner time telling me that she would be back in an hour. I spent the next three days calling and texting her phone without getting one response. Sometimes the phone was dead; sometimes it was accepting my advances.

Oddly, this fact is what kept me from going completely crazy. If the phone was dead and stayed dead either she was too impaired to charge it or she was even worse. But the fact that it was dead and then alive told me that she was at least okay enough that in between whatever no good she was up to, she could charge the phone.

You are not living a right life, I tell her. *People should not live this way. There is no excuse for this. You were raised better than this.*

I know I should not be saying all of this. It is all too much. Even though they are all the right words, this is not the time, place, or manner. But I cannot seem to help myself and my finger continues to type, punching at the defenseless letters on the keyboard of my phone. The only defense I have is that I have had the last four days to rehearse these words and I am desperate to deliver them.

My words are a bipolar mix of support and understanding, condemnation and criticism. Nowhere in any book or manual instructing you about how to talk to an addict will you find this approach as a suggestion. But I seem to be married to this method and continue to barrage Natalie with insulting compassion…if there is such a thing. My excuse is that I am a distraught mother. That is always my excuse.

You need to get away from these people. These people that you are calling your friends are trash. They are bad people honey. And you act like trash when you are with them. You are better than all of this. You are capable of having a wonderful life. Just come home. And let Dad and I help you. That's what we are here for. That's what parents do. Dad says that maybe we all need a week in Rehoboth or New York City.

Peter did not say this. He actually said that we all need about five years in rehab or even longer in a funny farm. These are my added touches because these are mine and Natalie's two happy places. I know these suggestions are ridiculous and that the calm of the beach or the glorious hustle and bustle of the energetic city will not solve anything. Because if they truly could, they would have by now. And if there was even the slightest chance that going to these places would help, Natalie and I would, together, become mermaids and never leave the water and I would pitch a tent in Times Square. But because these are the only carrots I can think to dangle, I wave them shamefully in front of Natalie's face.

Really?! she texts back.

I note her use of double punctuation and almost dance. Good God, she bit the carrot! Maybe with these promises, I can actually get her to come home! I experience a fleeting moment of guilt at my hollow promises, then assuage these feelings by telling myself that I really do mean what I am saying and will actually take her to the beach or the city, but after she comes home, goes to rehab, gets well, and stays well for a bit.

I do not add this, of course.

Another troubling part of all of this is that during previous trips with Natalie to the beach and the city, while breathing a sigh of relief that she was safe and away from all of the bad stuff and horrible influences, she had made connections, finding drugs there as well. They always find each other.

Of course! I exclaim and add an emoji that looks like a wave to me. Or is it the wind?

I am old. And emojis are new to me, and my eyes are old as well and not the best. Once I am on the emoji screen, I can never remember how to get back to the letter keyboard. But I am on a winning streak and venture to this emoji-land that I don't navigate well and may never return from. I am searching desperately for a big city symbol or something like it when Natalie texts again.

I gotta go.

Wait! Why? What do you mean? I press send.

I'll see you soon for sure, she tells me.

Define soon, I demand.

I am being confrontational again. But I am panicking. I am losing touch with her and know that she is drifting away.

Tomorrow for sure, she types.

Natalie no!! Now!! I screech out loud and via text.

You are doing the wrong thing! Come home so that I can help you.

Soon. I promise, she tells me.

I am livid. *I am furious with you!* I tell her.

Sorry Mummy, she texts.

I am still beyond angry but when I see the word "Mummy" typed out like that, I can almost hear her voice saying it and my heart squeezes.

I sit there watching the screen, waiting for her to say something while trying to think of some compelling magic words that will make her come home. Why isn't my pull, the might of her own mother, stronger than the pull of these horrible people and the drugs that they provide?

Natalie!! is all I can think to type, desperately trying to keep the dissolving connection between us alive.

Gotta go Mom, she types. *Bye.*

I am still angry, but devastation and heartache are overtaking the feeling. I sit there holding my phone in my hand, fixated on this magic electronic box that sometimes provides my only connection to my daughter. I think of what to type next. Is there anything left to say? I know that for the time being, I have lost her. But I won't let it just lie there like this. That's not how mothers operate.

I pick up the phone, clean the smudged screen off with the sleeve of my shirt, and on the fresh glossy screen, I type the three words that I will always say. I express the one thing that will always be true. The one thing that I want her to know she can always count on. When she doesn't respond, I retype the same words.

I love you.

I do this because, simply and no matter what, the last text should always be I love you. I wait an excruciating seven minutes, doing nothing but staring at and polishing the phone until the conversation bubble appears and the dots begin to parade, marching in their designated pattern, relieving the painful pressure that I am feeling in my heart and chest just a tiny bit. I count the dots. There are seven of them on the screen at the same time. The dots halt, then disappear, and Natalie's words take their place.

Love you too, she says. I know she does this because she also believes that no matter what, the last text should always be I love you. Just in case.

The dog and I are home alone. I am trying to distract myself by watching TV. We are watching *The Waltons.* Jeez, how I love these people! I want to live on a mountain. But specifically, I want to live with the Waltons on Walton's Mountain.

Specifically, I want to be Olivia, the mother. I want to successfully juggle six children, as well as a couple of wayward nieces, nephews, a husband, and in-laws. I want to learn to crochet, and I want to make apple pies with apples that I peeled myself and leave them out to cool on the kitchen windowsill. I want to live in a more uncomplicated place in a more uncomplicated time.

Olivia is explaining to Mary Ellen that she will realize her dreams of being a doctor one day when the screen flickers, the sound goes out, and then almost instantly, a new picture appears. The volume is blaring.

"For just ten dollars a month or one hundred and twenty dollars a year, you can become a member of the church!" the preacher on the screen tells me from his stage. The camera pans the crowd of thousands in front of him who are all hooting and yelling their encouragement for him and for God. I am perplexed as to how the television got onto this channel and search for the remote buried somewhere in the comforter that I have wrapped around me.

I discover the remote under the dog's foot. He must have stepped on it and changed the channel. I take the remote and hold it outright and am just about to change the station back to rejoin Olivia and Mary Ellen in Mary Ellen's floral bedroom when the preacher on the screen ropes me in. He reaches out of the television and grabs me by the heart.

"Pray for yourself!" he instructs. "Pray for someone else! Have a struggling child? So many of today's youth are lost! It is not their fault. The Devil has made them stray!"

"Yes," I say out loud, agreeing with him.

"We can help you get them back!" he promises me. "We can lead them back to the church and Jesus! For only ten dollars a month or one hundred twenty dollars a year, we will lead your baby back to the Lord."

This last part is hitting below the belt. Calling anyone's child their baby pulls at a parent's heartstrings. I wonder if this guy thought to say this himself or if someone else did by speaking into the earpiece that is attached to his microphone. As he continues his sales pitch, I study him. He is a nice-looking guy, immaculately groomed and wearing an expensive suit. I am not sure that he is actually representing God well or has God's ear like he is claiming, but he certainly is putting on a captivating show.

I keep watching and listening. He's promising me instant results. I am thinking that he means that I will get my results as soon as he gets authorization on my credit card or my check clears, but he doesn't say this. How nice of him to take checks.

When my kids were really little and they were doing something good, I would tell them enthusiastically, "You are making God smile! He is smiling right now just because of you!" I, unfortunately, also turned this around and sometimes told them, "Aw, look you are making God frown. Please stop that."

I believe in the power of prayer, both my own prayers and the prayers of others, but I also know that this is not the way it works. I don't claim to know exactly how God answers us, but I know this is not it. I feel compelled to tell him that he definitely is not making God smile right now. I want to tell him that, furthermore, I am pretty sure he is making God frown. I actually believe that he is making God roll his eyes, and that he should consider a different career path.

I know he is not going to heal my Natalie. I know what he is say-ing is not true. I know that no matter what I pay this guy, he is not going to heal my broken daughter. I know he is just trying to take my money so he can buy more expensive suits.

I don't believe a word he is saying because I am smarter than this. So, why I reach for my purse, take out my cell phone and credit card, and authorize a payment of one hundred and twenty dollars, I am not exactly sure. I guess I just don't know what else to do.

I want to hurt everyone I love,
So, after I'll never hurt them again
Whether brother, father, or mother
Or simply just a friend

I see the pain I cause you
Every single day
And those are the moments when
The voices start to say

Stop being so selfish
Give them a break
To ease so many
Only one life you must take

—Natalie

I walk into Natalie's room after calling countless times up the stairs and find her sitting on the floor in the fetal position. I guess she didn't quite make it all the way to the bed. She is shivering while at the same time her skin is glistening with sweat. She is wearing only her bra and panties. She is impaired.

"What did you do, Nat?" I ask her. "What did you take?"

She had been pretty good for a while, or it seemed that way anyway. But now, we are back to this.

Predictably, she mutters, "Nothing," in response to my question.

"Yeah, you never take anything," I grumble back.

I start to feel guilty for my snideness, then decide I am entitled to this. I don't like how she looks and am not comfortable dealing with it without guidance.

I go out into the hallway, call Peter on my cell, and describe the situation as I see it. He allays my fears and tells me that she probably needs to just pass through it. But tells me to call again if I need to.

I go back into the room and help her onto the bed. She is groggy, and I practically have to lift her. I am not strong enough, so I end up pushing her. I cover her up with the blankets and look around the room, trying to find a place to sit amongst the mess. There is no place, so I push a pile of clothes to the side and sit on the floor with my back leaning up against the bed. I should clean and make better use of my time in this room while I am in here. But that's another thought and inclination that I ignore, and for the millionth time I wonder how we got here. How did we get in this horrible place?

"Mommy," Natalie moans as she stretches and turns. "Stay with me," she whines and, with her eyes still closed, reaches outward with her hand, wanting me to grab it.

I am less worried now, realizing that Peter was right and that she would gradually sleep it off, which it appears she is doing, and I am now becoming angry. So, I do what most mothers I know would do first in these situations: I yell at her.

"You need to shape up! Things need to change! You need to get help! We CANNOT continue to live this way!"

I watch her on the bed, waiting for her reaction, which is stupid on my part because she is far too impaired to comprehend what I am saying, let alone care about my words or feelings.

"I know," she manages weakly, appearing to drift in and out of consciousness.

I realize that she does not mean these words now nor will she remember these words later. She still has her eyes closed, and her arm remains outstretched with her hand dangling, waiting for mine.

"Love me," she whines. I shake my head and sigh, then take her hand and hold it in mine while saying, "Of course, I love you. I always have and always will. And I'm not going anywhere." She nods, then drifts further away.

Sitting on the edge of the bed this way reminds me of the times that I would sit at her bedside when she was little and had chronic ear infections. I would give her the medicine and sit with her late into the night. She would be groggy and exhausted, drifting in and out of sleep, moaning and whining fragments of sentences—mostly, "Mommy."

I knew then that she was not awake and didn't appear to be hearing me and would not remember anything of this night in the morning. But I just could never bring myself to leave the room and go back to bed. When someone calls for their mother, she should answer them, whether they know she does or not.

Remember my intentions,
My dreams and my hope
When I'm gone, do what you need
Whatever helps you cope

Remember when I tried
Not only when I failed
Remember the fun times we had
Not just when I bailed

Remember our conversations
Way late at night
Don't remember me losing
Remember my fight

Remember how I held you
So very close
Forget when I lied
Just to get a dose

So, remember how I loved you
So very dear
Remember the difference I made
During my time here

—Natalie

"Please don't make me bury you," I say to her, understanding that this is an odd statement to make. A very blunt request that people don't often let themselves think, let alone say out loud.

"Please," I add.

"I'll try," Natalie responds with, in my opinion, a lackluster and less-than- adequate answer.

"Natalie," I scold.

"I said that I am trying," she tells me.

"Are you really?" I say, getting a little mad.

I regret these words and my tone because they will change the trajectory of the conversation I was hoping to have. I don't want to argue. We have been doing too much of that lately.

"I'm terrified that you are going to have me putting you in a box and then have me putting that box in the ground," I say. She doesn't respond at first, and I wonder if she is contemplating the unsettling picture that I painted with my last words.

When she does respond, I know that she heard me, but I cannot tell if what I said rattled her or not. It doesn't appear to have, by the nonplussed way that she answers.

"Then don't," she says simply. I don't know what to make of these words. I can't tell how she means them. Is she saying, "I don't care?" Like, "I don't need you to bury me. I'll show you and bury myself." Or is she saying something else?

What she says next has me realize that she is telling me something else. "I don't want to be buried."

"What do you mean?" I ask, pretty sure that I do know what she means. I am not sure I have the strength for this conversation. I am tired. "I'm asking you not to die. I'm asking you to try harder." Even to me, my voice sounds weary.

She ignores these requests from me and says, "But when I do, I don't want you to bury me."

I am troubled by the fact that she chose to say "when" instead of "if." I am regretting starting this conversation and backpedal, trying to get out of it.

"Well, let's not talk about it," I say. Right then, I am wondering if she remembers any of the conversations we had about death when she was very little.

I have never asked any of my children this question but would like to. Death is one of those subjects that they asked more about when they were very little, less so as they grew, then not at all once they were entering adulthood. I wonder if this is because the answers that I gave them to these tricky questions were enough. I hope so.

"It's not going to happen. Nobody is burying anybody," I insist.

Then I sit there resisting the temptation to say something I would always tell my children when they were little and asked if I or they were going to die.

I used to tell them that I will live to be one hundred. "I will have lived a wonderful life," I'd said, "Mostly because of you. I will be very old and will be ready to begin again, healthy and happy in heaven." Then, before they would have time to ask or get sad, I would tell them, "And you will know this and not be too sad."

They would invariably then ask about their own mortality. I would then tell them that they would also live to be one hundred. They, also, will have lived a wonderful life. Not because of me. But because they were simply wonderful. And then they would go to heaven, starting happy again.

But instead of all of this, I just repeat, "Nobody is going to be burying anybody."

I realize that I am actually trying to console myself just as much as I am trying to be consoled and am doing a pretty good job of it when she says, "I want to be cremated." I manage a nod and a grimace simultaneously.

This combination of expressions is a unique skill, and I am pretty sure is becoming my signature look. I don't know what to say and can only think that if this horrible day ever comes, I selfishly want it to be about me. And I will want to have a place to visit. God! Why does that sound so horrible? And morbid! Does this qualify as morbid? And it is not like I can justify my choice with some compelling wealth of evidence or plea that putting someone you love in a box in the ground and then covering that box with dirt is somehow better than burning them up and putting them in an urn to put on top of a mantle and hope not to knock it over when you dust, so I just say honestly, "I'd like a place to visit."

This time, she nods with understanding.

"If I am not mistaken," I tell her, "Pap kind of wanted to be cremated, I think. But he didn't actually insist upon it."

"Good old Pap," she says.

My father was an unselfish man when it came to things like this. Even if he did feel strongly about being cremated versus being traditionally buried, he would have made it about us and put our preferences over his. The only time that I ever doubted my choice and second-guessed it for a bit was the first night it rained after he died, and I wished that he was safe in the house with me.

"Yep," I agree, missing my father and thinking that I haven't been to the cemetery in a while to visit his grave. I should make more time to visit him. Maybe he could help. But I do believe that he can hear me from anywhere I am and not only when I am standing in front of his gravestone. Maybe I don't need a place to visit as much as I think that I do.

Natalie shrugs and maybe this bothers me more than anything. She is a fighter, a debater, an arguer. She does not give up on her opinions regarding the issues she believes in. Has she given up? Is she so sure she is going to die that she doesn't care anymore? I feel helpless and need to say something brilliant right here but for the life of me can think of nothing even close to smart to say.

"Nobody is going to die," I say just to fill the silence because the quiet is uncomfortable. "Not me. Not you. So, no one will be burying or cremating anyone."

She says nothing for a moment, but then she looks at me with weary eyes and asks, "Not even when we are one hundred?"

I am at church. It is a regular Sunday morning except that I am fascinated by the back of an older man seated about ten pews ahead of me.

The back of his head looks just like the back of my father's head. The hair is the same color grey and he even has the same bald spot, a swirl of hair that looks just like my father's did before he died. Do all old men go bald in the same pattern?

How neat it would be if, when the guy turns around to offer the people beside him the sign of peace, he actually ended up being my father? I am so consumed by this thought that I forget to sit down after the opening hymn and, for a moment, I am standing alone inside of the church.

I hurriedly sit and duck a bit in the pew, knowing that of course this man is not my father but distracted by the idea of my father coming back for a visit. I decide that, although this guy is not my father, he is indeed a sign.

During the first reading, I am wishing I would have spotted him sooner because if I had, I would have sat in the pew behind him. During the second reading, I scan the pews between him and me, and decide that depending on just how married the other parishioners are to their present seats, I just might be able to fit right between a middle-aged couple and another lady in a red dress.

During the alleluia, I get brave and make my move. I excuse myself from my present pew and seat, whispering apologies as I climb over the family of five to my right. "Sorry," I repeat five times, one for each of them as I wiggle out of the row.

While the priest begins the gospel, which is an important part of the Mass and not the time in which I should be jockeying for a new position, I scoot up the aisle and almost to the row where my sort-of father is.

The guy behind my kinda-dad does not notice me at first. Or he is ignoring me. Either way, he is looking straight ahead at the priest, just like he should be. I wait for him to glance sideways and before he does, a man standing behind him motions for me to sit next to him. He thinks I have just arrived and wants to be gracious. I smile and nod in a declining sort of way. I don't want him to feel rejected, but I am on a mission.

Finally, my target notices me and gives me a sort of, "what do you want?" look. I am tempted to volley back a "what do you think I want?" look, but we are in church, so no need to get snarky. Instead, I smile at him and point to the seat next to his wife who either doesn't notice me or is ignoring me. "May I step by you?" I whisper, still smiling.

He hesitates and gives me a not-so-Christian look. This isn't totally surprising; people are on their most Christian-like behavior during church—until you ask them to give up their seat or move an inch in any direction. I am sure there is a perfectly logical, personal space, psychological explanation for this, but I don't know it. All I know is that by the look on his face and by the way he nods at the seat to the left of his wife, he is communicating something like, "We are here. We are in church. So, at least for this one hour, I am going to do as Jesus would and let you sit down; but don't think for one second that I am going to make this easy. I'm just going to let you uncomfortably crawl over me."

He nudges his wife and steps back a millimeter, and I smile bigger and thank him. The Gospel has been read and the priest is now starting his homily, so they sit as I creep over their knees. Once I'm past them, I plop down, now positioned between his wife and the lady in the red dress, which also positions me behind my pseudo dad—but not directly enough to guarantee that he will shake my hand during the offering of peace. I need to be where the lady in red is.

So, while the priest talks, I wiggle a bit closer to her, thinking that my theory of personal space will not fail me and that she will move away a bit and allow me to shift closer into position. She does. But I still need a few more inches. So, while we are standing and reciting the Our Father, I shove my purse right up against hers so that when we reseat ourselves again, she takes exception to this.

She gives me a look then that suggests I might be a pickpocket, and she harrumphs a little, but she grabs her purse and moves down. Success! I am right where I need to be.

I was not wrong. The up-close look of the older gentleman's head is just like I expected. Perfectly like my dad's. I nearly crumble into tears when I realize that his aftershave has him kind of smelling like my father, too. I wait anxiously as we get closer to the offering of peace and become a little worried that maybe he isn't big on this ritual. Maybe he won't take part at all or might only offer to those beside him without ever turning around.

My worry is for nothing. At the sign of peace, I keep one eye on him and quickly offer my hand to the wife on my right (I ignore the husband; he doesn't want to shake hands with me anyway), and then to the lady in red to my left. I am efficient because I want to be ready to receive peace from my father.

He does not disappoint me. He not only offers his one hand to shake but with a little bit of an elderly quiver holds my arm with his other hand. He smiles beautifully and says, "Peace be with you, darling." My father used to call me "Darling."

I nod and can barely choke out the word "peace" in return. But I know I am smiling and hope he notices the gratitude in my moist eyes. We hang on to each other for just one second longer than is usual.

I spend the rest of the Mass staring at his beautiful bald head and soaking in his scent.

"Remember, we need to be fun," I tell Peter as I apply an extra layer of lip gloss to my already super-shiny lips. It's something I do when I am nervous and need courage. Some people correct their posture and offer a firm handshake. Superheroes strap on a red cape. I add glitter to my lips. I have no idea why, but it makes me feel ready and more prepared. "We are not fun," Peter points out in a very bland way that seems to illustrate his point.

"I know that!" I snap, taking a moment to glare at him in between doing my top lip and my bottom lip. "But we need to be fun if we are going to have friends."

We are getting ready to go out to dinner with friends—something we hadn't done in ages. Without really meaning to or even knowing that we were doing it, we had somehow let go of all of our friends. When you are in the middle of a family crisis like we had been with Natalie, it's easy to focus on only that at the expense of everything else. We were dealing with the emergency of Natalie's addiction exclusively and had no energy left for other things. If your house is on fire, you put the fire out before you do anything else. Our house had been on fire for quite some time now.

The problem is that we underestimated the problem, its giganticness and its persistence. Addiction is a multilayered, complicated issue that defies quick and easy fixes. When people ask how Peter and I are still standing and how we are managing other things, I always say that we are learning how to live around the mess. For survival, you need to learn to do this.

Sometimes, I will find myself out somewhere—usually someplace pleasant or festive—I will look around at everyone else there, and I will try to imagine what secrets their lives hold. What sad things are behind their smiles? No matter what I ever imagine other people to be going through, I always seem to feel sorrier for me and end up feeling sure that I am the owner of the most shameful, ugly secret. This feeling always leads me to feel that I have no right to be where I am; at a nice place, having a good time. Instead, I should be home, putting my house in order, taking care of my business, fixing my daughter.

I have come to realize that this is not true. I have spent nearly all of my time and energy on helping my daughter. I always do and I always will, without regret or resentment. But just like they tell you if you experience an airplane emergency—put your own oxygen mask on first and the other person's mask second. I not only deserve to live a little, I *need* it.

"All I am saying is that we need to be fun, because no one wants to go out with or be friends with people who are not fun," I say as we are getting into the car. "So, no dismal talk; no talk about kid problems."

"No crying?" Peter asks jokingly as we head onto the highway toward the restaurant.

"Of course not!" I admonish.

Forty minutes later, we are sitting across the table from our friends and we are crying. "I'm sorry," I say, dabbing my eyes with a white linen dinner napkin that I wish was black instead because it is stained with my lip gloss. I am contemplating stuffing the napkin in my purse, taking it home, laundering it, and returning it to the restaurant later the next day.

"But we are okay," Peter says, rubbing my back with his left hand and pouring wine into the glasses of our guests with the other.

"Yes! Yes!" I chirp, my voice muffled through the napkin, my nose beginning to drip. "We are actually fine."

"We are fine," Peter says, this time emphasizing each word.

I turn to him and try to smile encouragingly, thinking that if he reads my signal telling him to smile, and we smile as a unit, our dinner mates will fall for our act and be convinced that we are anything less than devastated. The problem is, when I look at Peter, I can see that his eyes are moist. And he either does not read my signal telling him to smile or he is unable to because his words say one thing, but his face tells a different tale.

But it doesn't matter because my smile has disappeared, so even if Peter does attempt a weak smile, mine is no longer there to accompany his. We are failing at working as a unit at the moment. I swallow and it hurts because my throat is unusually dry and feels swollen; I feel as if I need to take in a big gulp of air. The sight of Peter's damp eyes destroys me. It's strange how I can ugly cry for hours and it's not as pathetic or heartbreaking as seeing the slightest glint of tears in my husband's eyes.

Our friends, who I am pretty sure will not be remaining our friends for much longer, are staring at us and occasionally nodding. They look nothing short of horrified at what we have just told them. And I can't blame them. It is kind of unfair. They had only asked, "How are the kids?" Did we really need to tell them? We could have just said, "Good, good." Or if that was too much of a lie, why not an "Oh, you know kids; ups and downs," and left it at that.

But *nooo*, not us. We caved and crumbled and were honest. Peter and I have often said that we would not be great at pursuing a life of crime together. Or playing poker. We would be bad at both. We would confess to a murder and our faces would announce a poor hand of cards equally as fast.

Our guests still look horrified and I think that the husband is resting a supportive hand on the wife's thigh. I feel bad to have done this to them. They glance at each other uncomfortably like married people do when they are faced with a conversation that is plagued with land mines. I feel even worse for putting them in this position. We really hadn't intended on divulging all of this when we left the house. But it is always on our minds and haunts our thoughts and consumes us and somehow when someone extends a genuine how are things, we sometimes cave.

"But really, we are doing okay and, and, and…" Peter says stuttering. Peter never stutters and my heart threatens to break a little more. "…and Natalie is a strong, smart, beautiful girl, and she will beat this."

We all jump in with a chorus of supportive comments like "Of course, certainly," and, "Yes, for sure." And try to collectively regroup as the waiter sweeps away the salad plates. Did we really do all this before the entrees were served? Then I think of something to add: "Many people do!"

It is a lie, but it was something to say. More collective offerings of support follow. And as a limp piece of cod is set in front of me—I should have ordered the steak, to hell with the calories—I lay the messy red, tear-stained napkin on my lap and prepare to carry on. Reading my mind and knowing exactly the correct thing to do, the wife tells the waiter to bring me another napkin. And the husband pours more wine into Peter's glass. They are really good friends, and I like them a great deal; I just hope they will agree to have dinner with us again.

On the way home, I ask Peter if he thinks they will. "Probably not," he says. "I don't want to have dinner with us again; do you?"

"No," I admit, looking up into the night sky. I sigh and think that maybe I will phone the wife tomorrow and tell her how sorry we are and that if they give us another chance, we will do better. Or then I think that maybe I will just send them an apologetic fruit basket instead. Nothing says sorry like apples and bananas. And everyone likes fruit, right?

Why doesn't anyone ever send me a fruit basket?

"Natalie!!"

My eyes open to the sunshine "Nat!!"

"One sec!" I manage pushing myself up off of the closet floor

"I can't even do that right." I chuckle

My head pounds with memories of the night before

Pills and Gin.

More and more.

Despair and depression

Slipping away

Drifting further and further

I cannot see I cannot hear

The voice saying

"Just take one more step

Just take one more step"

"Natalie! Let's go!"

My head hurts

I take the belt from my neck

Toss the empty gin bottle into the closet

Kick the stray pills under the bed

Slide my bare, thirteen-year-old feet into my tennis shoes

"Coming!" I call

I join the world that I had just tried so hard to escape

—Natalie

When I was busy preaching about saying "please" and "thank you" and the importance of chewing with your mouth closed, I should instead have been talking about drugs.

If I could turn back the clock and be given the opportunity to choose, I would trade in all of Natalie's pristine manners and exchange them for a girl who didn't stick needles in her arms.

The other parents of addicts that I have met who don't talk to their children much about drugs explained their hesitancy in the same way; they were afraid that telling their kids about drugs would put ideas in their children's heads that were not there.

I have to admit this was my reason as well. In addition to being kind of afraid of doing it wrong, I think that, selfishly, I didn't want to have such unpleasant conversations. Not knowing much about drugs, I didn't believe I was qualified. I know now that I needed to make myself qualified. I needed to become educated in the same way I would have about anything else. Just like I did when I needed to learn about soccer, the saxophone, or frogs for that science fair project.

Fast forward years from when I should have first started talking about drugs to Natalie; we now talk a lot about drugs. But unfortunately, when we talk, it is Natalie who knows everything, and it is me asking the questions.

It is true what they say about addiction being a family disease. Natalie's illness certainly has affected Peter and me and her brothers profoundly. I always joke and tell people that this makes them the bravest boys on the planet.

Like all families, we share. We share our ups, downs, successes, and lesser moments. And none of us resent this. We are a family and by definition, for us, that means we are in all of what this life puts before us together.

But having an addict in the family and loving someone with illness certainly has provided the four of us with knowledge and skills and habits that not everyone has. These are also good and bad.

We celebrate her not being impaired. We enjoy the moments when she is "her." We are grateful for small accomplishments. And we take very little for granted. We know that the victories and joy are often in the small stuff. We know the difference between good breathing and worrisome shallow breathing. We have stepped on needles. We have stood by horrified as Peter chased and tackled Natalie, wrestling a syringe out of her hand as she tried desperately to put it in her arms. And we have, terrified, crept into her room, worrying that our worst fear has come true, to make sure that the sister and daughter we love so much is still breathing. We spot dilated pupils quickly. And notice bloodshot eyes and grey skin color at a glance. We are too good at understanding slurred speech and know how to use Narcan.

And we also know how to offer unconditional love, how to support someone in their worst moments, and how to forgive.

I never worried about Peter and myself or all that we had to deal with. We were grown-ups and we signed on for these parenting duties, which I still believe is a privilege. But there were times that I worried about Natalie's brothers, Jason and Trevor.

I worried a lot about Jason. He is Natalie's older brother and takes this role seriously. And has often expressed that he feels that he should have stopped it and stood in the way of it all. That he should have known sooner and then when he finally did know, he should have done something, anything, to stop Natalie from this horrendous path and her horrific choices. I believe his guilt to be unwarranted and undeserved, but I know that I have not lessened or alleviated it.

Once when Jason and I were talking and he was down on himself for not helping Natalie more, not knowing what else to say, I offered a hollow platitude, saying Natalie was the owner of her poor choices, and we are not our brothers' keepers. He correctly shut me down by saying, "I think that we are supposed to be." I would have disagreed with him except that he was right.

I did worry about Trevor more. He was younger, more impressionable, and I worried that he was more affected. I didn't want him to think that just because our situation was normal for us, that it was normal at all or okay or acceptable or something to be tolerated. I would try to point all of this out to him while in the next breath explaining that we do tolerate it all and hang in there because families just don't throw their troubled loved ones away. I began to worry less and began to believe that maybe it is true that adversity does make you stronger and better. When we were talking once and I apologized for a difficult patch that we had been going through with Natalie, he said, "It's no problem, Mom, as long as she does what she does, we do what we do and hope that we win. Sometimes, people need saving from themselves. There's good in her."

I feel it unfortunate that because of all of it, Natalie's brothers learned some pretty unsettling and sad things. But it is obvious they learned to be compassionate and understanding humans. So that's an okay trade.

We did all of the regular things that families do. Peter worked hard and I ran myself ragged trying to arrange all the world into a perfect childhood. I swear, one minute we were on top of the world and the next minute, we were watching the walls come tumbling down...and ducking.

People always ask if I can pinpoint what the first sign of trouble was; I cannot. I always think that, somehow, a good mother could. If I was a better mother, I would have seen that very first sign of trouble and thrown myself down on the tracks in front of the train like a heroine and stopped this entire thing. I did not see what I was supposed to and did not sacrifice myself in a glorious fashion.

Instead, I am afraid, I stood holding Natalie's hand on the side of the train tracks, pointing at and encouraging her to look at the pretty train. This is not a movie or a fairy tale. Which means a happy ending is not a guarantee.

It's funny how every personal quality in a person that you can name can be a good or a bad one.

Natalie is intelligent. But is she too smart for her own good? She is strong-willed. So, she's stubborn. She was a precocious child. A smart aleck. She was curious, courageous, and fearless—but was she too curious, courageous, or fearless?

If you google "personality traits of addicts," the lists often include: impulsive behavior, compulsive, inability to handle stress, grandiose feelings, nonconformity, lack of patience, low self-esteem, and denial. I can come up with specific instances when Natalie was each of these.

She broke her ankle jumping off of a concrete wall. She always puts exactly two tablespoons of butter and one quarter cup of milk in her mac 'n cheese. I had to visit the school at lunchtime in second grade to calm her down when the other little girls were unkind. She never felt the rules were for her. She wanted to wear blue clothes as a toddler, all the while that I was stuffing her into pink ones.

She wanted black roses instead of red for Valentine's Day, she wants everything "right now," thinks every other girl in the world is smarter and prettier than she is, and thinks she is not an addict when she is.

But can't the same be said for us on occasion? I have bought expensive shoes on a whim. I press 2:22 on the microwave when heating up my tea instead of just 2:00. I have been treated for anxiety. I have walked too confidently into a mammogram. I did not take dance lessons like every other little girl in the world and never liked Mary Poppins like everyone else. Every other woman in the world is smarter and prettier than I am, and I did not think my daughter was an addict when she was.

Maybe if I would have looked at the list earlier, I would have been on this sooner and, possibly, derailed the train or at least redirected its path and Natalie would have learned to like red roses and I would have grown fond of Mary Poppins. But as it stands, Natalie still prefers black and I continue to be annoyed by a woman flying around with the help of umbrellas.

Every year before one of my children entered kindergarten, we attended a late-August "getting to know each other" picnic. As the children played nearby, the parents were left to introduce themselves to one another. There we'd stand, a clump of strangers huddled together for the next two hours in a park. We knew that, for at least the next 180 days, these strangers were the parents of our children's friends, therefore making these same people our friends, too.

So, standing there with the children hooting and hollering around us, we introduced ourselves. Then, we talked about our children.

And if you listened in you would have heard things like, "I'm worried. My daughter is shy. But I'm kind of shy, too."

"He's not chubby, just kind of big-boned like all of us are."

"Excuse me, I need to go put sunscreen on him. We burn even when it's cloudy."

"I keep telling her that one day she will love her red hair." "I know! He's a tall one! But my brother-in-law is tall!" "I always hated math. I'm sure that she will, too!" "I was the only one who couldn't climb the rope in gym class. My daughter doesn't have a prayer there."

I think it is natural for parents, in private, to comment on a cute little nose or feet that seem to be growing at an alarming rate, to wonder where these features in their children come from.

If you look hard enough through the leaves of the family tree, you will be able to find someone that had that same straight hair or talent for music that you hadn't been expecting.

What you wouldn't have heard at that picnic, if you would have been a fly on the potato salad, was, "I'm hoping he knows when to stop. My dad never did. Alcohol ruined his life." Or "I'm really praying that she doesn't end up an addict like my sister."

While we all have a predisposition to be certain ways and we are likely to become like our families, life is full of exceptions: those people who are amazingly unique and wonderful with talents and gifts and, yes, faults and quirks all their own.

We watch these people achieve great things and say, "Wow! I didn't see that coming!" or "Where did that come from!"

I believe that while we inherit much, we end up being more us than anyone else. No one ever looked at a newborn baby and said, "We better brace ourselves, he's got Uncle Joe's nose. So, he's pretty much washed up." Instead, we look at the baby hopefully, wonder what is special about them, and dream of them doing great things.

Discovering your DNA has become very popular now. People search to find out more about their ancestors, but even more so, they are eager to discover more about themselves. Some people dive right in, spitting eagerly into that tube and sending it off with swift service, anxiously awaiting the results. While others, like some people I know, spit more tentatively and choose regular mail, hoping their submission might get lost so they don't have to know anything more than they already do. When the results do come back, they ask someone else to open the email, instructing them to only tell them what they want to hear and already knew about themselves.

But when our DNA storybook comes back to us, we shake that family tree, and end up pulling off and discarding the leaves that hold the qualities that might make us less while embracing, polishing up, and further securing the leaves that contain the gems that boost our confidence, leaving us to create a better and more beautiful tree than we ever dreamed of.

No matter how we are created and come to be on this Earth, one thing for sure is that it is not like creating a Mr. Potato Head. There is no such thing as a Build-an-Addict Kit that comes equipped with poor judgment, risky behavior, syringes, and packets of heroin. Someone does not hold us in their hands and say, "Let me make this one addicted!"

Natalie is not what people often expect when they meet her. When you say the word "addict," she is not the common image people conjure up. People visualize someone bold and brash, rough and scary and harsh, and honestly, a lot of people expect evil. They do not expect a pretty, petite, charmingly quirky, funny, easy-to-smile young lady. When people know Natalie's history and meet her, if they allow themselves, the good things are what they will see and notice first. Only after being made aware of her history, do people expect her to be something other than what she is.

My daughter is a beautiful person inside and out. I know this for sure. She may have her issues, but she is one of the most kindhearted people I have ever known. While I like to think that I had a bit to do with this and take pride in it, I probably don't deserve any credit. The kindness in her eyes was there from the moment that she arrived.

Children teach their parents and make them better people. Natalie has taught me so much. With her outer shell being a little harsh and often a poker face, I assumed that she didn't notice or simply didn't care about the criticizing looks she received from strangers when we were out in public together. In reality, she was just doing exactly what I had always taught her to do: turn the other cheek.

These looks affected me very much, wounding me greatly. And I would often become defensive and, I am ashamed to say, would glare at these judgmental people, hoping that they could read my telegraphed message filled with unkind words and that it would hurt them like they were hurting me.

I would rant in my head, telling them the virtues of my sweet girl as well as the sinfulness of their feelings. But with me, in reality, saying nothing, all of my words manifested themselves as the angry, hurtful tears that pooled in my eyes. I would warn them not to fall and betray me.

But at the same time, I hoped that Natalie didn't see me glaring, because I didn't want her to feel bad. But, of course, she did notice the unkindness. Sometimes, simply saying quietly to me, "Let it go Mom."

I never knew what to say when she said this and usually said nothing back. Once I managed to mutter, "Sorry."

"No worries," she told me softly. "I'm used to it."

I remember thinking to myself that maybe that was part of the problem. Once we were out to lunch together, and a very troubled looking girl came in. She was disheveled, with blue-and-green streaked hair, dark, overdone makeup, a black trench coat, and combat boots. I swear I wasn't being critical, but I did probably look longer than I should have.

As the young lady walked near, Natalie chirped, "I like your hair!" The girl's face unexpectedly came to life, breaking into a very pretty smile.

"Thanks. And your piercing is cool," she said, remarking on Natalie's lip piercing. "I want one," she explained. "But I'm scared." She giggled. This surprised me. She didn't look like she could be afraid of anything.

"It's not that bad," Natalie encouraged. Natalie and this kindred spirit shared a grin and then the girl smiled at me. It was easy for me to smile back at her.

After we watched her turn and walk away, Natalie looked at me and said, "Don't be judgy, Mom. It hurts."

I knew by the way she said it that she spoke from personal experience. I am proud of me and I am proud of her. I am not a mean girl and I didn't raise one either.

When Natalie was two or three, she would watch me intently as I put my make-up on. Her head would dart back and forth from my face to the mirror, double-checking my progress.

When I was done, she would pull me down to her level and inspect my lips. After approving, she would lean in and kiss my lips, hoping that some of the lipstick from my lips transferred to hers.

Then she would stand on her toes to view herself in the mirror, puckering her tiny lips.

There is nothing that is scarier than hope
Especially when your life's run by dope

Hope that things will be all right
Hope there will be no more reasons to fight

Hope that the scars will begin to fade
Hope I can survive the choices I've made

Hope that my family will forgive my lies
Hope that my friends will hear my cries

Hope one day my heart will be whole
Hope one day my life will be full

—Natalie

chapter *four*

Anything?

I was staring at myself in the mirror, noticing how worn-out and older I looked. Peter noticed and asked, "What are you doing?"

"Nothing," I told him. "I was just thinking of how much I looked like the 'after' picture."

Peter stopped and turned back to look at his own reflection in the mirror. He frowned and said, "Me, too."

Dealing with something like this either makes a marriage stronger or tears it apart. While neither of us is perfect, Peter and I make a really good couple. I'm proud of this and together we work on it. But I believe that what we are individually makes us the strong unit we are(Basically, we believe in kindness. And if being nice to one another is at the root of all that you do or say, then it works.)

We talk about everything. But one thing that we did not speak about was hanging in there together. We had wordlessly somehow decided this. Maybe, just by not leaving.

When Peter leaves work in the evening, he could head to the bar or to a younger, perkier, problem-free version of me. But he doesn't. He comes home. And while I have plenty of time while he is at work to pack everything I own and flee, I do not.

So, every night when I hear the garage door going up, I pinch my pale cheeks and try to put on a less worried expression. And by the time he drags his tired self up the stairs, I am ready to greet the less worried expression he is faking for me.

Our barometer is different than most people's. If nothing tragic happened that day, then it was a good day.

Dealing with all this often is paralyzing. When we greet each other, we can't move on to anything else until we verify with each other that nothing horrible has happened. We do this with just one word. "Anything?" we ask each other upon greeting, usually while we are still leaning in for a kiss. And when the other confirms, "Nothing," we both are able to breathe.

Now, the definition of "anything" is broad. So, "nothing" just means nothing horrific. But we will take it. And until, as my father would say, "the cavalry arrives to save us," this is good enough.

We were out to dinner one night with people who know of our struggles. They complimented us by telling us that they admire our unity as a couple. We thanked them and assured them that no hero-ics are involved in our union. And that simply, we will be together forever because we agreed that whoever leaves first must take all three children.

Peter and I met on a Hallmark-ish blind date. He was the handsome young doctor. I was the Catholic school kindergarten teacher.

It was love at first sight; we dated a year, were engaged a year, and got married surrounded by family. A year of wedded bliss and a son, Jason, followed almost exactly a year later.

The only logical next step to follow all of this perfectness was to give birth to a baby girl. I did my part by being glowing and pregnant for nine months while Peter doted, kissing my belly for luck every morning and evening.

Late one March, under a scripted pink-and-blue sky, Natalie cooperated and appeared as a girl. The pregnancy average, the delivery typical, but the bundle wrapped in pink was anything but average or typical.

She was insanely cute, funny, and smart from the start. We were perfect and did it all exactly right. We followed the invisible rule book to the letter. Nothing would go wrong. How could it? The only thing ahead of us would be an idyllic life full of magical moments.

Is it better to be left
Or is it better to be alone?
Is it better to go out with a bang
Or with a moan?

I crave unconditional love
So terribly so
But it's something
I do not know

So do I open my heart
And open up to hurt
Or close myself up
Until I'm in the dirt

It's a balancing act
Of give and take
But too much hurt
Is what will make me break

—Natalie

"How about this one?" I asked holding a photo of Natalie in Peter's view. He glanced up and waves his hand, dismissing it.

"Too harsh," he said, continuing to rifle through the pictures in the large cardboard box we were both hunched over.

Natalie had been out of contact for more than two days. Unfortunately, this was not too rare, but usually by now, we would have received a moment on the phone or a one- or two-word text. This time, her phone seemed to be dead and we had no idea where she was. We had decided that it was time to file a missing person's report with the police.

We knew nothing about filing a missing person's report except what we knew from watching *Law and Order*. So, we had no idea what we were doing except that we needed a recent photo of her.

Was this really a thing? Did real people do this kind of thing? I wished that we had a script. But that probably wouldn't have helped. The desperate parents don't usually have many speaking parts on TV anyway.

I continued rifling through the pictures, trying hard to ignore the ones of Christmases, birthdays, trips to the pumpkin farm, and dance recitals. I knew that if I did look at these photos, they would make me emotional and melancholic. Who was I kidding? Emotional and melancholic? If I looked at them, they would knock the wind out of me like a kick in the stomach, leaving me in a weeping puddle on the floor. That's why I was avoiding them.

But when I happened upon a picture of Natalie at Easter, I couldn't help myself and I paused. It was probably my favorite photo of her. She was about four years old, dressed in a blue-and-yellow floral dress, Mary Janes, and an Easter bonnet. She was holding a patent-leather white purse and smiling brightly.

A lump formed in my throat as I stared at it, lost in the memory. "Stop," Peter told me. I nodded but couldn't pull my eyes away from the photo. "Stop," he repeated firmly yet gently this time, taking the picture from my hand and tossing it back into the box. I was grateful he did this. We took turns saving each other like that. "Here," he said. "This one." His voice a little more firm.

Slumping, he sat down on the ledge of the fireplace and ran his hand through his hair. I joined him, viewed the photo he had chosen, and nodded my agreement. She certainly wasn't wearing a flowery dress or smiling brightly, but still, somehow, I was able to see the little girl I saw in the other pictures.

The photo met the criteria we had previously discussed. She needed to look clean, friendly, and wholesome. She needed to look like the girl next door. The police looked eagerly for the girl next door. Did they really look for drug addicts? We weren't so sure. The girl next door was the girl the police wanted to rescue. The girl next door was the girl everyone wanted to find. The police looked with effort and regular people shared her photo on Facebook, lit candles, and organized Saturday morning search parties.

We were not so sure that people looked so eagerly for IV drug users. In so many of the photos we had of Natalie, her overdone black makeup and tough-girl expression was masking the sweet girl she actually was.

Peter sighed and looked toward the ceiling. I let my head fall into my hands and we each took separate moments before uniting again and reaching for each other's hand. Just as our fingers touched, the sound of the front door opening startled us. We both froze for a second. Squeezing each other's hand again, we both let out the breath that we had been holding. Natalie was home.

We shook our heads as we heard her call, "Hello." We stood and walked toward the foyer. Peter led, but I lagged behind and snatched the Easter photo from the box. Some nights, it helped to sleep with it under my pillow.

"Young hearts beat. It's what they do," my husband says after I asked him, "How can she still be alive after all she has done to herself?" We are lying in bed in the middle of the night. This night, we have stayed awake together waiting for her to come home. Natalie had come home minutes before. Peter greeted her wordlessly, locked the front door, and joined me back in the bed.

Of course, I thank God every minute of every day that my daughter is alive. But knowing what she has done to her body and all the risky behavior, she's a little bit of a miracle.

"But so many like her, even some of her friends have died," I point out. "The body fights to stay alive," he tells me, settling in under the covers. "Thank God it does," I say, thinking of all our close calls.

Peter reaches for my hand and squeezes it. "Good night," he says and turns.

I lie there in the darkness. I mean to leave him alone. But I am trying desperately to grasp a thread of comfort.

"So, young hearts beat. It's what they do," I say repeating his words, hoping that he will say them again. He doesn't. This disappoints me. But he doesn't take them back either.

I am just about to take comfort in this. I am pretty sure Peter is asleep now. Until I realize he isn't asleep and tells me the other part of the truth. "Young hearts beat," he says. "Until they can't."

Unable to speak, I nod that I understand. I'm sure he can't see my face crumble in the dark.

Swallow me or snort me
Whatever you like
Or simply give your drink
A little spike

Take this pill or that pill
Whatever you may please
Until you can swallow
Them all with ease

Pack me and smoke me
So, you won't go mad
Just tell yourself
It's not as bad

Dilute me then shoot me
However you desire
Just know that you
will never put out this fire

—Natalie

It is 2:32 AM. I know the exact time because I have just rolled over and checked the clock on my cell phone. I set it back down and wait for the light that is now illuminating the room and causing pretty patterns on the ceiling to dim, then disappear. It does.

I wiggle farther under the covers and close my eyes. Then I hear him. I freeze and listen more closely, not wanting the ruffling of the covers to keep me from hearing. I must be mistaken. I need to be mistaken. Please let me be wrong. But there it is again. I am not wrong. The sound is undeniable. And right now, the sound is breaking my heart.

"Hey," I whisper softly into the dark room. I turn and reach blindly, and my hand lands on his shoulder. I begin to stroke his arm gently.

"Sorry," he apologizes hoarsely.

Few sounds are as heart-wrenching as waking up in the middle of the night to the sound of your husband crying next to you. The strong, solid rock of a man that dries your tears, keeps you safe, and holds you in his muscular arms and assures you that all will be okay is sobbing in the bed beside you.

"Don't say you are sorry," I scold him quietly. I scoot closer to him and wrap my arms around him, trying to create a cocoon. Trying for once to be the strong one.

"She's going to be okay," I tell him, trying to sound more confident than I really am. "I just know it."

Of course, Peter knows me well enough to also know that not only do I not know this but maybe I don't even believe it. But he does know that I wish it and want it to be true with every fiber in my being and so does he. So, I lie because it is the kind thing to do. And he pretends to believe me because that is polite. It's the middle of the night, and we are exhausted.

I hold him a little more tightly, wanting him to feel my love. He allows me to hold him.

"She's going to be okay," I repeat. "And so are we." Another wish spoken as fact.

I wait until his breathing is regular and I am sure that he is asleep. I give him some space and settle into my side of the bed. I feel cold, or just maybe scared, and shudder.

I reach over and pick up my cell phone. I press the button and it lights up the room. It is now 2:38. Only six minutes have passed. At times, every minute seems to pass like days. I stare again at the shadows above me. They don't look pretty anymore.

Peter and I lie. Sometimes we lie together, sometimes we lie independently, but we lie.

My father used to always say, "You never know what other people have in their lives." I heard him say this often. I just never really thought about it much.

Lately, I find myself thinking about it a lot, especially one evening when my husband and I went to a work function for his job. We were late, harried, and haggard. We arrived at the table of ten, taking the last two seats, smiled our plastic smiles, greeted everyone, and plopped down into the chairs.

"Nice of you to join us," someone joked, playfully calling attention to our tardiness. "Where were you two?"

We hesitated before answering, not sure that a response was actually required. *Don't want to jump the gun and lie needlessly.*

Often when people throw a question like this out, jokingly, with a glass of wine in their hands with an audience of other people with glasses of wine in their hands, they don't really care.

Experienced at fielding such fly balls, we hesitated and ramped up our smiling while adding a jovial shake of the head (my husband did this) and eye roll (I was in charge of all rolling eyes). These accompaniments were our jovial way of exclaiming, "Oh, life! It's busy! But what a joy!"

As we settled into our chairs and placed our napkins on our laps and grabbed our wine, trying to catch up with everyone else, blend in, and become comfortably invisible, my husband gave my knee a comforting squeeze. He was in tune to the stress I was feeling and trying desperately to hide. The touch also said, "Hold on. Maybe we won't have to answer. I will handle this."

Still smiling so much that I knew his cheeks were aching, Peter surveyed our tablemates and while some of their interest seemed to have already waned, enough of them were still focused on us and it didn't look like we were going to get off the hook without a fib.

"Ruptured appendix," Peter said with a sigh that, being an honorable doctor, signaled that although this event was an inconvenience, caring for this unwell organ was a privilege.

I supportively reciprocated and gently touched his thigh, making a mental note to tell him to use gallbladder next time because he had used the appendix excuse last time. (It was best to mix it up a bit for variety and believability.) I made some nondescript expression appropriate for a doctor's wife, just in case anyone was looking at me, that was meant to convey my complete unselfish support as well as promote my role as best supporting actress in this drama that is my life.

With Peter's comment, everyone became distracted, eager to share their own gripe and less interested in us. Peter and I relaxed, he sipped his wine, and I became lost in my thoughts, scanning the table and wondering what was in everyone else's lives. As they laughed, I hoped that they were as happy as they were acting right then. And that their lives were only as complicated as the minor inconveniences that they were sharing then. I knew that this probably wasn't the case. Everyone has stuff. More stuff than they let on. But I don't wish our stuff on anyone.

"Make this guy take some time off so that he gets you to these things on time, Christine!" one of the guys called across the table.

Shaken from my reverie, I perked up, making sure that I was smiling, realizing that my cheeks ached and that I probably hadn't unsmiled since we got here. (I need to remember to turn it off and on). No response was required, so I just nodded, still smiling.

Peter wasn't the reason we were late. I wasn't either, not really. We left on time but had to go back home because I had forgotten to turn the dryer off. I ran inside while Peter waited in the car, assuming this would just be a quick detour. But even the most mundane things are never that. I first had to get something the dog had in his mouth. It wasn't a shoe or a stray sock. He was carrying a syringe.

In retrospect, this incident was a defining moment for me. It told me we were in a seriously bad place. I chased the dog for ten minutes before I caught him. And that is why we were late.

When the party was breaking up and everyone expressed their tiredness and desire to get home to crawl into bed, take a warm shower, or relax in front of the TV, I didn't bother mentioning that the first thing that I was going to do when I got home was to make sure the dog was okay.

Just when I believe
I have a solid grasp
I hear the siren song
Of the next relapse

Maybe the pressure
Is becoming all too much
Maybe I just feel
Like I am losing touch

Losing sight of
What I thought mattered
Slowly becoming
More tired, more battered

So how can you expect me
Not to give in
With this burning
Right beneath my skin

So just when you
Can't seem to find me
I'll be in the past
I thought I was free

—Natalie

"This is not your fault!" Peter is all but screaming at me, which he never does. "She is not your fault!"

I am tempted to tell him not to call Natalie a fault. It seems particularly unkind to refer to a human being that way, much less our daughter. I am in a very guilt-ridden place. I am feeling like the worst mother ever and am having a hard time snapping out of it. It's really not self-pity as much as it is regret. Some days, I can find a way to accept blame and regret for everything. This is one of them.

"You did nothing wrong!" he insists. "How about me? How about this is all my fault. I was never here! I spent too much time at work and should have been home!"

"But that's better!" I squeal back. "You were doing what you were supposed to do and building a career." And I truly believe this. "I was here. I was doing it all. And I did a horrible job. I failed." In my mind, right then, it seems more acceptable to have not been around much than it is to be the one who blew it.

"We should have been doing it together," he sighs.

"I could have done better," I sigh.

"I'm not sure that you actually could have," he tells me. "You were —are—a wonderful mother. A lot of mothers would have given up on her by now."

I want to tell him that I doubt this is true because leaving is nowhere in the job description of motherhood.

"Nobody does more momming than you," he tells me. "It's what I do," I say.

So, we remain there at an impasse in our on-going fight, trying to decide if doing a job poorly is worse than not doing it at all or vice versa while simultaneously trying to badger the other one into admitting he is blameless. I guess there are worse ways for a couple to fight.

"Stop being Pooh!" I say.

"Stop being Eeyore!" he counters.

I am not sure what it says about a couple that exchanges Winnie-the-Pooh insults. At the very least, they should apologize to A. A. Milne, because I doubt he intended his beloved characters to be used as weapons.

It starts one Saturday evening. Peter and I need a distraction and decide to go to a movie. We scan the list of what is showing and negotiate.

"I can't do anything sad," I tell Peter. He crosses a couple of movies with potentially unhappy endings off the list.

"Too much death here," he mutters, deleting a few more. "And of course, no drugs, incarceration or suicide," I say.

When life itself is so difficult, the last thing we know we need to do is spend our leisure time watching anything that could unsettle us even more. While you wish TV shows and movies with tough plots wouldn't feel like they are speaking directly to you, they do.

I guess this is why these subjects are explored. Because they are real and do resonate with so many people. So, in that way, they are valuable and probably helpful. Maybe they educate those who are not experiencing these very real struggles. Maybe it will make them more sympathetic and understanding. But to those of us who are living some of these nightmares, watching a replica of your life on a humongous ninety-foot screen can be pretty unnerving. And honestly, it hurts.

When these depictions are so accurate, I always wonder just who involved in the movie has had that experience. Is it the writer, the director, or the actor? But when it hits so close to home, I know that somebody is the real deal. Us real deals can spot one another.

So, when we go to the movies, Peter and I are looking to be entertained and to get as far removed from our present situation as possible, which is how we ended up seeing *Christopher Robin.*

It is a pleasant and enjoyable film. I am a Winnie-the-Pooh fan from way back. When the kids were little, we had the stuffed toys, little plastic figures, and many of the DVDs. The movie depicted a make-believe world and a pleasant time. And these movies existed in a more pleasant time in my life, too, which I'd like to think wasn't make-believe. I am happy to share this with Peter as, with our buckets of popcorn in our laps, we are experiencing the Hundred Acre Wood.

Peter is a little bit of a novice in all things Pooh and has a lot of questions, such as, why the name "Sanders" is above Winnie-the-Pooh's door. He's extremely intelligent, uber curious, and needs to understand and make sense of everything, which I love. I, on the other hand, accept a lot of things just the way they are, without inquiry.

I whisper that Mr. Sanders was the prior resident of the house where Pooh now lives and that when he says that Pooh lives under the name of Sanders, he's just being kind of funny.

Knowing how his mind works and anticipating his next question, I tell Peter that Winnie-the-Pooh's last name is not Sanders. I am expecting this to continue to bother my man of fact, detail, and science while it's just funny to me.

Peter begins to speak, and I am pretty sure that he is going to ask me why Pooh just doesn't change the sign above the door, but I shush him. I have to set limits or he will never stop. And besides, I have already had to make him okay with the fact that Pooh only wears a shirt and no pants.

"He would never get away with this in this day and age, even in a cartoon," he insists. I am tempted to tell him that Daffy Duck never wore pants either, but I know that he has told the kids that "just because more than one of you do it, it doesn't make it right" and will surely give me this same explanation, so I don't bother. And besides, the people sitting behind us, who have three tiny children and who are practicing better movie manners than we are, seem to be getting annoyed. The mother is now explaining, I think more for my benefit than theirs, that it is impolite to talk during the movie.

Eeyore appears on the screen, talking low and slow like he does. "He's suffering from depression," Peter mutters to me.

"Just enjoy it," I whisper. He has already diagnosed Tigger with mania. And Pooh with delusions. "You're not working. Punch out."

"Twenty milligrams of Zoloft. Twice a day," Peter mumbles, writing Eeyore his prescription.

Having occasionally suffered from depression, I take exception to this and tell him to leave Eeyore alone. "He's me," I say defensively.

When Peter agrees by innocently saying, "You are," I become even more defensive and indicate that he is often delusional by saying, "And you're Pooh."

Realizing what he has done, he says, "Sorry. I didn't mean it," as he reaches down and gives my hand a squeeze.

Not over it, I tell him, "I did," and take my hand back.

"So, did I," he corrects striking back. There is a pause. Then we both dissolve in laughter. We laugh louder when the woman behind us shushes us.

How can I want to go back
And supposedly want more

If this has always been me
And nothing more

How can you want the old me
The me that is clean
When I know that is someone
You have never seen

How can I take the leap
And try and see
How much I can change
Without losing me

—Natalie

Before all of this, I used to wonder if a person could actually die of a broken heart. I don't wonder anymore. I know they can. I don't need to google this question or ask a physician.

It's funny, if you google a symptom, you will probably come up with much more on the topic than any conversation you will get from your average physician. But I think this is only because doctors aren't used to being vulnerable and this question leaves them wide open and they don't like that. Peter, of course, is a doctor and walks a tightrope, juggling the delicacies of this question well, so that he somehow doesn't betray his peers nor my feelings. I am certain that if a colleague were to question him on this possibility, he would answer with a definitive no.

But when we were lying in bed one night, I did ask him if he believed this to be true. I knew that he probably didn't before I asked him. And he knew that I definitely did before I asked.

But I know that people most certainly can die of a broken heart. It all gets physical. The headaches and stomach pains, the shortness of breath all add up. But the way my own heart feels tells me for sure that it will give out one day. It usually starts with a feeling of tightness in my chest that turns into an ache. This ache is nagging and always present so I can't ever forget. And often, my breathing is compromised. And no matter how deeply I breathe, I can't seem to get enough air. I am not a medical person, but the combination of the two can't be good.

But I ask anyway, maybe it is just my way of telling him that I am hurting very much. "I don't know," he sighs in response through the darkness of our bedroom. "Some people believe they can," he points out, expertly sidestepping this trap I had set.

I have the urge to launch a barrage of my symptoms and evidence at him, pelting him with them like a hailstorm. But I fight it. He doesn't deserve this. So, I simply tell him, "I am one of those people."

"I know," he tells me as he turns to hold me in his arms. He is quiet for a moment, then adds, "And I'm not sure that they are wrong." I guess maybe this is his way of saying that he is hurting very much, too.

Natalie is not the only one who cannot escape her thoughts. I am the owner of a very busy mind myself.

Like all things, there is good and bad to it. I am thoughtful, insightful, compassionate, and creative. But I am also overly sensitive, obsessive, fearful, and worried much of the time. I believe that we all live two lives: one when we are with others and the other when we are alone.

There is the outside of us, the part that can be seen. And there is the inside of us, the part that is invisible to everyone else. This is where we hide our most private thoughts...hopes, dreams, insecurities, and fears. This is where we have those private conversations with ourselves. The really, really honest ones. It is in these conversations that I often console myself, scold myself, yell, scream, swear, and confess. This is where I tell people off, extend apologies, admit things that I don't usually, verbalize what I won't when people are around, and dare to say things that scare me. But it is not always an unhappy place; sometimes I give myself accolades and compliments, and crack myself up. Sometimes, I am quite funny.

A woman I used to work with would always say, "You can't un-ring a bell." While I knew what the phrase meant, I never really understood it completely until experiencing what I have with Natalie over the last few years.

I know I will never be able to un-hear, un-see, or un-feel so many of the things I have seen, heard, and felt. I know I will forever hear the words "Mrs. Naman, your daughter is an addict," and "Mrs. Naman, this is the ER, we have your daughter here," ringing in my ears. I know that the sight of Natalie's swollen, blue, and lifeless face from an overdose will never be erased from my mind, and I will always shiver at the memory of first realizing how deeply addicted Natalie was.

But I also know that I will forever be able to replay Natalie saying, "Thanks, Mom, don't know what I'd do without you," in my head when I am feeling discouraged and need a boost.

I will forever see the vision of Natalie's sweet, easy smile when she is well. And I will cherish the way that the memory of her laugh makes me feel genuinely happy inside. The same woman who wisely told me about the bell used to always say, "You have to take the good with the bad." She was right and that is what I will do.

"Ouch!" I shriek. It's early morning and I am in the bedroom alone. The dog hears me and runs to see what's happening, looking concerned. I grimace in pain and don't know what is wrong. But I bravely say, "I'm okay." Satisfied with my answer, he happily wags his tail.

I have just gotten out of the shower and am dressing for the day. I am pulling up my panties when I get an excruciatingly sharp pain in my private area. I slide the underwear back down and am horrified to discover that there is a syringe stuck inside of me and it is dangling between my legs. "Jeesuz!" I say. Bracing myself, I reach down and pull the needle from my skin, cringing in pain. I hold the needle up to examine it.

"I can't believe this is happening!" I say in a horrified whisper to no one because the dog has already lost interest and left the room. I had just done laundry the day before. As usual, of course, I do the family laundry together, including Natalie's. There must have been a used syringe in one of her pockets and somewhere in the mix of doing all of the washing and drying, the needle attached itself to my underclothes. I discard the panties, choose another pair; I then limp to the closet and decide against the stiff jeans I was planning on wearing and instead I grab a soft pair of leggings.

After frantically yanking them on, I grab my cell and dial Peter's cell in a panic. But it goes instantly to voicemail. *Call me!!!* I text him. I don't know who to call next. All I know is that I should call someone. *I should call my doctor! The gynecologist, right? Yes! That's it! He should know! This is a medical emergency! What if I am infected?* I dial the first three numbers but freeze. *What in the world am I going to say? How can I explain this? My friend Denise, I will call her! She will help me!* Again, I stop before pressing the entire number. I don't think that I can get the words out.

Before I finish putting on the rest of my clothes, Peter calls and I answer before the first chime is done. I don't say hello, instead, I practically screech into the phone: "You will not believe what just happened!" And then I am off in running with my story, pacing as I recount the experience in detail. Peter is sympathetic, but he cuts me off. He's in the middle of something, he tells me and says goodbye.

I am worried about what I might have been infected with by this needle as well as pitying myself. With no one to talk to, I turn to go out of the room and almost trip over the dog who, apparently sensing the tone of my voice, has come back to investigate. Even though the usual expression on his cocker spaniel face is one of concern, I let myself believe that he looks a little more worried than usual. I am grateful that he has respectfully ceased his tail wagging, waiting for my tone to lighten to give him the go-ahead signal.

I finish telling the dog the story I had begun telling Peter, including all the ramped-up emotion. The dog listens attentively and seems appropriately horrified. Then, because I feel sorry for him, I purposely lighten my tone and tell him that everything will be okay. Consoled, he resumes his tail wagging. I just wish that my tone was genuine enough to console myself.

Pain is . . .
The voice inside my head
The one that's always saying
You are better off dead

The voice that creeps in,
In the middle of the night
The one that's always there
In the dark and in the light

So consuming and loud
It takes all the space in my head
So heavy and haunting
It drags me down like lead

I do what I can
When I'm able to break free
I wish I could show you
That this isn't me

—Natalie

I am getting ready to be with a group of women I don't know very well, and I am in the car rehearsing my family story. I always decide in advance if I am going to tell the truth or not.

This day, I have decided to lie. It is true that lying is more difficult than telling the truth. When you are telling the truth, you don't need to keep such a good account of what you are. Telling the truth is easy.

But when you lie, you need to keep track of what you have said so that you remember to say the same thing. Being a good liar is a skill and takes practice. Who would have thought that such a good Catholic girl would ever consciously strive to perfect this talent?

I am sitting in my parked car, watching the rosary beads that I have hung on my rearview mirror sway back and forth. Transfixed by the glistening beads that are reflecting in the sun, I wonder if tiny Jesus hung on His tiny cross is enjoying the ride while wondering if using the word "awesome" would be overdoing it. I decide to be all in and that I might even add "super" to "awesome." I stop the swaying rosaries, thinking that Jesus might be getting nauseous, touch His head for luck, and get out of the car.

I walk across the parking lot, wondering what it feels like to be normal. I am instantly envious of the mix of people who are going about their days, walking in and out of the restaurants and shops, because I have decided they are all my definition of normal. Maybe not problem-free. But with lives that are peppered with just enough problems and concerns so that they feel grateful for the rest of their circumstances that are better. I am trying to remember if I was ever normal. I believe I must have been at one point because I wasn't always dealing with such serious things, but I can't exactly remember when that time was.

I find my group in the coffee shop and offer a cheerful wave and huge smile (which in itself is a lie). I am clumsily worming my way out of my coat when they ask how everything with me is. As I fall into the chair, I tell them, "We are hanging in there."

Wait! Where did "super awesome" go? I sigh at my own failure as I order a drink and blame that darn Catholicism for bubbling up again.

It is a bad morning because I have spent a restless night tossing and turning, chasing a solution to our problems that keeps running from me in my dreams. Realizing that our answers seem to run even faster in the light of day, I eye the plastic container of Holy Dirt. It was a gift that a friend bought me on a trip to Mexico, and now I decide to give it a try.

I know how to use Holy Water, but I am not sure what to do with the dirt. I wonder how to use it. Where exactly do you put it? I am thinking I should dab it on me like Holy Water, but it is dirt; if I do, won't I end up looking like the chimney sweep from *Mary Poppins* or one of the orphans from *Oliver?*

I remove the plastic lid off the container, being careful not to spill any. If this dirt is as powerful as I hope it will be, I don't want to lose any of it. And considering our current situation, I will need all of it, plus another truck load.

I dip one finger into the center of the container and swirl it around, generously coating it. I decide to put the dirt close to my heart, so I rub it on my chest. As I go through the day, I check and recheck that it is still there.

Every time Natalie walks out the door, I am afraid it is going to be the last time I see her.

The news is flooded with stories of addicts who don't go home. Their mothers end up on the news, tearfully pleading for people to understand. I understand.

Because I am afraid this will someday be me, I look at her closely when she walks out the door, trying to take a snapshot of her in my head. I file it away so that while I am crying on television, I can tell everyone what she was wearing, how she was wearing her hair. I am hoping that all the mothers who are judging me from the other side of the screen, making dinner for their not-troubled daughters as they watch, will at least give me credit for knowing these things.

Good mothers always know this kind of information. I also try to know the names of the people she leaves with. But they make this difficult. They all seem to go by initials. I hardly think the police will find me telling them that she left with "D" or "L" useful.

When I can, I try to remember license plate numbers and car models even though I don't know anything about cars.

I worry about being on TV, though. What if I do it wrong? What if I can't cry? Will people think I don't care? Will they think I deserve to be sitting there in pain? What if I ugly cry too hard or too much? Will people think I am being dramatic? How much makeup should I wear and what about my hair? Up or down? Will anyone understand?

But maybe also making dinner and watching me will be the other mothers, those who unfortunately *do* understand. Mothers who are fearful and in pain just like me. Mothers with children who have not come home. Mothers who worried one time when their child walked out the door that it would be the last time. And it was. They will understand all too well.

Every time I find light
The darkness pulls me back in
Every time I think I'm free
It's back under my skin

It seems so futile
To even fight
There's just so many things
That won't be set right

How can I fight
With so little power
Everything sweet in my life
Has begun to sour

Everything seems covered
With an endless cloud
All I want is silence
With my thoughts so loud

Thoughts tainted from
The voice inside my head
The voice that insists
I'd be better off dead

— Natalie

My cell phone rings and it jolts me like it has an electric cord attached to my heart. I know that my heart skips a beat or two. Or maybe it beats extra? I'm not sure which. But the sound is connected to my heart anyway.

I have tried changing the ringtone to one that might be less startling, something friendlier. But it didn't work. It was on this same ring when I first received the call from the school that Natalie was caught with drugs there. When it rang then, the tone was harmless enough and pleasantly jingly. But when it was the school principal on the other end speaking kindly while at the same time speaking the most horrific words to me…words that started me on a nightmare of a journey…words that I will never forget because they will be forever etched in my memory. *"Mrs. Naman, this is the high school. We need you to come immediately. Natalie is in significant trouble. The police are involved."* The first truly bad *Oh my God!* news, the ringtone became my enemy.

I have actually upgraded the phone twice since it became my enemy, childishly thinking that changing the device might help. I made the two young men selling me the new phones play each of the ring choices slowly and twice for me before I chose one. They seemed confused when I asked them which one sounded less terrifying to them. They were equally stumped when they asked me what feature I wanted most in a new phone and I told them "one that was kind." Apparently, their phones only deliver good news. I am not friends with my phone like most young people are. My phone and I have a painful history.

They say that no news is good news. And that bad news travels fast. I haven't been able to sort this out yet. Personally, I have suffered the anguish of silence when Natalie is missing. And I was late to the ER during one of her overdoses. So, I have an argument both ways.

But anyway, the phone rings. It sounds ugly. I should have chosen another sound. And my heart is doing that thing it does. Instantly, I look down at the screen. It's Natalie! I pick up, and she is calling from the police station. It rings and it is Peter. He got the bad news first and is calling to break it to me. It rings and it is one of her brothers. She called them for help and they don't know what to do. It rings and it is the emergency room doctor. (The doctor only calls when it is really bad. The doctor tells you to hurry but not hurry so much that you are his next patient. But still hurry.)

It rings and it is a random number, a stranger telling me where to find her body. My phone rings and no matter who it is, my world instantly begins crumbling. And it does this all before the second ring.

The guilt is immense. You were given a perfect, healthy, precious baby. That baby was yours to raise: to teach and love; to fill up with goodness, kindness, knowledge, and morals; to have the ability to not only know the difference between right and wrong but the ability to do right and not wrong. And you failed.

She was born perfect and you messed her up. She was the baby. You are the adults. She is not to blame. You are. The guilt is all-consuming.

My husband and I share this guilt, but somehow instead of sharing the burden of our portion of this suffocating emotion, leaving each of us with less, just half the full amount like you would think, the guilt has multiplied and seems to have grown.

There is Peter's guilt. My guilt. Then the guilt that we share. There is always guilt. Sometimes we even feel guilty for forgetting to feel guilty, those rare occasions when we laugh about something.

Sometimes we suffer together. Sometimes we suffer alone. But we are always suffering.

There are things Peter feels he should have done better. And there are things I feel responsible for.

We have each labeled ourselves the bigger, badder guy and have given the other one the pass. Neither of us deserves the title or the pass, but we are kind people. So, we offer them to each other. Sometimes, we struggle at the same time, sometimes he is okay while I am struggling, and vice versa. But sometimes we are low at the same time. This is not good because when our despairs collide, it is dark and quiet.

Throughout the day, we are in touch often through a couple of calls and texts. When we ask, "How are you?" we mean it.

And because we love each other truly, we brace ourselves for the answer, always hoping the other is better than they are. Some days, we explain where we went wrong and apologize to the other. "If I had been a better mother..." "If I had been a better father..." "It's all my fault. I wasn't home enough." "It's my fault. I was the one who was there." "I think there is some of this in my family...a cousin maybe." "I think there is some of this in my family...maybe an uncle."

But the guilt in its purest form with its truest definition is suffocating and it hurts. *Guilt: (noun) the fact of having committed a specified or implied offense or crime.* Pick your poison. It's all bitter.

And again, because we truly love, we try to shoulder the bigger part of the blame. But in the end, we own our part. Justified or not. "We should have watched the music, the movies, the internet more closely." "We should not have been so tolerant of the friends." "I should have ironed clothes more and made her birthday cakes from scratch." "I should have been the French tutor instead of hiring one." "We should have made her continue with dance, join the band, or keep up with gymnastics." When you are desperate for answers,

somehow the ability to do a proper somersault or play Happy Birthday on the fluta-phone seems important. You oddly wonder if these
skills would have helped.

Natalie feels guilt, too. One evening, Peter and I were getting ready
for an evening out and she asked who we were dining with. I told her
who, then added, "He is the doctor who delivered you, you know?"
Her reaction surprised me. I smiled, thinking back at that precious
time, but I noticed that she was frowning.

"What's up?" I asked her, giving her hair a ruffle.

"Tell him that I'm sorry," she said softly, with genuine sadness in
her eyes.

Why was I looking back at her birth with such fondness and she
with such sadness? How could we be viewing it so differently? "What
does that mean?" I asked, quietly hoping that she would confide
in me.

"He handed me a perfectly good start and I messed it up. I was a
clean slate back then," she told me regretfully.

My heart sank and I fought to not become unglued by her words.
"What I have done with my life is kind of disrespectful to a lot of
people, him included...you."

"People understand," was all that I could think to say. "Life is about
starting over."

As she walked away from me, I added, "That was one start; make
another."

Hey are you there?
I know you know it's me
Back again
With money and a plea

Can I get something
That will ease this constant pain
I only have so much to give
And so much to gain

So just let me know
The where and the when
And for just a little
We can pretend we are friends

I need the release
Your medicine gives
I need to silence the place
That my demon lives

So please, please answer
You're my only hope
I need my medicine, my relief
I need my dope

—*Natalie*

My pregnancies ended up with three beautiful children, but they were actually quite difficult. I started out okay physically and emotionally. I looked fit on the outside and what people couldn't see, my mental health, matched this. The two were in synch.

As the pregnancies continued, I struggled emotionally but stayed physically healthy, gaining a considerable amount of weight—fifty pounds each time—which made me appear healthy and sturdy. When I was at my weakest and most fragile, I looked my strongest. By the time I was ready to deliver, I was truly an emotional wreck and fragile. But my outer shell betrayed me.

The same thing happened to me when Natalie became ill. I started off fit inside and outside, able to deal with the challenge. But as time wore on and the damage of addiction wreaked its havoc, I got physically lazy and, as they say, "ate my feelings." But no one could see the pain I was in.

I saw a Facebook post that depicted something similar so well. The post showed six photos of famous individuals who took their own lives due to depression. The post was captioned, "This is what depression looks like." I am always grateful when social media is used this way.

I walked through the latter days in my pregnancies the most vulnerable and weakest that I had ever been in my entire life. And people couldn't tell me enough how wonderful and healthy I looked. (I won't even go into the beautiful "glow" they imagined me to have).

And the same happened within the nightmare of Natalie's illness. I was falling apart but never looked stronger. I would stand before people as they complimented and gushed about my pretty appearance.

"What kind of makeup is that? Did you color your hair? You look slim!"

And while I was graciously thanking them for their genuinely well-meaning words, I would be crying inside and screaming in my head, *I am not sure what you are seeing! But it is not the truth! It is all a lie! This is drugstore make-up! Look closer. I am going gray! I have gained thirty pounds. I am weak and pathetic and fragile! I am in pain. Please see my pain.*

I am driving in the car. It is therapeutic for me. I am writing Natalie's obituary in my head.

I had just read a touching obituary that had been circulating on Facebook. It was written by another mother whose daughter was an addict. She had penned a moving, sweet send-off to her child. I admired her for this and made a mental note to put both her and her daughter in my prayers. Maybe one day, I would even reach out to the mom. After reading her words I couldn't help but wonder what I would write.

Driving in the car, I am composing a rough draft in my head. I wonder how many words the newspaper allows, hoping that there isn't a limit. Mine is getting quite long and I am not even close to my destination. There really shouldn't be a word count requirement on obituaries. After all, you are saying goodbye. You should be able to get it all out. And someone—everyone, actually—should hear you.

I get to thinking about the reason for publishing obituaries in the newspapers. With the original and practical reason being to let people know and simply announce a person's passing. A last chance to say goodbye.

The other reason would be to honor the loved one. Everyone deserves a few good words to be spoken about them after they live the life they are given. Whether it was the most obvious of stellar lives or a quieter, simpler life, they tried. While I believe every life is stellar in some way, not every life gets the recognition. We all do the best that we can. So, somebody should say something.

For me, I would want to let people know and honor, but I believe that writing an obituary would help me say goodbye properly (or see you in a better place, as I believe). I also would want to thank those who should be thanked and maybe even let those who are not thanked notice that, too. (Small of me, I know.) The last reason, I guess, would be to explain.

One day, I would like to publish a book of obituaries that people would like to write to their loved ones. No rules: no word limits or time constraints. But they could send the people they hold dear off, knowing that their thoughts and words were released into the universe. Hopefully, that would help.

My mind drifts back to what I have written in my head so far. I had started from the beginning and told of the day she was born. Specifically, the sun rising and the perfect pink-and-blue sky that was above us as Peter and I headed to the hospital. I told of how cute and perfect she was and how she looked at me like she knew me. And I told, of course, how she owned my heart immediately.

I thanked the people who helped her arrive safely: the doctors who delivered her. I mentioned her pediatricians who had watched her grow and helped us through the years, as well as her adult doctors—ironically, the same doctors that had cared for me when I was pregnant with her and had seen her at her best and most hopeful, and then years later, when she was troubled. I acknowledged the therapists, psychologists, and psychiatrists who listened and counselled.

I ended by thanking the ER doctor who, when she was at her lowest and had overdosed, arrived in the room and said, "I am sorry that you are here. But I am happy to treat you." There was a mention to the medical doctor (during another overdose) who took the time to object when Natalie had stated that she was nothing but a junkie, by telling her that he was sure she was much more than that.

I thanked her schools. From the doting preschool, the elementary, middle, and high school to the community college that didn't go so well.

I thanked her first best friend, a three-year-old preschool classmate, who, being from China and only temporarily here, spoke not one word of English except for Natalie's name, became someone we both loved, and made those years a joy.

I thanked the few elementary school friends who enjoyed her spunk and quirky, funny personality. And the fewer friends after that who saw the good in Natalie. The ones that while they moved on with their healthy lives still keep in touch every once in a while, caring to think about how she is.

When the obituary is complete, I let my mind fantasize about all those I would hug and cry on the shoulders of in the funeral home, as well as those that I would ask the funeral director to escort out, or better yet throw out myself. (I am finding this quite satisfying.)

There are a couple of people that I hope show up to pay their respects or, more accurately, their lack of respect, so I can ignore them to let them know I saw them clearly.

But there are a few others who I will leave my daughter's side for just the time required for me to place them on the sidewalk. I know that Natalie will be proud of me then.

I want the girl who made her cry in third grade by showing up to school with party invitations and ordered all the other little girls to stand around her in a circle so that they could receive their invitations. When there were two little girls'left, Natalie and another, and just one invite remaining, she held the envelope out to Natalie. Natalie, exuberant to be included, reached for it. But when she did, the girl quickly snatched it back, saying, "I'm sorry, my mother and I decided that you didn't make the cut." And handed the last invitation to the other child. Actually, the little girl can simply be escorted out, after all she was just a kid. But I want to physically toss the mother out myself.

Excused from the wake will also be the teacher who, in an effort to make the other students laugh, commented on Natalie's messy hair one morning when we were in a rush. It became a thing with the kids and was jokingly repeated often. It's not like you can show up to school without your hair. I apologized to Natalie and was sure no matter how short on time we were that we saved an extra couple of minutes to tame the tangles. We did this without conversation, but while a child, she was far from stupid, and I wondered what Natalie made of us succumbing to the criticism. I should have thought of something to say. But at the time, could not. It's difficult to come up with the right words when you are being bullied by the teacher.

The preteens who got together for sleepovers and stayed awake all night calling her cell phone only to giggle and hang up while texting her to kill herself, they will be tossed out by me.

As well as those who advertised themselves as the only ones who truly loved her because, after all, she was pathetic and just a junkie.

But on the list of those who will get extra-long hugs is the elementary school friend who hugged her joyously every morning at the doors of the classroom, exclaiming, "I can't do this without you, Natalie!"

The boy who took her to her first dance, his mother taking the time to tell me that she was pleased with his choice.

The high school friend who was almost as troubled as Natalie was but stuck by her anyway.

The stranger who saw past the black eyeliner and face piercings and told her, "You look like a winner to me!"

I am planning what I will say to Oprah and Morgan Freeman, who, of course, will hear and come to pay their respects as well.

I will welcome that one really inappropriate comedian from the show that I can never remember the name of that she loved, the girl who was always in those scary, horrible movies that were too scary and horrible for me to watch, and the two rappers that I can never remember the names of but will be sure to remember then.

With things pretty much figured out as I arrive at my destination, I don't actually remember the drive. I think I am satisfied and a little less stressed and anxious than when I started.

I don't really care
For living this life
In my defense
It's one that's been filled with strife

It's usually just apathy
Not an active thought
But that quickly changes
When my mind gets caught

Caught up in how this world
Has left me behind
Caught up in the dark thoughts
That cloud up my mind

Will I end up okay
Before it's too late
I will never truly be all right
And have a clean slate

Please give me one reason to stay
When I have so many to go
Will I ever have a reason?
Is what I want to know

—Natalie

I wake up every day one of two ways, suddenly with a jolt or slowly emerging from a hazy fog. While that part is different, the next thing that happens is always the same. I reach from the bed and ritualistically touch the heads of the statuettes that sit on my nightstand, asking them to watch over all of us. There are three of them: Jesus, Mary, and St. Jude. Next, the cold reality of where we are becomes clear.

There is a split second of denial before the truth of it all either socks me in the stomach, taking my wind away, or slowly seeps over top of me covering me like poison. In just that single moment, I am not sure that all that has happened has *actually* happened, that maybe it was all just a bad dream and we are a normal family with regular manageable problems and concerns instead of a family who shares their life and home with a vicious monster.

I woke up for a while this way after my father passed away. It took me a minute to realize that he had passed and was not in the world with me any longer. Just then, hope and despair share the same moment.

The result of either way I wake is the same, though. I am no longer protected by the cocoon of sleep. I am up and present and aware. My daughter is an addict, and I am the mother of an addict. That is the kick in the face and the poison. But the fact is while either can kill, it has not yet, and she is still alive.

There is no second button, option "B" or opportunity to press zero for an operator to help, so I have no choice except to get up and face the day.

I tried once to not get up and made the decision to stay in bed for the rest of my life. I quit. I considered rising just one more time to post a sign on the front door announcing my withdrawal from life just to keep people from ringing the doorbell. But that would be it. I lasted twenty-three minutes before I got up, brushed my teeth, and jumped in the shower.

To save face, not fully commit to living or betray myself, I defiantly skipped my blood pressure medicine that morning. Maybe I will get an easy out and explode. I am not sure if this qualifies as a failed attempt at suicide or not. I ended up taking it at noon, so probably not.

After the waking up and the arrival of the truth, I hit the beast head-on because he is blocking my view of everything else. And as I prepare for the day, I decide my plan of attack. It always involves rehabs and programs, letting go of the past and beginning again. I will read and study and research, find the elusive solution to this riddle, the golden key that unlocks the golden door, the last letter in the crossword, the antidote.

I will locate the right doctor, medicine, and therapy. And make this all right. I will also practice what to say when, invariably, people ask how my daughter is.

I spend a few moments baring the teeth that I just brushed, trying to look genuine and natural. Before facing the day and what it will bring, I practice my smile. Before leaving the bedroom, I glance back at the bed and am tempted. I am already so tired.

It's three o'clock in the morning and I have been to the window dozens of times, looking out into the black night. Funny how some nights seem darker than others. I'm actually a little afraid of the dark. For me, the world gets scary when it's cold and dark.

I'm a tiny bit comforted by the fact that Natalie is not afraid of the dark. But she is out, with no good reason to be, so I'm uneasy.

It's quiet torture. I vow to stay up until she gets home. But it's an old story and has happened too many times.

She left at five in the afternoon, promising to be home in an hour (she says she is just going to comfort a friend in need), but here it is ten hours later and there is no sign of her.

Again, her phone is dead and goes directly to voicemail…a voicemail manned by a mechanical voice. I always wonder if the mechanical voice is truly a machine or if it is an actual person who sounds kind of automated. This does not matter, but I will google it in the morning anyway.

I wish she would record her own message so I could at least be comforted by that. (If you need to be rejected, another actual person should do it.)

Breaking my promise to stay up, I usually drag myself up to bed around midnight or so. I believe the saying that nothing good happens after midnight, so Natalie is up to no good. Because the cold and dark have invaded the house at this hour, I feel safer next to Peter's comforting rhythmic breathing.

Now that I am in the bed with the covers pulled up to my chin and around my ears, in lieu of my vow to stand guard on the first floor, I promise to stay awake while I lie there. I break this promise as well. Exhausted by worry, I drift in and out of sleep. And that is simulated torture: the repetition of awake and sleep causes nightmares to appear and disappear in and out of my mind. Thoughts of where she is and what she is doing haunt me.

When I am in between one of these nightmares, the sharp sound of jangling keys, which echoes more like crashing glass at that time of night, jolts me awake. You might never think that such a harsh, startling sound could cause comfort and relief, but it does. I bolt up, and this makes Peter shift and turn over.

I wait for the sounds of her entry into the house and the thud of the closing of the door. There is a brief pause, then I hear the pound of her footsteps on the stairs. These are the sounds of impairment. I am a master at recognizing them.

There are five steps, a small landing, then eight more steps. I count until she is at the top. Impaired but less so than other times when I have found her asleep in the middle of those stairs. She staggers down the hall, and with more clamoring, she enters her bedroom at the end of the hall. The sounds are always the same, disturbing and comforting at the same time. Impaired but alive. Devastated and grateful.

Unique to this night is the sound of a tiny yelp from the dog; she stepped on him. I can hear her slur, "Sorry." At least she noticed and really does love him.

She slams the bedroom door shut like it is the middle of the day, and I wait for the thud of her fall. Sometimes she lands on the bed. Sometimes she does not. The nightmare is over, just for tonight. She and I have survived.

I sigh and settle and pull the covers more snuggly around me. The house is warm, but I am still cold. Peter, somewhere in between awake and sleep, turns and mutters, "Did she come home?"

"She did," I tell him. "All good." I lie. I wait for him to drift away again and I am afraid to move. I get that terrified feeling a person gets when you have just witnessed something horrible almost happen, but it didn't, and you escaped tragedy by a hair. My body involuntarily shivers. I reach over and touch the heads of Jesus, Mary, and St. Jude to thank them. Then I fall asleep.

How can I adore the person
The one that broke me?
How can I still love you?
How can that be?

How can I doubt myself
When I tell our story?
How did I stay so long?
No matter how painful and gory

Why did I always try to build you
When you just tore me down?
I tried to be your life vest
While you left me to drown

Why did I see your good
As you pointed out my bad?
How did I think I was happy
With you always so mad?

But I made it out
Bruises and all
How did I make someone so big
That made me so small

—Natalie

"I am afraid of losing her," I tell him. Even though it is such a bad thought, it feels good to say it aloud. I clear my throat and speak the words clearly.

My words come out blunt and harsh and seem to be kind of echoing. The voice is mine but doesn't sound like mine. I don't sound like I normally sound anyway. I usually choose my words more carefully, more politely. But with him it is not necessary to be careful about what I say. It's refreshing not to have to be so guarded or lie, which I often do. Not everyone needs to know the truth.

It is just the two of us in the room, and when I say such things out loud, I have actually physically shuddered involuntarily. I ask him if he is cold. He doesn't answer so I turn the thermostat up two degrees for my own comfort, knowing that it won't help. It never does. It is a different sort of chill. It's a scary movie kind of feeling. But for a second, I admit that I do worry that saying it out loud increases its chances of happening or makes it real. I feel a tinge of regret, worrying that this is true.

I've known that some people feel the same way about saying the word "cancer" out loud. They think it is bad luck or a curse. People at funerals don't say, "I wonder if I am next?" out loud, even though everyone is questioning this in their mind. People on planes don't talk about them crashing into mountains and people on boats don't speak of them sinking. It's actually illegal to speak of bombs in the airport. This is good, though. It's not always necessary to spread your fear and crazy, even though sharing these extremes is very therapeutic. Even though after something happens, everyone likes to say, "I told you so!" Or, "I was worried about that!" Everyone likes to be right, even if it's about something horrible. Except me, and this, of course. With this, I am happy to be mistaken.

I push this thought and feeling away. If what I fear actually happens, it's not like anyone can track the cause back to me and my fears anyway. I decide I don't believe that this is true.

I am, by nature, a talker, and if everything I ever verbalized came true, we would all be dead by now. I always tell people that it is amazing that Peter's ears haven't fallen off because of all the thousands of words they are forced to absorb in an average day.

This is why it's great that I have someone else to talk to besides Peter sometimes. This way, I can vent to someone else instead of Peter, and I can get some of my horrendous thoughts off my chest. This way, maybe I will manage to talk about something else, anything else, during my and Peter's time together. "I am afraid that she will die, and I will have to bury her. I am afraid that she will disappear, and I won't know what happened to her and I will spend the rest of my life looking for her and she will be where she is being held by someone thinking that I am not trying to find her. I am afraid that she will end up dead somewhere and I will never have a body to bury. I am also afraid that I *will* have a body to bury."

He says nothing, but his eyes tell me that he understands. He is really easy to talk to because he never judges. I am pretty sure that he thinks and fears the same things in his own way. He shows it all differently than I do. He's less dramatic than I am. He is not a talker, but he has very sweet, concerned eyes. Through our eyes is how we connect. He is the quiet one. I am the noisy one. I find him staring into mine all the time. He lacks words, but his kindness pours from his eyes. He gives me the benefit of the doubt and thinks the best of me, even when I don't exactly deserve it.

Strange how the most unlikely of friends surprisingly gives you the most comfort. He tries hard to be there for me even though his abilities are limited. He is a patient listener and never seems to get sick of my rambling and repeating. He understands and never tells me to "Get over it."

"If someone were to ask me my biggest fears," I tell him. People seldom ask other people what their biggest fears are, but I think that they should. I always welcome it when people ask me.

"So, if someone were to ask me...those would be mine," I conclude. It feels good to tell the truth to someone. I always tell him the truth. I know that he can take it. I never lie to the dog.

One of the things I feel guilty about is that while Natalie is the addict, the ill one, the one who is falling apart, I seem to be falling apart right along with her.

Good mothers don't do this I kept telling myself when I felt myself falling into a depression of my own. *Good mothers rally and become stronger and more capable when their children get sick. Good mothers turn into great mothers, going into mommy overdrive.* While I was sliding further into my own depression, one of the things I kept thinking about was all of the inspirational stories that I read in magazines and newspapers about average moms turning into superhuman moms with abnormal strength when their kids were in need, doing things like single-handedly flipping cars over to free their trapped children.

Okay, maybe that isn't for me. But why aren't I at least marching around Washington, DC, or even my congressman's house, which was only a few miles away, with a homemade sign, demanding laws and regulations that would lead to a cure for Natalie?

One day, trying to focus my practically lifeless self, I sat down at the kitchen table and tried to make a list of all the tasks I needed to accomplish to help Natalie. It was my Fix Natalie To-Do List. Good, productive, energetic mothers organize and focus themselves. These mothers jot numerated notes on floral paper and hang them on their refrigerators with inspirationally appropriate magnets.

On my list, which I entitled "Help Natalie" with Natalie's name written in pretty curly script that I decorated with hearts, flowers, crosses, and butterflies, I wrote specific tasks. Clean out and organize her room, help her delete harmful contacts from her phone, help her apply for a part-time job and enroll in classes at the community college, and clean the house so it was trigger-free, removing anything that might lead to temptation.

On the list I also included names and phone numbers of doctors, rehabs, and clinics to call and talk to and make appointments with. I then listed recommended books on addiction written by specialists that I should read.

When I was finished creating the list, I eyed the paper with all of its prettiness like an enemy. I hated every single word I had just written. I did not feel organized and the longer I looked, the more the words seemed to blur and swim on the page. I felt defeated without even beginning, and every task seemed like a mountain to climb. I felt exhausted and depressed.

For a few minutes, I let my tears drop on the paper, watching how the liquid made the ink bleed, causing the colors to run into one another as they combined, creating muddy colors. Then I crumpled the paper into a ball and tossed it into the garbage. Even though it was only noon, I went up to my bedroom, got into bed, and forced myself to sleep for eight hours.

I found out later, after only seeking care for myself, that as unique as I felt I was, I was more typical than I could have imagined. Research has shown that depression and anxiety among the family members of addicts are common. And if you think about it, how could it not be? Considering all of the stress and pressure that the family of an addict is under, as well as factoring in the responsibility we feel, how could we not be affected?

I once had a psychiatrist tell me, "If you weren't feeling a little like you do, that would actually be kind of odd."

The key for family members of addicts is to get help for yourself. While you are running around making monstrous to-do lists of all the ways to help your addicted loved one, don't forget to put helping yourself on the list, too.

And as far as those lists, it was suggested to me not to make them quite so huge, and to break them up into smaller portions. As I always used to tell my children when they were faced with a big job, "How do you eat an elephant?" One bite at a time.

Just like the flight attendant tells you when giving you the emergency instructions, "If there is a problem and we are in distress, put your own oxygen mask on first before trying to help anyone else." Lord knows, many times throughout all of this, I have felt like I couldn't breathe.

The physical health of the families of addicts is often compromised as well. I can attest to this fact, too, with firsthand experience.

During the time that Natalie suffered from addiction, I gained forty pounds. I didn't need a formal study to tell me why I felt sluggish and unmotivated and why I had let myself go, leaving me physically less well. Once when a doctor pointed my weight gain out to me, I did not explain, but instead sat there red-faced and embarrassed, wishing that I could tell him the reason why I was struggling but stayed mute while in my head, saying, *Be me for five minutes, then see how much you feel like going to the gym or eating celery instead of pizza.*

But I can also tell you that help can help. When I finally realized that maybe I needed some care, too, and sought that care, getting myself in both better physical and mental shape, not only did I feel better, but I became better able to help my daughter.

chapter *five*

Hi God! Got a Minute?

I am a person of faith. I love God and I believe in Him. And I want to believe that He believes in and loves me, too.

But I have to admit, sometimes I do wonder about both. When I was younger, I used to think that this signified a lack of faith. But now that I am older, I realize that this is just a part of the faith journey. So, I give myself a pass because I think that the fact that God and I have not been on a five-decade honeymoon just makes me normal. (I am not exactly sure what it says about Him.)

We have our ups and downs. We enjoy the ups and power through the downs. Because I have always found comfort in my faith, I have tried to pass my religion on to my children.

Where Natalie really stands on religion is a bit of a mystery to me. As much as we talk about everything, we maneuver around religion. It is safe to say that she is not headed to the convent any time soon or building a shrine in the backyard. But she doesn't disregard it all or disrespect it either. I am aware that the only reason for this just might be that she knows that outwardly doing either would hurt me. I am grateful for it and will take it.

And me, I take the coward's way out. Because I am afraid to know her deepest feelings, I don't ask. But because it is pretty clear that Natalie and God's relationship is strained, to say the least, right now I am the intermediary and everyone's lawyer. I tell Natalie to just try to believe and trust and to not take everything so personally. (I have no idea what that means, by the way. And I understand that it is pretty difficult to not take one's own life personally. But I am a mother and sometimes we specialize in saying stupid things when we are desperate to persuade our children to believe as we do.)

I have, conversely, on more than one occasion, demanded a meeting with God, trying to explain Natalie's side of the story and telling Him that He is sometimes pretty difficult to defend.

So, if he could at least lighten up or, better yet, shape up, I would appreciate it. For now, in our present state, I continue to accept His ways, trying not to question. And I work on accepting His best work, Natalie, just the way she is.

I have exposed her to and encouraged her to embrace God, and I have always told her that while she can't really see it, I believe that His arms are out and open, and if she would simply reach out, He will reach right back. They both just might need to stretch a bit to make this work. I say that I am a believer, and this is a fact.

The whole truth is that I believe in both of them.

I am in church, it is right after Mass, and as is my custom, I am lighting a candle and lingering in the back as the rest of the congregation—all filled with fresh hope and inspiration—file out.

I always hang around a little longer than everybody else and sneak back into the empty church, hoping to steal a private minute or two with God. I know that He is probably tired, having just spent all of His energy and patience trying to impart His goodness and grace to people who are waiting for the hour to be over and whose minds are somewhere else while they are wishing their bodies were, too.

I understand that this is the end of His workday and all He is wanting to do is get back to his big chair in the sky. The one that is surrounded by fluffy white clouds and floating angels.

I deposit my three dollars. Which I believe is highway robbery, an awful lot to charge just to light a candle. But somehow extremely cheap to fix even one of the problems in my life. So, I pay the price, deciding that the person who set this price thought it through and knew I would fork over the money. I always light the candle in the bottom right corner. This is part of the ritual. I choose this one to light because it is the one closest to me.

When I was little, my mother used to tell me that when someone offers you something from a tray or platter and there are many to choose from, you should take the one closest to you, not the biggest one or the one that looks the best. Reaching for one over the others makes you look selfish. But taking the one nearest to you is polite.

I take the candle from the sandbox that it is stuck in and light it from one of the others. This is a concern as well. I used to never know which other candle to light it from, worried that I wouldn't choose a lucky one. If the person who lit that candle has a lot of luck, maybe that good vibe will somehow burn and seep into my candle and bring me some relief.

I decide to follow my previous policy with this choice, as well, and light the flame from the next closest candle. Is it weird that I worry all week long if the bottom right candle is already lit and I have to choose a different one? I note how quickly my candle lights; if it struggles, I am disheartened, and if it has a false start and lights for just a moment then goes out, I am devastated. The height of the flame matters and means something as well. Sometimes during really troubling times, I stop in during the week to visit the candle and make sure it is still lit.

Some weeks are so bad that I hesitate with fear, my eyes closed as I approach the display, sure that my candle is not lit, extinguished along with any hope I had when I lit it in the first place. Gratefully, the candle has always still been lit.

After I light the candle, I touch the toe of Jesus, who is suffering and cradled in his mother's arms. I always choose the candles in front of this particular statue, the Pieta, partly because it was my father's favorite statue and partly because the fact that Mary, the mother, is holding tight to her struggling child.

I am a mother holding tight to her struggling child, as well. Mary and I have a bond. I silently ask her to intervene. I would for her. We mothers need to stick together.

I look around. The coast seems clear with almost everyone having exited the church and now speeding away in their cars like they are getaway drivers in bank robberies. They are hurrying to beat each other out to get in line first at the local breakfast places. The only Catholic competition more fierce is the fight to get in line at a Lenten Friday Fish Fry.

I leave my candle and will visit it once more before exiting. I am just rounding the corner to go back into the church that I am sure is now empty, and I run smack into a family I know from when my kids were in elementary school.

We all do that jumping and whooping thing people do when they almost run over each other. We laugh and greet each other. "Oh, hi!" I chirp, wishing to be swallowed up by the carpeted church floor. Why am I not on my way to breakfast?

"Chriiiistiiine!" they say. They are a couple and are with their three children.

It's been a few years, but I remember them to be nice people. I'm pretty sure they are Ed and Ellen, which is a cute couple name, but I don't want to blow it, so I call them "you guys," and ask how they are.

They are great, he tells me and reintroduces the children. Lilly, who is older than all of my kids. Jack, who was in Natalie's class. And little Eva, much younger than any of mine.

I ask about them, hoping that they will tell me quickly and hurry off to secure their place in line. They are not in a hurry and tell me that, "you know, life keeps happening." I try not to grimace as I agree.

Not bragging, they tell me that Lilly just completed her second year of college (a good one). And that Jack will "fly from the nest" as well, and with a loving, fatherly hand resting on Jack's shoulder, Ed predicts that Jack will make them proud and soar. I strongly—maybe too eagerly—agree with this, hoping my compliance will equal speed and move this conversation along.

We move on to Eva and thank God that she is still young and around to keep them company. Eva, apparently knowing her importance and having heard this before, basks in her preciousness and emphasizes this with a pirouette right there in the middle of the church. I am actually impressed. She somehow pulls this dance move off well, remaining delightfully precocious instead of obnoxious.

I attempt to move on to "how great it was to see all of them" but in addition to being nice, they are polite, too. "Tell us about your gang!" they demand.

"All good," I insist, hoping to get away with this catchall. Then I speed talk my way into my stock speech. Peter is great. Working hard. Jason is well. Trevor, also great. And Natalie is…hanging in there. Struggling a bit, but hanging in there. Their faces drop. The husband momentarily bows his head. "Struggling" is parent-speak for "not good at all."

While they glance at one another and regroup, I notice Jack's head is down and he is looking at the burgundy carpet and his black dress shoes. He knows. I am not surprised. Kids—especially teenagers—live in an underground world of their own. A world that their parents are not usually privy to. I know that it is not always good. But I kind of respect how they keep some things private. The parents appear to know nothing about Natalie. I would bet that Jack knows things that I don't.

"We all struggle!" Ed proclaims.

Ellen agrees with aggressive nods. "Life works out!"

I am tempted to use the expression "from your lips to God's ears," but while I wish it, I am afraid this might be too dramatic. So, instead, I think it to myself and touch the gold cross I wear around my neck.

"Hey!" pretty-sure-Ellen exclaims, coming alive with excitement. "Jack and Natalie were in the same class! They know each other and were good friends!" This is an overstatement but kind. "Isn't that right Jack? You remember sweet Natalie! We always loved her! Still love her," she amends quickly. "Isn't that right Jack?"

Jack looks up at me with a genuinely sympathetic, knowing

expression that really touches me. I am pretty sure that my baby girl won't be soaring anywhere anytime soon, but I truly hope that Jack flies high.

"She's a nice girl," he tells me. I am almost overcome and feel my eyes mist over. I need to end this. I offer Jack a weak smile that I hope expresses my gratitude, good wishes, and especially my feeling that I've decided he's a good boy.

"Thank you," I tell the parents. "It will all work out!" I hope I have made them feel like they have fixed my life.

We stand there awkwardly for just a split second too long and I am tempted to resurrect the phrase about my lips and the Almighty's ears, but instead I apologize for being rude and holding them back for so long and actually take a step to move through the huddle of their family.

"No, no," Ed protests. "So great to see you Kar—Christine!" Our conversation has him so rattled that he misspoke my name.

I smile so brightly my face hurts and tell them goodbye. They smile back, grab Eva, who had been spinning in circles by her hands, and exit the church, with Lilly and good boy Jack following dutifully. I wonder if Jack will tell them the truth about Natalie in the car on the way to breakfast. It doesn't much matter.

Exhausted and warm, I shrug off my coat and plop down in the center section of pews, last row, end seat. There is no complicated rubric or ritual involved in this choice of seat except that being closer feels too confrontational and off to the side seems too casual. Sitting in the center, I am more likely to get noticed and from the last pew I can hear anyone entering behind me as well as see any prayerful stragglers.

I sigh loudly, more loudly than I like to, but it feels good to do so. I need the air. I guess a sigh is not exactly the best way to begin a conversation, but I don't care. I am frustrated and, honestly, annoyed. And at this moment, I don't think I care that He knows this.

Since He is supposed to know everything anyway, He already does. It's hard to know where or how to begin. It seems like you should start all things from the beginning, but He and I are not strangers. We talk all the time and know each other well. So, instead, I feel free to start in the middle and begin with a question. "Why?" I mutter in a whisper, looking up at the altar. "I mean, really?!"

He and I have been through the whole "God doesn't give you more than what you can handle debate" too many times to revisit that theory. I have previously expressed that I am not sure He isn't wrong about this and cite examples of numerous people I know of personally who have been done in by their struggles and sadness.

I always also counter with the idea that maybe the bigger question is if He somehow gives people more than their fair share of strife. Maybe we should talk about that. And while He and I are at it, please give me the appropriate email and complaint form to fill out to get my excess retracted and this entire mess cleared up.

Peter and I always joke that if we demand loudly enough one day with our faces turned upward toward the sky, like you do in a restaurant when you have received poor service, God will show up to make it all better, apologize, and give us a free dessert and a coupon for a replacement life.

I begin by trying to pray. I need to make up for the Our Father and Hail Mary that I daydreamed through during the regular Mass, and I attempt an Apostle's Creed because I don't remember saying that, either. I think I was trying to remember if I locked the front door during that.

My effort to recite these rote prayers fails as my mind jumps erratically from the events of the week. It had been a difficult seven days. When Natalie was not passed out cold, she stumbled around impaired. I found remnants of drug use everywhere. There were syringes, plastic bags, and lighters. More jewelry is missing. As I think of these things instead of calmly sorting them out in the quiet tranquility of the church and coming to some sort of peace with them, I find myself becoming angrier and angrier, feeling myself quite the unjust victim.

A priest once told me if you cannot pray conventionally and traditionally, then just talk to God. So, I sit back in the pew and say, "Hey, it's me. We need help. All of us but especially her. I know that she hasn't exactly been here much. But I have. And I am asking for her. And that has to count for something. I have been pretty faithful," I point out, realizing that I am defending myself and justifying my request. "Almost devout!"

"So anyway, please. Please, please."

I am tempted to tell Him to just do what He can but decide against this. Now is not the time to sell myself short and settle for less; He might be in the mood to perform a miracle and do something miraculous. A sudden thought pops into my mind. I think I remember the priest saying something that caught my attention and seemed important, but because I was distracted, I don't remember what exactly it was.

Maybe it was something in one of the readings! I grab the book in front of me and quickly find the passages for the day. But when I try to read them, the words swirl on the pages and I am unable to concentrate. I scold myself. Why don't I remember? What if this was that really important something that I needed to know, and it was right there in front of me and I missed it? Did I miss the golden key to the golden door? The magic answer? I sit for a few minutes with my eyes shut, hoping that whatever it is that spoke to me will return unexpectedly like things do when you are relaxed and least expect it.

But I quickly realize that I am both the opposite of relaxed and very much on guard and expecting it. Now I am getting mad. "I'm furious!" I tell him. "Stop ignoring me! I don't deserve this and neither does she! Okay, maybe in some ways I do, even though I don't think I deserve *all* of this. But for sure she doesn't! She is just a kid and you of all people should know her heart! You know how good she is! I know we are not perfect. But jeez! And I know that you are supposed to be perfect...everyone says so anyway. But truthfully...okay I'm not even going to go there! Just stop it! Please."

My mind races. "Chocolate! I love chocolate! I will give up chocolate! That's a sacrifice!" I don't know exactly where, but I am sure that somewhere in the Bible there is something about sacrificing something and getting something in return.

Certainly, bad things don't happen to people who sacrifice. I need to remember to look this up in one of those religious apps. People don't eat fish on Fridays during Lent for nothing, right? But it has to be something you love or it doesn't count. Which is why shrimp and lobster in place of the usual burger for a couple of days seems a little suspect. But anyway, I am covered. I adore chocolate. Chocolate it is!

The only problem with this plan is, some days, a gigantic cup of tea and two pounds of chocolate is the only thing between me and insanity. I will have to look this up in the Bible as well. Maybe there are exclusions just for chocolate.

I give up, and I grab my coat and purse and exit the church. "You're not listening," I grumble. "Even if you are, you apparently don't care."

I all but storm out of the church. I plan to head directly to the car but cannot resist the urge to visit my candle. I stand there assessing it. The flame is tall and strong. That cannot be denied. I watch it flicker, winking at me. I'm a sucker. I begin to soften in spite of my attempts not to. I don't know how long I stand there, mesmerized by the golden colors. A wave of unexpected, fresh hopefulness washes over me. Thoughts of better things sneak into my head.

"Maybe it will be a good week," I sigh.

And instead of heading straight out to the car, I turn and go back into the church for a minute to say I'm sorry and to tell Him that I am willing to give Him another chance.

There's that popular question: "If you could have dinner with anyone living or dead, who would you choose?" I'm pretty sure that I would pick Jesus. And not just because Jesus is the obvious choice. I mean, let's face it, you are supposed to pick Him. You are supposed to want to be with Jesus more than you want to be with anyone else. So, no one can argue with this decision. Choosing Jesus as your number one dinner date is a popular, politically correct move. And, after all He is the obvious choice. I have considered others; I'm kind of fascinated with Oprah. The idea of having Miss Winfrey all to myself for a couple of hours excites me. I have so many great ideas and projects that I really want to turn into realities; I just need her help in launching them. For some reason, when Oprah and I have dinner, it is always at Olive Garden. I would like to have dinner with Morgan Freeman and Robert De Niro. Morgan Freeman reminds me of my dead father and Robert De Niro was my father's favorite. I guess we could all go; I just don't know if they get along. But ultimately, I would most likely choose Jesus. Mostly because I believe that I have more questions for Him than I do for anyone else. I guess, if the truth were told, I really just want to ask Him why. Why me? Why Natalie? Why us? I would want to also ask Him how we are doing, and sometimes when I long for this conversation, I simply just want to know "When will it stop?" I can see myself begging for a happy ending. The question is, who wants to have dinner with me? And at the end of the dinner, my last question would be, "Would you like to have dinner again?" "Or if maybe not a long dinner again, then, how about a quick lunch?"

I do talk to Jesus all of the time, though, and I do believe that He hears me. And while I do believe He even answers on occasion, with subtle signs and graces, face-to-face contact with some concrete answers would be great. As many times as I have had this conversation in my head, I have never been able to guess what He might say to me. I imagine myself pouring my heart out, explaining how painful this struggle is even though I believe He already knows. I know that I will describe the pain to Him just in case. I also wonder what He will order, what He will drink (I'm guessing wine), and who will pick up the check. I've decided on the salmon and rosé (you know, kind of like the wedding at Cana). If I am to be completely honest, though, I do kind of fantasize about Him apologizing, or even about Him giving me some sort of enlightening answer to my questions that has me saying, "Oh, my! Really? That's the reason? I'm sorry that I asked. Very well, then, carry on." But for now, I read my Bible over my usual lunch of pretzels and Diet Coke, searching for answers, studying His words. Then I try to incorporate His teachings into my life with my words and actions. I do this hoping to live in just the way that He would wish me to live, so much so that someday, when someone asks Jesus what person in the world, He would like to have dinner with, He chooses me.

"Maybe it's not your fault," he whispers quietly.

"It is," I answer him in a voice just a little louder than the one in which he spoke to me.

"I don't think it is," he counters.

"I know it is," I tell him, instantly and firmly.

I know he didn't come here to fight and neither did I, so I should not be arguing with him. I know I have frustrated him because while I cannot see the look on his face, I can hear him sigh.

We sit in silence in the darkness of the confessional and I wonder whose turn it is to speak next. I have been particularly tortured lately and am searching. It seems that my searching often leads me to God, and while I am not sure why on this particular day, my sorrow has led me to confession.

It is true that I feel guilty over everything that has happened to Natalie and I believe myself to be at fault. Even if I have not pinpointed specifically what I did wrong, I still feel as if I didn't do all that I could have. I thought that by going to confession, I might be able to ease my sorrow and my hurting heart.

When I first entered the confessional, I had no idea what I was going to say, but once I got going, I completely let the unsuspecting priest on the other side of the screen have it. I wasted no time telling him that I had sinned, that my poor daughter was an addict, and it was all my fault. I all but said, "Here I am! I am the guilty one, let me have it, give me penance of twenty thousand Our Fathers and thirty thousand Hail Marys. Tell me to deliver all of my worldly possessions and my checkbook to the rectory by tomorrow morning. Tell me that it is too late. Tell me that I am not absolved from this sin because it is too bad. Tell me that I am the one person that God has decided not to forgive. But stop telling me that it is not my fault because I know that it is!"

After more silence, I hear the priest clear his throat and shift slightly on the other side of the partition; he is getting ready to say something, so I wait.

"I just don't believe that it is your fault," he says again. "Can you tell me why you are so sure that it is?"

This is useless, I think to myself, but before being done with him, I decide to tell him very emphatically why I am now and will always be the one to blame.

"I am her mother," I seethe. "It is my fault because I am her mother."

I am just about to tell him not to dare tell me again that it isn't when he takes me off guard by saying something in the confines of a confessional that you don't often hear from the priest.

He says, "I'm sorry."

I once saw a bumper sticker that announced, "God Is My Co-Pilot." I always felt this thought to be backward. We should not be driving God anywhere. He should not be in the passenger seat. We should be the one in the passenger seat and God should be the one at the wheel. The bumper sticker should say, "I Am God's Co-Pilot," and if the bumper is long enough, it should also say, "I Am Happy to Be His Passenger and Along for the Ride."

Heck, if I ever looked over and saw God sitting beside me, I'd be scared to death knowing that I was horribly unqualified to drive God anywhere and was in way over my head. I would immediately pull over and switch seats with Him. I would then sit still and quiet in the passenger seat with my hands folded politely on my lap, not even touching the radio dial and resisting the urge to ask, "Are we there yet?"

I would be happy to wait patiently to see where He was taking me. My faith is strong enough that I know that no matter where God is taking me, for sure it is a great place.

I will fix you
Even if it brings me pain
I will fix you
Even when I have nothing

I will fix you
Even if you treat me like dirt
I will fix you
Even when it's all hurt

I will fix you
Any time of any day
I will fix you
As long as you'll stay

I will fix you
If you stay with me
I will fix you
Until you see me free

I will stay
Even if there are problems we can't atone
I will fix you
Just anything but being alone

—Natalie

There is a parable that tells of how in life, each of us has a cross to bear. And how we all believe that our crosses are heavier and harder to carry than everyone else's. It says that if we had the opportunity to unload the cross that life had given us and put it on top of a pile of crosses that others had discarded, that if we could choose another cross to carry through life, we would ultimately decide to pick up our original cross again and carry it.

Having been given the cross, the heartbreak, of being the mother of an addict, I've often believed that my cross is heavier than most. I've often wondered how I can take such a heavy cross and have something good come of it.

I believe that each of our crosses is individual, meant only for us. We might not be able to decide which cross we receive. But we can control what we do with it.

It's Halloween. I hate Halloween. I have tried to analyze exactly why this is the case and the only explanation that I can come up with is that we do it in the dark. I am afraid of the dark, so going out into the black abyss and walking the streets, fending off strangers dressed as frightening things, unsettles me. I am honestly grateful that my children are older and my participation in this event is limited.

I don't mind staying home and handing out the candy, though. Over the years, I have earned the reputation of being that nice lady in the nice house who gives good candy; in fact, I have become pretty popular. Our house sits up on a small hill, so I needed to up my game and give full-size candy bars for the trick-or-treaters to find it worth the climb.

Priding myself on being an equal opportunity candy giver, I welcome all ages and offer my fuss equally. I know that some people aren't as welcoming to the older kids, thinking that they shouldn't still be trick-or-treating. But sometimes I think they need it all the more. Sometimes people lose sight of the fact that under that unsavory teenage exterior is an overgrown child.

So, if they take the time to dress up, walk the neighborhood, climb the hill, ring the bell, and chant "Trick or treat!" to me, they get a big Kit Kat bar. And in some cases, depending on how needy they look, they may get two.

On one particular Halloween, I had just finished gushing over a very large gorilla, Freddie Krueger, and a bleeding zombie. They seemed particularly awkward, so they each got a candy bar and a dollar. I only resort to money in extreme cases and only the most downtrodden have me running for my purse. I could smell their teenager-ness as soon as they appeared. Their mothers need to address this.

It was the end of the night, so why not get rid of the candy? When I give money, I used to say, "Don't smoke it or drink it," but Peter says that I shouldn't because maybe it will give them ideas. I have stopped, but I believe they already have plenty of ideas. I honor Peter's request and satisfy my worry by whispering *don't drink it or smoke it* instructions to myself like a prayer as they are turning away, muttering the little gratefulness they know how to express.

And I am beginning to close the door when tiny Natalie appears in the doorway, taking their place. Where they completely filled the door frame, her minute being looks dwarfed by the space.

It is actually not Natalie, of course. Natalie is nearly twenty now and off doing God knows what as I am answering this door.

But this little being is staring up at me with the same dark beautiful eyes that Natalie has and had as a child, and they are melting my heart. She is dressed in a pink princess costume that I am pretty sure we also owned at one point. Her dark brown hair is spilling in disheveled tangles out of her bedazzled silver crown and onto her shoulders. The gown that she wears is too big for her, which makes it even cuter on her.

"Hi," I say, kneeling down to her level. "You are simply amazing."

Her mother, who is giving her space to complete this chore on her own and is standing about ten feet back, nods and smiles gratefully, letting me know that she can hear me.

"What's your name?" I ask. She mumbles something inaudible and I look to her mother for help. She mouths what I think by reading her lips is the name Emma, and I ask, "Are you Emma?" The nod of her head confirms this.

"Hello, Emma. Thank you for coming," I say, deciding that she is probably three. She looks up at me with big doe eyes and seems to suddenly remember her part in this choreographed event, sighs, and says, "Twick or tweet." I am melting.

"Yes, yes!" I answer, coming to life and remembering that I have a part to play as well. "Trick or treat to you!" I say, fulfilling part of my obligation while reaching into the candy bowl and pulling out three candy bars. I put them in the plastic orange jack-o'-lantern that she is carrying. They are too big for the bucket and I have to push the black handle out of the way to wedge them in.

"Say thank you, Emma," her mother prompts.

"Sank you!" she chirps. I have decided that she should keep this adorable speech impediment forever. No need for correction. It is completely becoming.

"Wait!" I protest when she begins to turn away.

I scramble for my purse on the steps behind me, fish furiously, sending some of its contents flying, and locate a dollar bill. Not enough. I dig more and locate a five. Deeming this unacceptable as well I fish around one more time with both hands and pull out a ten.

"Here, this is for you, too," I whisper. "Maybe your mom will take you to get something special."

Emma peers into the pumpkin, and I am glad that she can tell, even with only the dim lighting of the outdoor light and the moonlight, what I have placed on top of the candy. She looks up and smiles at me. It is amazing how young they realize the sight of money and its value.

Emma pauses just long enough for me to stuff the rest of the remaining candy from my bowl into her bucket. It's the end of the night. I am out of energy, and, besides, she deserves it.

The mother smiles gratefully at me and takes her daughter's hand. I watch their silhouettes as they make their way down the steps. I want to call to the mother to be sure to hold onto her daughter's hand tightly and to always keep her just that close, but of course, I do not.

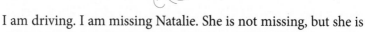

I am driving. I am missing Natalie. She is not missing, but she is gone.

She spends her days sleeping, and when it is time for me to go to bed, she is coming to life and going out to who knows where. Even when I do catch her awake, she is unhappy and disinterested. I try, but I am unable to talk sense into her. And I feel like I am losing her.

I am beating myself up over and over, asking myself how I could have possibly let things get this bad. I miss her. My heart actually aches, longing for the little girl she once was. I want the old her, the old me, the old us.

I stop at a red light and something flittering in the air catches my attention out of the corner of my eye. It is a tiny hand waving from the car next to me. I squint to see that the delicate little arm belongs to a beautiful blonde girl around three years old. She smiles brightly when she realizes she has gotten my attention, which was probably her goal. How precious it is to have such hope and confidence in a complete stranger that you wave wildly at them for nothing more than a wave back.

I smile and wave at her. I exaggerate both my facial expression and my gesture, putting everything I have into it. I want her to know I am grateful.

She amps up her grinning and waving, and I do the same. I am so fixated on this little girl that I almost don't notice the mother in the driver's seat. "She's beautiful!" I say out loud, knowing she cannot hear me but hoping that she can read my lips. She does, and I nod when I see that she mouths the words, "Thank you."

I can tell that the little girl says something to the mother by the way her mother tilts her head backward and says something. The mom turns back to me and takes the collar of her shirt in two fingers and pulls it. She is trying to tell me that her daughter wants to show me her shirt. I nod to both of them with an expectant look. I watch as the little girl climbs up on the seat so that I can see all of her through the window. Proudly, she sticks out her belly and points to the pink glittery script that is written on the shirt. It says, "Brave and Beautiful."

I smile and nod as big as I can. She grins and wags her head. I give her a thumbs-up and she offers the same to me. I watch as, at her mother's direction, she climbs back down, sits, and replaces the seatbelt. The light turns green and we exchange final smiles and waves. She throws me a kiss and I throw many furiously back to her.

I wish for both me and Natalie to be a little bit younger. I could buy (or make!) her an entire closet full of T-shirts with phrases like, "Brave and Beautiful," "Wild and Wonderful," "Flawed but Fearless." Definitely one that simply says "Loved."

The time for glittery clothes has passed, but that doesn't mean that I can't go home and tell her I believe that she is all of these things.

I turn the car around and head home to do this.

No one can ever hate me
More than I can
This is not how it was supposed to be
This wasn't the plan

My family still loves me
Their resentments they shelf
I wish I could say the same
I wish I could love myself

They have taken me back in
Time and time again
So I try and be there
When one needs a friend

I hope they know my intentions
Are always pure
As I fight this disease
Without a cure

So if I leave this earth early
I hope that they know
I wouldn't have had it any different
And how much I love them so

—Natalie

Like all mothers giving birth to their babies, I felt it with my own body. I felt the moment that Natalie came into the world. I am sure that I am not unique in remembering this moment. It was painful but somehow okay at the same time. It was an appropriately significant moment.

I have often wondered if when a child dies, the mother somehow feels this within her own body, too. Many mothers, and others included, often speak about having a feeling that something has happened to someone they love.

But this is not what I am talking about. I want to know if they have some random inkling. Fearing that it might be rude to do so, I have never been brave enough to ask a mother who has suffered this cruel loss this question.

I visualize myself in this position often and have decided that I hope if Natalie passes that I do feel something at that moment. And I want it to be painful. I am not talking a little twinge or a Braxton Hicks contraction. I want full-on pain.

If my baby is leaving me and the world, I want to know this undeniably. And I want to know this at that exact moment. That moment in time should be significant, too.

I think that while losing a child is never fair, it would be fairer this way.

But in this case, I want to feel pain. Maybe if I do, the pain will be in my heart and I will feel a piece of my heart being ripped out, or shattering to pieces.

Maybe if Natalie ever leaves me and I feel her leaving me, she will somehow know that I am feeling it, too, and she won't be going alone.

It is the night before Thanksgiving, and I have cooked myself silly. The food is made and jam-packed into the refrigerator, waiting to make its grand appearance the next day.

I cooked alone in the kitchen for hours, hoping Natalie would join me. But this wasn't meant to be; I was pretty sure she was impaired upstairs in her bedroom. I called her a few times, telling her this would be a great time for us to spend some nice time together. But after the third round of begging and pleading, I gave up and attacked my work alone. I cannot compete with Vicodin.

Finally, five hours later, I am all done and the kitchen is cleaned up. I am rewarding myself by strategically smooshing two pieces of double chocolate cake together so that I can tell everyone, including myself, that I practiced self-control and only ate one piece of cake. I am also using a fancy dessert plate as a reward. And if the universe makes sense at all, and I believe that it does, I am only absorbing the calories of one piece.

Natalie comes into the kitchen. I always eat my dessert on special plates even if it is just a regular day and not a holiday. I feel I deserve this. I am wrestling with life and so far, life is a worthy formidable opponent, pinning me to the mat several times. But I give forth a courageous effort.

So, a treat every day is my just due. Toward the end of every day, if it looks as if I have made it through, I reward myself. And I use the fancy dinnerware because I will make my mini holidays when I can. And dessert should always be an event.

Things have been horrible lately with Natalie. "Hi," she says and sits down to join me. She looks at the cake on my plate. Knowing me well and what I have done, she smiles. "I love you," she tells me, laughing approvingly. I smile back.

"Anything new?" I ask. She shakes her head that nothing is. I am glad that she has settled comfortably back into the seat and is not in a rush to disappear and do something that she should not be doing. I take a sip of my tea.

"I have a question," I tell her, thinking of something that has been on my mind. "Where did you go last Thanksgiving?"

Holidays seem to only be days that exaggerate our difficulties and unhappiness. They add to the pressure. When life is tough, trying to keep the turkey moist, the mashed potatoes lump-free, and coming up with the perfect gift for everyone, while at the same time chasing away drug dealers, watching for overdoses, and ditching syringes, things get stressful.

If given the choice, I will take a regular uneventful Tuesday over a holiday any day.

When things are bad and your only prayer for the day is that nothing horrific happens when most people are wishing for the day to contain magical moments or miracles, it's sad.

Most days, I feel lucky if we escape tragedy. And when I get out of bed, I am grateful that we avoided tragedy throughout the night and pray that when I lie back down in that same spot at the end of the day, I can say the same about the day I just lived.

But the holidays happen whether you want them to or not. Sometimes, that's a good thing; sometimes, not so much. One thing the special days do, though, is get me thinking… Things that you never think you would do, think or feel, people you never thought you would meet, places you thought you would never be, life is made up of these like a puzzle.

Last Thanksgiving, Natalie had promised to help me, and after spending the majority of the morning trying to rouse her from bed, she was finally helping me a bit. For a few minutes. But then, without warning, I heard the slam of the front door. And she was gone. She did not return until the next day.

"To get stuff," she tells me. I nod. I guess I should have known this. "Sometimes it's hard on holidays."

"What do you mean?" I ask her. I am so naïve.

"Well," she begins, "It's a holiday and all of my dealers are celebrating the holiday and with their mothers and stuff."

This statement practically startles me so much that it makes me flinch. The thought of these people celebrating holidays with their mothers. Or even having mothers, for that matter, surprises me. "So, they are closed for the day?" I ask her. "I don't get it."

She smiles. We find ourselves doing this, smiling or laughing about things that should not be joked about. This conversation should definitely be filed under this category. "Pretty much," she tells me. "I mean they need a day off, too, I guess."

I am so dumbfounded by the thought that a drug dealer should need time to rest from doing his evil that I let the statement pass and don't bother to comment.

"They are usually with their families and they don't want you to come there," she clarifies.

"So, what do you do?" I ask her, knowing that she is so severely addicted that she cannot do without these drugs for an entire day without suffering horrendous withdrawal.

"If you pay extra, they usually let you come if you meet them a few streets away or something," she tells me. The thought that she is paying extra and probably begging these guys nearly kills me.

"So, it is kind of like the reverse of a holiday sale," I state. Supply and demand.

"I guess," she grins amused by my analogy.

"I may not know this particular business," I admit. "But I do know shopping. Do they ever have sales?"

"Yes," she says. Apparently, this is not as dumb a question as I originally thought.

"I've gotta hear this," I admit.

"Well, if they are not your regular guy and they want you to be, sometimes they will give you a break to steal your business."

"Do they raise their prices once they have you as their customer?"

"Yes," she tells me. "But moving from one to another is risky." I can tell she is speaking from experience. "If you try to leave the new guy you moved to and go back to your first guy, your original guy will be pissed and charge you more because you tried to leave him."

"That is some sort of scheme," I tell her. "I just can't remember the name. Any other sales?"

"Lots." She smiles with a look that is asking me if I really want to know all of this. I do, so I nod for her to go on. "Well, if they are getting ready to go to jail and need to get rid of their stuff, then they sometimes sell it cheaper."

"Good God!" I exclaim, abandoning my effort to remain calm or cool. "A going out of business clearance sale!" Natalie laughs heartily as I shake my head. "What else?" I demand, acting as annoyed as I should be but less than I actually am.

"They often give you stuff cheaper after they have been in jail and have come out and want your business back again."

I drop my head, letting it fall onto the table. "Okay…" I say sarcastically. "A grand opening special!" I raise my head just so that my rolling eyes can be seen. "Everything but free samples."

Then I get a glimpse of Natalie's face. "Nooo," I say flabbergasted.

"Tell me they don't!" Natalie nods her head in the affirmative.

"Sometimes, they will give you stuff free to get you hooked. Then once you are, start charging you. A lot."

My stomach suddenly feels queasy. I wonder if with such horridness going on and with so much working against us, we will ever be able to get out of all this. There is another battle waiting every time we turn around. I get up from the table, give my tummy a pat, and head to the dishwasher to put in my dirty dishes.

"What's wrong?" Natalie asks innocently as I purposely turn my back to her.

"Too much cake," I lie.

For those who died young
But are still breathing
I know how you feel
You get to a certain age
Where everything's just so surreal
You weren't supposed to make it this far,
And yet here you are
So lost, it's like you're in the driver's seat
With someone else steering the car
Hold on to the wheel if you dare
Try and make a plan
I know you,
I am you...we just do the best we can

— Natalie

I am terrified. Natalie has been barricaded in her room for days at a time lately, and while I prefer this to her being missing, I am still nervous because I have not heard sounds from her room in too many hours.

I am a coward. Time passes without me hearing anything, so I call up loudly from the kitchen. Nothing, so I call up louder. Then I resort to calling her on her cell phone. But I do not go into her room. I am petrified at what I might see behind that closed door, so I stay on the other side, begging for any noise that signals she is okay.

Selfishly, I wish Trevor was home. He has accompanied me into the room on several occasions when I was in this situation before; he is far braver than me. And to be truthful, he has always stepped in front of me and gone first. I wish he was here to take charge.

I did try to call Peter, which I try not to do because he deals with so much at work on a routine day anyway, but he didn't pick up. In the OR, I guess. I am left to myself.

When my children were little and they were facing something difficult, some scary or hard challenge or task, they would occasionally ask if there was someone who could do whatever we needed done. They would ask if there were people to call. I would always explain, "We are those people." And this problem was theirs to solve.

I think of this and tell myself I am that person and to get on with it. I gather the dropper full of courage I do possess but find a way to procrastinate for just a couple more seconds by picking Natalie's dirty clothes up from the hallway floor that have been there for days.

While I do this, I call her name. "Natalie!! Matlie-girl!" I yell. Still, no answer.

I am being cheerful to will good karma into this terrifying moment and act casual. Who am I acting casual for exactly? Maybe myself, like a personal pep talk. I gather the clothes, toss them into a pile, and stand before the door.

I have already rehearsed my plea to the 911 operator. I want to be able to give them all of the information they need to get to us as quickly as possible, and because I am a disaster under pressure, I am worried I will blow it.

I wonder if I will sound like I am supposed to. I have watched my fair share of *Dateline* and have heard the police remark that someone did not act the way a distraught person should act. I have no idea what that means or how panicked people should behave. But I think it's like when people who are claiming to be sad, cry without tears. These people always become suspects.

I knock on the door lightly at first, then rap louder. There is no response. I turn the knob and the click of the handle, while not very loud at all, startles me, and it jolts me so much that I actually pee a little. I decide to go for it, and with one swift motion and call out of her name I push the door open.

Natalie is on the bed, motionless, and my last effort should have surely woken her. The room and especially the bed are a complete mess. She is surrounded by hordes of stuff. And my stomach instantly feels sick when I see what I have grown to know is the cap of a syringe on the bed next to her.

There is an empty stamp bag of heroin with the word "hideous" on it. *You can say that again,* I think to myself, picking up both the cap and paper sack and placing them into the pocket of my jeans.

"Natalie!" I call again. She doesn't respond, so I reach out and touch her arm while calling yet again. *Does her skin feel cold? Oh my God! Is she cold?*

"Natalie!" My voice is shrill and urgent.

Then finally, gratefully, she moves. It's just a little, but she does move. Then slowly she comes to life, her face contorting and forming into a grimace while she stretches and reaches down blindly for the covers to pull up over her naked body. She is cold. But not that kind of cold. For the first time, I notice the window is open.

"NATALIE!" I shout with all my fear now turning to anger. She opens her horribly bloodshot eyes and squints at me through their narrow slits.

"What?" she groans, annoyed. I am livid! How can she actually have the audacity to be irritated by me?

"What?" I bellow. "What do you mean, what? *What* is that the way you have all of us living is disgraceful! That is *what!*"

I want a response, but know I will not get one because she is back to sleep or whatever you call this kind of knocked-out impaired state she is in. I glare down at her, wanting her to know how furious I am with her, but I don't make any more attempts to tell her this.

I have been so angry at her during other times similar to this that I would yell and scream at her, trying to express my fury, and Peter encouraged me to stop, telling me that I am wasting my breath. "You cannot talk sense into an impaired person," he always points out.

Hearing his words in my head, I turn to walk out of the room. I take a step and plant my foot squarely on a used syringe. I yelp in shock and pain. Natalie moves slightly and offers a small groan at the sound. I am angry that she is groaning because the sound of my pain is disturbing her slumber and not because of any sympathy she feels for me.

I reach down and pull the needle out of my skin and examine the pinpoint hole. I take the needle. I fish the cap that I found out of my pocket and replace it, then carefully place it in the same pocket that I put the empty stamp bag in.

I walk out of the room and kick at the pile of dirty clothes that I had just gathered, scattering them. I only make it to the top of the stairs before I have to sit down so I can have a good cry.

I am out of bed, which makes me a hero. It has been a difficult week with Natalie. A week that included an overdose. Things are calmer now—or maybe less tragic would be more appropriate words—and I am feeling sorry for myself.

I have managed to leave the bed and the shower, and make my way to the local Panera. I like the flurry of people that the coffee shop holds at lunchtime, and sometimes, I believe that the energy emanating from their bodies seeps into mine and gives me a lift.

It takes all the self-control I have not to tell complete strangers, "Look at me! I am suffering and practically dead, but I brushed my teeth!" I pathetically want them to know how courageous I am being and want them to applaud me. I want them to see the bright red cape that I envision is flowing from my back.

But then I wonder how many of them are being heroic, too, just by being at Panera and are wearing their own costumes, signifying them as fellow superheroes.

I attempt to feel a little less sorry for myself and will any sort of feelings of humbleness that I can muster up and encourage them to bubble to the surface.

I buy an iced tea from a young cashier named Anna. This is Natalie's middle name, and was almost her first name. *Is this coincidence a sign or signal of some kind?* I plop myself down onto my favorite corner seat. *Is the fact that the seat is vacant another sign?* I sigh so loudly that the two guys in the adjoining booth look up.

I look at them with an expression that is an apologetic yet playful grimace. It acknowledges that first, I realize my sigh was too loud;

second, it has been a difficult morning; and third, I promise not to do it again. They smile back with simple grins of understanding.

The gentlemen return to their conversation and I go back to my pity party, deciding that there are no such things as signs. The cashier's name is Anna because her mother knew how to choose nice names and my seat was empty because in the winter it is colder than the rest of the seats, and in the summer, the sun shines too hot through the window.

I stare mindlessly out the window and am not consciously thinking about or listening to anything when my attention is drawn back to the two guys next to me. One clears his throat and says the name "Bethany" in a way that has me believing Bethany has given him a headache even before I see him reach up and massage the bridge of his nose.

The other guy repeats this name with a definite lack of fondness equal to the amount the man before had. Before they continue, I realize that whoever Bethany is, and whatever Bethany has done, she has made herself a problem and has done something less than stellar. The way that they have both spoken her name in a distasteful manner that most people reserve for spoiled spinach, I know that they are not there to discuss her promotion, commendation, or the best location of her employee-of-the-month photo.

I am so intrigued that I am almost giddy. Eagerly and unapologetically waiting for the gossipy details, I try not to blow my cover and sip my tea as if I am just another tea-sipping Panera patron. With this sip, I realize that my cup is almost empty, and I could use another Sweet 'N Low. But I would not leave my precious, newly lucky seat as I wait for what they say next.

"She needs to go," the one says bluntly to the other. I wait for the other man's reaction and at first, because of his silence, I am thinking that he is about to disagree. But when I glance over, I change my opinion and decide he is just thinking.

Not waiting for a verbal response, the one that spoke first adds, "She calls them junkies." I audibly gasp. I hate that word. It makes me livid. It is disrespectful and cruel to refer to people suffering from addiction as junkies.

I sit next to these guys, and I am hot with fury now, invested in how this plays out. I have never wanted anything more in my life than I want for Bethany to lose her job right then.

As I wait, trying not to make myself so obvious, I catch sight of the knapsack on the floor leaning on the leg of the table that I hadn't noticed before. These guys are from a clinic that treats addicts. My heart pounds and I realize that I am holding my breath waiting for the second guy's response. "Unacceptable," he sighs. "She needs to go."

Outwardly, I pretend to focus on things out the window. Inwardly, I am rising from my seat and applauding, giving these two strangers a standing ovation. I listen further as they begin to wrap up their meeting.

It is safe for me to study them as they gather their things. They have genuinely kind faces. They shake hands, and right before they part, one of them glances at me. He catches me looking directly at him, and my nod keeps him from looking away. That moment of pause allows me to connect.

"Thank you," I say quietly. He looks at me expectantly. "My daughter is an addict. So, thank you for what you do." My voice catches in my throat. Both men look down at me with kind sympathy. "I'm sorry," I say, "I didn't mean to be listening."

"No worries," the one tells me. "You hang in there." He fishes a business card out of his wallet and hands it to me.

"It's tough on moms," the other acknowledges. I smile gratefully at them both.

"Take care of you so that you can take care of her," the one tells me.

"And it is not your fault. Your daughter is sick," the taller of the two says.

I am incapable of words and can feel tears of gratitude pooling in my eyes. We exchange smiles and say goodbye. As I watch them leave, I wonder if everyone else in Panera can see the superhero capes flowing from their backs.

For anyone who is struggling
Just know you are not alone
And anyone who is sinless
Can cast the first stone

Our sins are darker
Our life's harder than many
We did what we had to do
And searched for love if there was any

So ignore those who judge you
They just do not understand
For anyone who needs you
Try and lend a helping hand

Some will take advantage
Others will use you
Learn from your mistakes
Find someone who is true

Learn from your mistakes
Try and make amends
Try and make your mark
Before your life ends

—Natalie

"Mrs. Naman, we would like to take a few more images. The doctor would like to see a couple of other views," the nurse tells me with just-in-case sympathy in her eyes. She guides me back to the mammogram room that I had just been in a half an hour before. "I'm sure everything is just fine," the nurse soothes, like she is afraid that I am going to break.

After she positions me in the machine and steps behind a glass window and a computer screen, she pushes a couple of buttons, then frees me. After I cover up, she takes my hand and squeezes it supportively. "I know this is a big deal," she tells me. "And you must be scared." I smile weakly back at her, giving her hand a reciprocal squeeze and thank her.

I go into the dressing room and before putting on my top, I look at my breasts in the mirror and frown. I think they should be called boobs instead. They are droopy. Somehow, calling them breasts makes them sound as if they are perky. They do not deserve this title. They are definitely boobs. They look like they should belong to me because they look as if they are just as sad and tired as I am.

As I dress, I think of the nurse's words. I am glad that I resisted the temptation to tell her what I am thinking. I am thinking that, first, everything is not fine. That things have not been fine for too long now. But not for the reason she thinks.

I am glad I didn't tell her that I don't really think this is a big deal. Not really in comparison anyway. And that if she thinks I am fragile and needs to talk to me gently, I appreciate this, but I am actually already broken. I am scared but for other reasons. I am actually not afraid of this at all. The only thing I wish I would have told her is that she would be surprised at how remarkably brave people get when the worst thing that can happen to them, has already happened.

I am fiddling on my phone. Peter and I share a phone plan and an iCloud account with the kids, so apps tend to appear on my phone randomly. It seems the applications downloaded onto their phones also sometimes appear on mine. I notice an icon on the screen that I have not seen before. It's called "Sober Time." I study it, instantly knowing who has put it there and what it is all about.

I think for a few moments, trying to decide if pressing it was right or not. It is private and Natalie is not expecting me to see it. But will she mind? She has been doing well and I am proud of her.

I click on it and watch the bright golden sunrise pop up. Nice touch. I blink. The numbers must be incorrect. I am surely reading it wrong. It says that she has been clean for three days, two hours, ten minutes, and six… seven… eight seconds.

I stare at it and watch the time tick upward. I am not reading it wrong. There is only one way to read it. I understand that any clean time is good and to be commended. So, three days is three days for the better. But still my heart falls into my stomach and I feel suddenly deflated and tired. She told me last night that she had been clean for twenty-seven days.

I pick up the phone to call Natalie. Not to confront her or yell or anything. But just to ask. But when I do, I lie and tell her that I just called to remind her to take the chicken out of the freezer for dinner. There is no sense in trying to talk to her now. I can tell by her voice that she is impaired.

"Hi," Natalie says perkily, appearing in the doorway of the family room where Peter and I are watching television.

It is a random Thursday evening with nothing much special about it. We are watching something mindless, a half-hour sitcom of some sort because it is before ten o'clock, which is my TV time. I control the remote, not that I get to press the buttons or anything. Peter still does that, having the actual controller to his left, which is on the other side of me. He has a need to have physical possession of it. But he does follow my instructions and put on the channel I request.

Different things soothe each of us and take us away from our reality. For me and TV, the dumber, the better. For him, the more intelligent, the better. So, before I go to bed at ten o'clock, we watch my stuff, and after ten, I give him a kiss good night and leave him to his own comfort and a documentary or flying show, where he will learn something new and interesting. My brain is too crowded and exhausted—it runs laps inside my head—to learn anything else.

"Hi Honey!" I greet her. "Hi Nat!" Peter says.

Things with Natalie have not been horrible, but they certainly are far from optimal. She's not in school and does not have a job, so she is doing virtually nothing with her life. Peter is completely impatient with this and I don't blame him. Natalie's IQ was tested once at over 150, and regardless of what she tells her psychologist and psychiatrist, she did not grow up in a house of horrors, so she has absolutely no excuse to be doing nothing. Because doing most anything that she would wish to do is within her ability.

I came from a middle class, traditional household, and while I was expected to accomplish at school and hold a job, it was all rather cushy.

But for Peter, who grew up in Beirut, Lebanon, in the middle of war, spent much of medical school dodging bombs as he went back and forth to class during the day, and studied by candlelight at night because bombs had knocked out the electricity, this is completely unacceptable. While I often campaign for him to be a little more patient with her, he is not wrong.

"What's up?" I ask Natalie while simultaneously telling Peter to "try channel four." He does as she begins to answer.

"Nothing. You know, just chillin'," she answers.

I don't look at Peter and don't have to to know that he is wearing a certain expression that he always does when he is extra annoyed. "No one should ever just be chillin'," he has said many times before.

"You need to do more than just chill," I tell her, making a conscious effort to accept the role of the bad guy in this new act of the play that we are about to put on. Peter has worked hard all day and he needs a break.

When you are dealing with an addict, you don't have the luxury of choosing the time and place for your battles. You need to have them when the addict is not impaired and is fully present to try to talk some sense into them. But when I am at my best—in the morning—she is at her worst because addicts mix up their days and nights. I cannot count the times in the evening that I have decided I would wait until I was fresh and centered the next morning to talk to Natalie rather than when I've had a full day and was exhausted. I would deliver the well-rehearsed speech that would reach her and turn her around—only to spend the entire day trying to wake her up from a stupor. Tonight, I am tired and take the low-key approach.

"I know," she agrees. "I've really been thinking about starting school again." I don't believe her and I doubt she does either.

"It's a start," I concede.

"You need a job!" Peter barks. Apparently, he still has some left-over energy from the day and did not get the memo that he was supposed to be playing the part of the good guy.

"You do," I reinforce. "You need to get on with it."

"You need to become physically and financially independent," he says, raising his voice.

I reach over and gently touch his arm to try to calm him. It is late and we are not going to solve anything right now. His skin feels sweaty and I worry that his blood pressure is soaring. We don't need another crisis. I wasn't sure he felt my touch but realize he did when he sighs in disgust and settles back into the couch. After twenty-five years of marriage, it is possible to communicate this way.

"Try channel two," I tell him, realizing that he has exited the conversation. He switches the station and squints at the TV.

"Mommy! I got you something today!" Natalie tells me. She knows for the moment that she has won, so she addresses only me, trying to engage me in conversation. I am furious at what she has done to Peter. An addict's manipulation skills are second to none.

"Dad and I are trying to watch a show," I say, simultaneously telling Peter that I am on his side and will not tolerate this for much longer.

"Try forty," I tell him. He doesn't. I knew he wouldn't. He often draws the line at channel forty, the Hallmark Channel.

"Okay!" she says cheerfully, fishing something out of her pocket. "I just saw this and thought about how much you would like it! It's a present!" She walks across the room and hands it to me. It is a key chain made up of colorful plastic gems made into the shape of a smiling frog hung on a gold-colored metal loop. It is not expensive, and she is right, it is exactly my taste. I like things blingy and fun. But it is difficult for me to keep the disgusted look off of my face. I take it from her and am unable to offer more than a nod.

"Dad and I are trying to watch this." I motion toward the television without even knowing what is on the screen.

She either doesn't notice or pretends not to notice my mood and tone. "Okay! You guys have a good night! I think I'm gonna go out!"

Peter shakes his head in annoyance and makes a certain noise in his throat that he always does just after Natalie leaves the room, and we sit there silently for a few moments before he says, "You didn't even thank her."

"No. I did not," I tell him emphatically, setting the key chain on the table next to me, not wanting it in my hands any longer. The frog's smiling face was annoying me.

"It wasn't nice that she thought of you and bought you a present?" he asks genuinely confused. "She still loves you."

I hesitate, deciding on my next words. Do I spare his feelings? Do I make his evening even worse? Just because my day has gone up in flames, should I set his ablaze as well? I sigh, choosing honesty. "She stole it," I tell him flatly.

He stops looking at the television and swings his head suddenly to face me. He doesn't say anything, but with his eyes he asks if I am sure. "Completely sure," I answer.

He hesitates, sighs, faces the screen again, and begins to flip through the channels. "Sorry," he says, and I know he really does feel bad for me because he turns on the Hallmark Channel.

Feeling like a criminal, I drive to the craft store down the street.

I am nervous and have a sick feeling in my stomach. It is true that they say your children turn you into different people than you normally would be. Because of your kids, I have very diverse experiences. Sometimes this is good. Because of my children, I have been to a coal mine, I've met Wiz Khalifa, and I learned to quilt.

And I know there are very good friends I never would have made had they not been the parents of my children's friends and I was thrown together with them doing some sort of mandatory volunteer work at the school or at some sporting event.

But sometimes, diverse experiences can be bad.

I park in the lot in the farthest spot I can find. It will be faster to get out of the lot if I park closer to the road like this. But maybe this is a bad move. Why is it that cars that are parked by themselves in not-so-crowded parking lots look suspicious?

I sit in the car for a few minutes before I do something that the old me, the before-kid me, would never even dream of doing. I gather a tiny bit of determination and courage and get out of the car, looking back at it and willing it to look less guilty. I do not want to call any more attention to myself than I have to. I walk across the parking lot and into the store.

The cashier and someone who appears to be a manager greet me. I greet them back, not knowing if I remembered to smile or not because I am too busy wondering if I look suspicious. Do people who look suspicious smile or not? I tell them that no, I don't need their help and that I know exactly where what I am looking for is.

This is a lie. I am a liar now, too. Pre-kid me never lied.

Actually, I don't know where what I am looking for is. But I do know exactly what I am looking for.

I grab a cart and begin methodically going up and down the rows of aisles. There are crafts galore. The pieces are here for anything you would ever want to make.

Peter doesn't get crafting because he says that you can buy for pennies at the dollar store everything that we are trying to make because the Chinese have already made it for us and even shipped it to us. He is not wrong. I made a wreath once that cost one hundred and fifty dollars. Target sold twenty just like it but ten times better for fifteen dollars. I tried to explain to him that it is all about the process, but he doesn't get this.

Natalie loves doing crafts and, honestly, she is quite good at it. And she does benefit from the process. Crafting gives her something to do with her time, keeps her hands busy, and allows her to be creative. I like crafts. I am creative and have good ideas and great vision, but I am impatient and need instant gratification. I hurry projects and don't follow directions well. When it says to dab the glue, I pour. And when they say to add tiny touches of glitter, I, well...I pour again. I defend the last one, though. More glitter is capable of making most things better.

I am about halfway through the store before I spy what I came for. They are hung on a rack at the end of an aisle. Someone once told me that the things they display like this are called "spontaneous buys" and are positioned this way for easy reach. People tend to choose them without much thought. There is irony in this.

I crouch down and look at them more closely. Yes, they are the right ones. I am just about to make my move when the helpful manager checks in with me again. I pop up and assure her that all is well. Stupid me! I should have at least put something in the cart in an effort to not look so suspicious.

I watch the manager walk away, disappearing across the store while leading an actually honest shopper to her items. I crouch down, this time bringing my purse with me. I check over my shoulders to make sure that the coast is clear. It is.

I open my extra wide bag, spy the pretty things hung before me, then reach into my purse and take the matching one that I have brought with me out and carefully place it on an empty hook, so it fills in the gap and blends with the others.

I stay there at eye level with them for another moment and look back at the smiling gem frogs that are smiling at me. I take special note of the one that I just replaced and notice that his smile does not annoy me anymore and he looks happy to be back with his friends. I am happy and relieved that he is back with them, too. I tell him goodbye and hope that he does not feel rejected. I decide that he does not. He is smiling too brightly for that.

I make my way to the front of the store and replace the empty cart as the cashier asks me if I found everything that I was looking for. I remember to smile this time and assure her that I did.

Just for a minute
Just come on baby
Just give in
Stop saying maybe

Lick it or suck it
Just for a sec
Come on baby
Give me some neck

Come on baby
You light my fire
I will give you the drugs
That you so desire

Come on baby
Let's make a trade
I already know, you know
How these deals are made

Come on baby
Just let me in
I'll pay for it
Every inch of skin

I have the drugs
Don't make me flaunt it
Come on baby
Pretend that you want it

—Natalie

I have never been to this part of town before. And I hope that I never am again. Not here in front of this particular house anyway. No. I take that back. I don't want to be anywhere near here again. It is a struggling development that points out clearly to me just how fortunate I am.

The buildings on either side have "Condemned, No Trespassing" signs on them and the one I am parked in front of looks as if it should. There are cracks in the bricks that zigzag down the front of the house, and there are imprints of shutters on either side of the windows where the shutters used to be. I see the shutters have found another purpose. They now serve as a ramp, leading from the sidewalk to the dilapidated porch where the concrete steps underneath them have crumbled. Ingenious, I think. Whoever lives there had that one smart idea.

While I am certain that I do not like the owner of this house, I oddly give him this credit. I also give him a point for the rotted potted plant hanging from a plastic hook to the left of the stand-in steps. He thought to hang it in the first place and it must have been alive at one point. Why am I giving this despicable person credit for anything? I have never met him, but I know I do not like him. Of course, he travels through life in disguise and simply goes by "J," which is stupid. I hope I never meet him, but if I do, I might tell him this. Okay, probably not. But I will surely be thinking it.

The door of the house opens, and I am momentarily relieved until I see that it is not Natalie who I am waiting for but instead three little girls all under the age of eight. The oldest holds the door open for the other two. Little girls are natural caregivers. They begin to play on the sidewalk. They are adorable and intrigue me for a few moments. Kids are kids no matter where you plant them.

The mother and teacher in me assesses them. I am grateful to see that they look clean, are appropriately dressed for the season, and although thin, they are adequate weights. Two of them even have accessories in their hair. I decide that they are well cared for and am relieved at this. Is J their father? I hope not.

I study the house in front of me. I bet its walls contain a lot of secrets. I check the time on my Rolex and think how wrong it is that the watch I am wearing could feed all three of them for years.

I have been waiting for Natalie for more than ten minutes for a task that she assured me would take only a second, and I am beginning to worry, then panic. What if she doesn't come out? What do I do? How long do I wait? Who do I call? It's ridiculous that I am even here. What kind of mother does this kind of thing? I answer my own question. The kind of mother I am, I guess.

Mothers of drug addicts drive themselves in their fancy cars to pay off drug dealers who are harassing their drug-addicted daughters. Mothers who are trying to save their daughters and feel that if they can just make this particular dealer go away it is a step in the right direction.

My speech to Natalie is familiar because I have delivered it before. I see the worry in her when she answers her phone. I notice the way that her face drops, and I insist on knowing the reason. She protests for a while, then tells me.

"He wants his money." This is where I yell and scream and insist that I am not helping because last time was the last time.

Then my imagination goes wild, and every time I turn on the news, an addict has been found dead under suspicious circumstances, and when I try to be distracted by the regular shows, I tune in to see some poor girl being tortured and threatened by an unsavory character demanding money, and I give in.

"How much?" I ask. And another question, "What exactly goes along with *he wants his money back?*"

It sounds like he is getting threatening. Now, if he is simply threatening that he will not give her any more drugs until she pays for what she has already taken from him, then great. I will not pay him. But my daughter is worried, and Natalie is not worried easily. So now, I am worried, too. Will he hurt her? Will he hurt our family? The dog? I have no idea what this guy's parameters are.

I am appalled at the amount of money Natalie owes him and am furious at her. How could she possibly owe him three hundred dollars?

On the drive there, I do not speak to her except to clarify the directions that she is giving me in leading me to this lowlife's home or place of business. I am not sure which.

My God, what is she doing in there? I am getting angrier by the second. Then anger gives way to panic. What if something is happening to her in there? I am paralyzed with fear and wonder if I am the kind of mother who will run into a burning building to save her daughter.

I consider the house in front of me to be in flames right now. Gratefully, I do not have to find out the answer to this question because the door opens again and Natalie appears.

My emotion is back to anger. She skates down the makeshift steps and onto the sidewalk. Before she can get to the car, the youngest of the little girls intercepts her. The other two look on expectantly. I am not exactly sure what the little one wants, but it appears like a proposition of some kind. I am anxious and I want Natalie to get back in the car so that we can get the heck out of there. But I am intrigued and resist a "let's go" beep of the horn and wait to see how it plays out.

I see Natalie nod her head. She has just agreed to something. But I don't know what. The girls nod as well. They've made some kind of deal. The girls begin to move, organizing themselves, and Natalie steps back, giving them the room to do this. They position themselves side by side, three in a row, an arm's length apart. Pause. They glance sideways at each other. Then with a nod of the oldest one's head, they begin to dance.

I break into a big smile. The dance is a combination of so many styles. They hip-hop, perform ballet, and tap. I even think that I spy a few steps of a tango between the older two that they must have seen somewhere. The dance lasts a good three minutes, and it is actually pretty good. It wasn't just thrown together. It is obvious that they have practiced this.

They are smart little girls. Natalie watches as attentively as I do. She is smiling as well. She used to take dance lessons. It was okay for a while, then as she got older, it got too competitive for Natalie's taste and a little risqué for mine.

When the dance is over, Natalie applauds wildly and hugs each of them. The girls are pleased with themselves. Natalie exchanges some conversation with them and actually steps back and does a moment of a dance step of her own. She is showing them which one she liked the best. I am proud of her. She is truly a kind girl. I smile when she shakes each of their hands, congratulating them on a job well done. Then before parting, she reaches into her bra and pulls out a pile of bills, peeling three off and handing one to each of them. They are not only smart children but enterprising, too.

Also, I realize that because Natalie has money left, she either already had the money to pay this debt or she inflated the amount so that she could pay it and still have some left to keep. Either way, she is not being completely honest with me.

Natalie hops off the sidewalk and jumps into the car. She waves to the girls as I back out of the spot. I wave to them as well, even though they don't care about me. We drive away.

"Done?" I ask her with a sigh, remembering the original task that brought us there.

"Yes," she tells me. "Thank you." I nod.

My mind is back on the little girls and Natalie's must be, too, because she says, "Cute dance, huh?" I agree.

"Beautiful children," I say.

"I love them!" Natalie tells me.

I can't stop my mind from thinking of these girls and wondering about their lives and about how much of our lives are dictated by simply where we are born and the opportunity that comes or doesn't come with this random location. Natalie and I must be sharing similar thoughts because she says, "I hope they end up okay."

I nod. "I hope we end up okay, too," I say. It is her turn to nod. It's Sunday; we should be in church.

"I'll just be a minute," I promise Natalie, maneuvering the car into a parking space a little too swiftly for an empty church parking lot. I put the car in park, grab my purse, fish out three crumpled one-dollar bills from the bottom, open the door, and jump out, slamming it as I dart toward the church. I am about ten feet away from the car before I think to turn back and call out to Natalie, "Hey, do you want to go in?"

I am sure that she is going to say no, but she says, "Sure," and jumps out of the car to join me.

It is a Tuesday afternoon and Natalie and I have been out to lunch before I decide to make a quick stop at church to light a candle before heading home. I have done this a hundred times while Natalie and I were together, and she has always declined my invitation to go into the church with me.

"Great," I say, willing my voice to stay even—despite the sheer joy I am feeling on the inside—and trying to keep a neutral expression on my face. I know I am failing when Natalie warns me, "Don't be so happy. It's too hot to wait in the car."

I grin, refusing to believe this explanation, grab Natalie's arm, and practically skip into the church. Arm in arm, we enter the dark church and allow our eyes to adjust before walking halfway down the aisle, genuflecting and sliding into a pew.

I am giddy to be there praying with my daughter, and when I bow my head, this is the blessing I thank God for first. I finish my silent prayers first and wonder what Natalie is praying for, glad she has so much to say. I bow my head for one more second and ask God to please give her what she wants, telling Him that He can easily dismiss my requests. "Just please hear her," I pray.

When she is done, she looks up and offers me a smile that I honestly believe is more peaceful than any smile I have seen from her in a long time. We then head to the statue of the Blessed Mother to the left of the altar to light a candle. When you really need something done, I used to tell the kids to go to Mary; she's got a direct line to God's ear. And every good son listens to his mother. I believe this, and I also believe that me talking to the Blessed Mother—mother to mother—helps, too.

I kneel, I offer a quick Hail Mary, light the candle, and deposit the bills into the receptacle. Immediately after I do all of this, I feel regret and think I should have let Natalie light the candle. I am about to say this and offer to go out to the car and get three more dollars when I turn to see Natalie fishing money from her bra. I am so shocked and amused that I struggle to not burst out laughing right there in the church. Smiling, I watch as she folds the money and stuffs it into the offering box.

Natalie kneels, prays, then lights the candle next to mine. She watches the flame for a moment, then looks up and grins at me. I'm done trying to hide my joy and smile back at her. We link our arms and start toward the exit. Halfway there, I don't remember the reason I am trying so hard to be quiet and allow myself to laugh with joy out loud, certain that God approves of happiness in His house.

And he says no one can love me more than he does
If that's true, "I'm royally fucked"
"Come on" he says "It's what you came for. Right?"
"You want it, get it!"
I look up from the floor at his hand dangling high above me
Three twenties pinched between his fingertips
Just enough to get me out of the physical torture
I am trapped
I rise on my tiptoes and give my best reach
He swiftly moves it away the moment
I graze it
"Please..." I beg "Don't make me do this"
He says "Junkie"
This humiliation at the man who is supposed to love me
The man that I am so vulnerable to
He teases me with the money
I reach, it is so close yet so far away
"Please, just..."
Tears stream down my face
In his eyes disgust
He smirks
He drops the money
I wait for it to float to the ground
Pick it up.
Eyes glued to the floor,
I hurry out the door

—Natalie

chapter *Six*

Looking for the Helpers

*P*eter works at the hospital that they brought her to, and they recognized the name. So, they called him first when Natalie overdosed.

When my phone rings, I feel the touch of panic that every ringing phone gives me. But I see it is Peter and I am happy. I was trying to decide between rice or potatoes as a side to the pork chops that I'd planned on making for dinner. I was happy that Peter was calling, and I would let him make the choice.

I am shaken out of my domestic reverie when I answer and hear Peter's voice, rushed and hurried. "I am in the middle of a case. She overdosed. Go to the ER."

My heart plummets into my stomach. I feel like I do not have enough air in my lungs, and I am light-headed. "Is she alive?" I ask. "Yes," he tells me and hangs up. I am less than a mile away, and I get there quickly, although I don't remember the drive.

I search for room number twenty-two and spot it in the distance. The emergency room is crowded and the staff are moving around busily but calmly. No one seems frantic but me. I head for the glass enclosed space that is called a room. The curtains are shut within the glass so I cannot see anything.

I draw in my breath, having no idea what I will be faced with when I draw back the curtain and see her. I brace myself. I pull the curtain and see her sitting upright in the bed. You would imagine that it would be quite the dramatic moment. It was not. She looks fine. The best of us do not look good under fluorescent lighting. But she does. She looks up and our eyes meet.

Now, this is the part where I think I am supposed to break down into grateful tears, rush to her side, and hold her in my arms as she cries, too. Except that I don't. Right now, I am not that mother. I actually don't do any of this. Our eyes meet and I glare at her from my spot in the doorway. I am furious. I say nothing but keep my eyes on her while moving to the chair. My chair. The chair reserved for angry mothers. I am surprised it doesn't have my name monogrammed on it like a director's chair. It should.

Natalie looks away first and wilts a little under my gaze. After all, I am still the mother and she the daughter. And as hard as she is, I can still affect her this way. I am glad I can. Because even I know that while, so far, she hasn't exactly been following my motherly advice like an instruction manual, she still does care how I feel, and if she ever stops caring completely, we are in a different place. We are in trouble. I sit in my assigned seat and open my mouth to say something.

But before the words come out of my mouth, a nurse arrives to check some of the machines behind Natalie. She offers a sympathetic smile to me, then says to Natalie, "If you need anything, hon, just ring the bell."

It was nice that she called her "hon." The nurse disappears and I settle back in the seat. I open my mouth again, but again the curtain is pulled open and I feel the blood draining from my face at the sight of him. He is a police officer, under-cover, dressed in regular clothes, and trying to look like the boy next door. He is not successful because if I recognize him as a cop, he is fooling no one. He already has his badge displayed for us to see. He ignores me and gets right down to business.

"Hi, Natalie. I would like to know who gave you the drugs," he tells her. I guess it was nice of him to use her name. But it makes me wonder how well he knows my daughter. I don't know why, but I sense this is not the first time they have met. I decide he is part of the secret world she lives in. The world that pulls her from my world. The world where she lives her other life.

I am invisible in my chair. I feel like I am witnessing something private between two other people that I shouldn't be. He looks angry and frustrated, and I wonder if he is angry that Natalie has overdosed or angry that some scum sold her the drugs. I wonder if he is that invested in his job or if he is just playing the part.

If it is the former and he really cares that much, then good for him! If it is the latter and he's acting, then he is doing a great job playing the part of the cop. I am not passing judgment. I am trying to figure out how to play the part of the distraught mother. I have seen enough episodes of *Law and Order* to know what my part is, though. My role is easier than his. The grieving mother just sits in the chair and weeps. I don't even have a speaking part. He, on the other hand, carries this entire episode.

"Tell me, Nat," he demands. Ah, he knows her well.

I wait in anticipation for her response. Natalie is doing a really good job playing the role of the addict by the way she pauses before answering. Then to prove that she has watched her fair share of crime shows, too, and to solidify her bid for an Academy Award nod, she looks at him and says, "I ain't no snitch." I am equal parts appalled and impressed. I got pulled over once for an expired sticker. I was so scared that the cop could have gotten me to confess to murder with very little effort. So, I can't help but be slightly impressed at her moxie. I didn't think people in real life said things like that. How did scared me give birth to such a brave creature?

The officer makes a sound that is one-part sigh and one-part growl. He makes a face and the sound again and tries to wait Natalie out. I have the urge to tell him that this method of dealing with her is futile and he is wasting his time. I once made her sit on a potty chair for an hour and forty minutes while trying to bribe her with a bag of M&M's to pee, only for her to get up and pee on the sofa cushion thirty seconds after I gave in. He doesn't even have any chocolate with him that I can see. But I say nothing, remembering that I am not supposed to be talking. I am supposed to be weeping. Why can't I cry?

The cop gives Natalie another annoyed glare and pushes back his wavy strawberry blonde hair. But I now realize by the look on his face that he is both invested in his job and cares, and is playing a little bit of a part, too. I am grateful for the first, and he deserves the other.

My guess is that he knew even before he walked into the room that his mission is useless. He knew that in order to help her, which

I believe he was genuinely trying to do, Natalie needed to help him. And he knew she wouldn't. Doing so would break the unspoken code between addicts and their dealers. They don't tell on each other.

"We don't want you, Natalie," he assures her. "You are sick. We want him." Natalie nods that she understands this. I want to thank him for acknowledging that she is ill.

The officer waits again, this time for a shorter time, makes his signature growl-sigh, and walks out of the room, dropping his business card on top of the bed. I leave my seat just long enough to rise up, snatch it, and put it in my purse. I glance at it. His mother gave him a nice name.

Natalie and I are alone for just a moment before someone appears in the doorway. It is her boyfriend, who was with her when she overdosed. Apparently, he saved her life by doing CPR when he heard her fall in the other room. In light of this fact, you would think I should rush to him, offering my thanks or at least rise from the chair. I do neither. To say that my feelings for him are complicated is a gross understatement.

We are not always a fan of each other. But we always respect each other. When each of us realized that neither of us is going away, although I believe that I will ultimately outlast him, we arrived at an unspoken understanding. We are two people who love someone in common and, in any other universe than the bizarre one we live in, would never choose to know each other.

Instead of getting up to greet him, I let him greet me, which he does by coming over to the chair and giving me a peck on the cheek. Our eyes meet and we exchange a strained look. He sits down on the edge of the bed without kissing her. They look at each other and both begin to cry, leaving me the only one in the room not crying.

I watch them as they quietly weep now, holding hands. "I saved your life," he sobs. *Yes, please. Go ahead and make this about you*, I say sarcastically in my head.

"I know," Natalie sobs back. *Oh brother*.

I think about giving them some privacy. Not for their sake but for mine because I am not confident in my ability to hold my tongue and not voice my disgust and intolerance of this entire event. They are now insisting on glorifying it like they have somehow heroically overcome some unexpected tragedy together.

I am dying to tell them that this is no one's fault but their own. That they both need to grow up and fly right, get out of the gutter they are living in. Stop living despicable lifestyles. And, who knows, do something crazy like the rest of the world and become law-abiding citizens. Get proper jobs. Get up every morning, shower and dress, and show up on time, do what they are told, stay the entire shift, and on Friday, get a paycheck that seems way too small for the amount of work that they did, gripe about it, then get up the next day and do it all over again.

I want to remind them that they have already been blessed by God with all they need to live a good life and that they should be grateful for this instead of disrespectfully throwing it back in His face.

And, of course, I want to tell them that they should be ashamed of themselves.

I do not say any of this. In fact, I've yet to say a single word since I entered this room. As many scenes as I stir up in my mind, I cause very few of them in real life. But I stay put. Part of maintaining what control I have over Natalie in the wrestling match that the boyfriend and I are constantly engaged in is by not retreating.

The boyfriend looks up at me to make sure I have heard that he did

CPR, which in his mind crowns him King in this play. I smile weakly, letting him know that I did hear and try to look grateful.

And in truth, I really am. And when I stop being catty, I do acknowledge there is true love between Natalie and the boyfriend. I know this is why I tolerate him. He does love her. And she does love him. The love they share is, in my opinion, the unhealthy type, but they have been together and stood the test of time, some time anyway. And while their trials are entirely of their own making, they have endured a bit and stuck by each other.

One of the reasons so many addicts die is that they are with people who do not care about them and fail to get them help when they are in trouble. I know that judging the quality of a relationship or a partner with only the expectation that they will not let you die isn't exactly the ultimate. But we are where we are. And we are who we are with.

Ironically, one of the things Peter and I would always debate was if this boyfriend would get Natalie help if she was in peril or if he would run the other way. I always said that if there was enough caring there, that he would. Peter insisted he would flee. He did not. I was right. So, I get to be right about another thing that I wish we would have never needed to know about.

Natalie and the boyfriend's pity party continues, much of it now supervised by the hospital staff coming in and out of the room, preparing Natalie for discharge. It is surprising how quickly someone who was technically dead an hour ago could be volleyed back into the world. Especially since they have proven themselves unable to navigate that world adequately.

Much to my embarrassment, Natalie and the boyfriend have added kissing and cuddling to their festival of sorrow. And I want to shrink from humiliation every time someone walks in. I am sure they have seen this all before and most of them pretend not to notice as they unplug her from the machines. Everyone but the nice nurse who called Natalie "hon." She smiles sympathetically, and I wonder if she loves an addict.

Usually, compassion like that comes from somewhere personal. I decide she is a woman I could have lunch with. This is how I measure other females: if I feel I can sit across a table from her and share a meal, then she and I can be friends. Heck, I'll even pay for lunch if she's the kind of girl who will take a minute to tell me I am not the worst mother she has ever known.

They patiently explain discharge instructions that I know Natalie doesn't fully understand. I listen attentively. They suggest rehab to Natalie and then, at the very least, the purchase of Narcan to the boyfriend. I will get some on the way home. Because I know he will not.

The cop makes one more obligatory appearance, as though he promised himself that he would check to see if Natalie has changed her mind. He goes only as far as the initial curtain and looks in. He sees the boyfriend and the affection and with a look of disgust walks away, not bothering to even walk back into the room. I do not blame him. He realizes he has lost. I feel bad for him. Probably more than I should. While I am sure part of him cares, I hope that he doesn't care that much.

I look at Natalie and feel like I have lost, too. I feel the urge to run after the cop and thank him. I also wouldn't mind explaining to him that I really tried hard at this motherhood thing. And that I am sorry for everything. What I really wanted to tell him, though, was that while he never actually looked at me, never allowing our eyes to meet, is that we have a lot more in common than one would think; we both fought and lost. And that no one wants to help her more than me.

We are almost ready to go. The little that Natalie arrived with is in a plastic drawstring bag and ready to go. She is disheveled and dirty, sitting on the edge of the bed with her filthy Converses dangling.

I sigh and suggest that the boyfriend go pull the car around. They are leaving together. They have plans. These plans do not include rehab or Narcan but, instead, Chick-fil-A. They have already asked for and I have given them twenty dollars. I will be leaving alone.

The boyfriend goes to pull the car around. It doesn't need pulled around. It is plenty close. But I suggested it because I want her to myself for a minute. We are finally alone. I sigh, and the anger I was feeling has dissipated, giving way to all of the emotions that would likely accompany where we are and what we are wrestling with. Sadness. Heartbreak. Fear. Are just a few.

"You need help," I tell her softly. "You need help now. You can't go on like this. You are going to die...you were dead."

She looks at me with tears in her eyes, looking very much like the ill, lost young girl that she is. Her tears inspire my own eyes to fill, and I get up from the chair, join her on the side of the bed, hold her in my arms, and stroke her hair as we cry a bit together.

The streetlights flicker
As I breathe in cold and snow
Where did all of my
Good days go?

As I lay on my back
And close my eyes
I miss the times when
People heard my cries

I poke and I prod
Trying to find a vein
In hopes that
The blood doesn't stain

Filling my lungs
With less air than smoke
Reminiscing on days
When I wasn't quite as broke

But nothing changes
By willing it away
The good days have left
Maybe the bad ones won't stay

—Natalie

"What did you wish for?" Trevor asks, knowing that my rule is not to tell and that I am not going to give up this secret.

"Not telling," I say and make some funny comment about all of them miscounting the number of candles as well as another remark about the house going up in flames.

The fact is that this is not a milestone birthday for me. It is a weekday, almost nine o'clock at night, and I practically screamed everyone into the kitchen and into place to "celebrate" me. Mostly so we could get it over with and I could go to bed. No one is in a good mood, especially me.

They say that a mother is only as happy as her least happy child. This is true for me and I guess that is why when I am by my three children and Peter and am blowing out the candles on my birthday, I am mentally trying to will any magic that might have been bestowed on me this day, during this ritual, onto Natalie. If I could only make her well and happy, I, in turn, would be well and happy.

I really don't feel like doing this, but I am superstitiously afraid that if I forego this tradition, bad luck—or *more* bad luck—will befall me.

Peter and the boys give me obligatory pecks on the cheek and file out of the room, their duty done.

Natalie goes to leave, forgetting this mandatory act of affection. "My kiss," I call, reminding her. She turns with an apologetic, weak smile, returns to me, and gives me a hug. As she leans in, I whisper, "My wish was all about you Baby Girl."

"Thanks, Mommy," she says, her eyes puffy and black. "One day, I'll return it."

We are at Christmas Eve Mass and I am scanning the faces of the people around me. The church is packed so I have more people than usual to choose from. While I am not proud of playing games at church, I always seem to find myself trying to read their expressions and guess what they might be thinking. I try to decide what their professions might be, if they are happy or not.

This Christmas Eve, even though it is too late, I am imagining writing my dream Christmas letter in my head. But I am having trouble. That week I had received many of them in the mail, written with care, folded carefully, and tucked inside Christmas cards.

Peter always tells me that, like Facebook, I should only believe some of what I am reading and that some people exaggerate and some people downright lie. I am struggling to find a way to realistically cheer up the part of the letter about Natalie. I am feeling frustrated, sad, and deflated. But I take solace in the fact that Peter always tells me Facebook is not real and the posted glee might just not be all that it seems. He reminds me that nobody posts the bad stuff, the same way nobody tells the truth in the letter they tuck into their Christmas cards.

I consider myself a pretty good writer, but I doubt that even I could spin our tale into an uplifting, inspirational holiday message. So, instead, in my head I begin to write a humorous letter about our past year. I decide on: *"Here on Newbury Drive, the Namans have survived two overdoses and avoided jail. Merry Christmas!"* I almost laugh out loud.

While standing for Gospel, I spot a doctor I did not know but recognize. Ironically, I have an appointment coming up with him this week that I am not sure if I am going to keep or not. I am nervous about it and am contemplating sharing some very personal information and am not sure if I can trust him or not. He is two pews ahead and I have him directly in my sight.

I stare at his back for nearly fifteen minutes, wondering what his green-and-brown plaid suit jacket says about him. I can't tell. I finally decide that I will make my decision whether to keep the appointment or not depending on what he does at the sign of peace.

At this part of the Mass, you are supposed to extend good wishes to the people around and next to you; I am most interested in what he will do with his wife, who is standing to his left. I decide that if he shakes her hand, he is a coldhearted fish. Any man who can't show public affection for the woman he is married to does not get to be my doctor.

If he hugs her, I will probably keep the appointment. I am going to try to time the duration of the hug, though. If it is too quick, less than three seconds, then it was just a formality and probably not heartfelt and he doesn't get credit for it. But if the hug lasts three seconds or longer, I will give him some points and probably keep the appointment.

If he kisses his wife, then he receives major points, all of them actually, and this will let me know for sure that he is a kindhearted, solid guy. And I will definitely keep the appointment, and he'll have won me as his patient.

As the priest instructs us to "Please offer each other a sign of peace," I watch him expectantly on tiptoes, holding my breath. That man not only leans in to kiss his wife but holds her tight for a solid five seconds. He is almost the best guy in the church. The only man who outdoes him is Peter, who holds on to me for seven seconds.

One early January morning, I was cleaning up Natalie's room. As I made the bed, I could feel paper sticking to my bare feet. The crinkle of the paper caught my attention. I sat down to pull the scraps away from my skin. When I went to set the paper on the dresser, the word "clean" surrounded in colorful squiggly lines caught my attention. Smoothing the paper out, I could see it was a New Year's to-do list that Natalie had written for the coming year. I think that I might have inspired this list.

I love the prospect of a new year. I like the idea of a fresh start, a clean slate, and the promise of what can come. Every New Year's night, after the holidays are officially over and I feel myself looking out into the year to come, I always find myself sitting in my oversize chair, wrapped in a big fluffy blanket with a huge cup of tea, making lists of the next year's goals and dreams.

Admittedly, I get a little crazy with my lists and, realistically, I could never accomplish so much even in a year's time. But it's fun for me to dream. My goals are lofty, and I tend to reach high. I know that I tend to organize myself on paper, but I never realized that I might have passed this habit on to my children until then. This is a surprise because my children poke fun at me for jotting down my regular chores just to have the satisfaction of highlighting them "done." And also for insisting they not leave the New Year's Day dinner table until they think of one life-bettering resolution.

I scan the list Natalie had made: stop drinking, get clean, no more stealing, don't lie, don't kill myself, and be happy. I sighed. It was sad that these were her goals while at the same time it was great that these were her goals. No nineteen-year-old's to-do list should include such things. She should have been making lists that include getting good grades in college and finding the boyfriend of her dreams.

But that list belongs to someone else. I found myself proud that she took the time to think it through and plan. I searched the dresser and found a pink crayon. At the bottom of the list, I doodled a heart, a cross, and a very poor attempt at praying hands and wrote the words

"I am proud of you, Love Mom." I added, "Go girl!" then set it on the night table for her to find.

One day, when Natalie and I were shopping at Target right before July Fourth, we ran into another mother and daughter we know. They seemed surprised to see us; I think they were going to avoid us at first and were going to just watch us from a distance. But we ended up at the check-out registers, side by side, so conversation was unavoidable. We exchanged greetings, then talked about how we were both there to pick up pretty much the same holiday odds and ends before we went home to celebrate.

I joked about the similarity of the items in our shopping carts, and you could tell from her expression that she seemed surprised. And her expression let me know that she was surprised. She was a nice woman and meant no harm or disrespect. I thought to myself, *See, we really are just like everyone else. Our days are just like yours, and the Fourth of July is coming for us, too.*

I was tempted to tell her these things and that also, just like her, we filled up our lives and kept on moving. No matter what was going on or how tough it was. And while we would rather drop out of life, email our resignation to God, illuminate a "Closed" sign, and hide under the bed, we do not. We get up every day, just like everyone else, and we carry on. We do this because, if you really take the time to think about it, there is no other option.

It is not always your birthday and there is not always something to celebrate. A perfectly dressed turkey with all the trimmings is not always what's for dinner. The majority of our days are "regular" days, and sometimes the only thing on the table is macaroni and cheese with a side of peas.

The mantra of most every self-help philosophy is based on the idea
of "one day at a time." I have to admit I wasn't always a big fan of this
phrase and I have never met an addict who initially was a fan either.

I think we all dream of getting quickly to the finish line first and
of get-rich- quick schemes. But honestly, it doesn't seem that most
lives work that way. And we are left with living life one day at a time.
And when things are really bad, one minute at a time. As the loved
one of an addict, this is how we live. And while we are not exactly
running through fields of daisies, we try to find the prettier of the
dandelions along the way. We slow life down and become grateful
for the bits of time when things are good and our addicted daughter
is okay. There are 24 hours in a day 1,440 minutes in that same day,
and 86,400 seconds. That fact never changes. Neither does the fact
that the sun always rises and the next day always comes. Even though
I have to admit to both thinking that the sun shouldn't bother rising
and wishing it wouldn't, it is good that it does.

$\sim$

"Look for the helpers…" Mr. Rogers famously used to tell children
when they were in crisis and were scared, they should look for the
helpers.

Well, we are surely in crisis and we have heeded Mr. Roger's
advice. We have looked for all of the helpers and have been blessed
to find many, many people who are trying to help people who are
struggling with addiction.

We have had the privilege of being cared for by countless professionals. We have had the support of psychiatrists, psychologists,
therapists, counselors, nurses, police officers, paramedics, emergency
medical technicians, principals, teachers, and others who have all
showered their gifts upon us and have tried their best to help. These

people have been our helpers. And in their own way, they have contributed to getting us at least as far as we have gotten.

Maybe Natalie is not perfectly well just yet, but I have confidence that one day she will be. And while she is not exactly healthy, I don't blame anyone involved in Natalie's care for her not being all that we need her to be.

And one day, I know she will be well. When I look back, I believe that it will have been the combination of all the talents that all these people have blessed us with to make Natalie whole again. Addiction is not an easy problem to solve. It is not like people are simply not trying.

Addiction is one of the fiercest dragons to tame and slaying this beast is an almost insurmountable job. But *almost* is the key word. It is not impossible. If you find the helpers.

When we think we may have found assistance, we always ask one question as we hold the hand of our broken child, dragging or carrying them toward the help. It is, "Does this work?"

The answer is, "I hope so." Which is more of a wish or a prayer than a definite answer.

We ask another question on the way out of the same door, thirty days later. We ask, "How long will this last?"

The answer to the second question is "Hopefully forever."

I have never picked up Natalie from any program or treatment when I was in the presence of another picking-up parent when one of us hasn't asked the other, "How long do you think they will be okay?"

The answer we are looking for is, "Forever." Hoping that this will then be followed up with something like, "That's it! Your daughter/

son is fixed! Ta-da! You do not need to return. They will now be drug-and/or alcohol-free forever! Congratulations!"

No one ever says this, though, because it is unrealistic.

You would think that the moment Peter, Natalie, and I realized we needed help, we would have stopped everything we were doing at that exact minute and stood together holding hands with our faces turned upward, screaming for help. We did not.

The realization of where we were and just how bad it all was didn't come instantly to us. So, we probably didn't run for help as quickly as we should have. But the nice thing is, when we finally did run toward the helpers, they were waiting for us with their arms outstretched and open.

I've just walked into our home office and closed the door. I am the only one in the house except for Natalie, who is passed out on the family room couch, but I really need to concentrate. I am determined to get her help. It has been a horrendous two weeks, and I have begged and pleaded with her to get help. I have screamed and yelled, cajoled and cried until my head aches and my throat is sore.

Peter and I are not speaking, but I don't think either of us are sure why. The only thing I can figure is that we are both mad. And while we are not mad at each other, we have somehow chosen to take it out on each other. The curse of availability.

I sit down at the computer and begin to google. I type in "addiction" and a million hits appear. I refine my search with the word "help." Even more hits pop up. I try once more, adding "help for families."

I am getting closer now, as hundreds of ads appear for rehabs. It asks me if I want to put in my zip code to find places close to me and

I agree, even though they tell you that sometimes it is best to choose a place away from where you live.

I think of all the songs I know that speak dreamily about better places far, far away. I, too, have fantasized about these places, and in reality, Peter and I have talked seriously about moving away from everything we have and know and taking Natalie to some random state and town and starting over. In our dreams, this place is always simpler and somehow seems more manageable than the complicated, gigantic mess that we call our lives here. I visualize the people simpler, too. Me and these fairy-tale people, passing blissful days together.

And of course, Natalie, the entire reason for the departure of the life that exists now, is living right there with us. She is thriving, achieving, and happier than me, Peter, and all the people in this make-believe town put together.

Instead, I begin clicking on the advertisements for rehab facilities in my area. I scan them quickly, trying to choose the options I will delve into deeper. I sort through them, quickly discounting some of them according to their criteria and some of them according to mine. Most of my rejections and acceptances are objective because Natalie doesn't fit the requirements of gender or particular addiction, which they very politely refer to as "your drug of choice."

There is a section that speaks directly to the addict and a separate one that addresses the families. Most of them call me a "loved one," so I qualify. I read both sections. I want to know that they are positive toward Natalie. And I wouldn't mind if they were supportive of me, too.

I accept some just because when I study the faces of the people in the ads, they look like genuinely nice people. If I am going to hand my daughter over to them, then they must be kind. I realize that the

people in the photos might be models, and I even think I see one particular lady in more than one ad, but I rectify this conflict by deciding
that at the very least, she probably wouldn't model for them if the
rehab wasn't staffed with nice people.

I narrow the list down to three and begin investigating more
deeply. I click on the staff directories of each. And one loses its spot
on my list because the doctors, nurses, therapists, and such are listed
only by their first names and last initials. I understand the reason for
this is probably to protect them for all of the reasons that I can think
of to protect them, as well as many scarier ones that I don't know
of. But if they need to know everything about Natalie and us, and it
seems that way by the lengthy and very detailed questionnaires that
we are required to complete for admittance, then we should at least
be able to know their last names.

After scanning the last names of the list of professionals on the
remaining two, I choose between them because most of the people
on one list have many more letters after their names, which I decide
makes them more schooled and qualified than the others on other
sites.

I do spend some time looking up the definitions of the groups of
letters after their names, and while I know what MD and RN stand
for, the others can be confusing and deceiving. From what I was able
to conclude, there are doctors, nurses, and therapists, and not-quite-
doctors, not-quite-nurses, and not-quite-therapists mulling around,
too. I dismiss all of the "not quites" and accept only the "real deals."

I read quickly through the schools, universities, and programs
they attended. And while I know nothing about this kind of thing
and can only recognize the really huge, prestigious schools and places
like Johns Hopkins and Harvard, I lean toward them and dismiss the

schools in what I view as great vacation spots. It would not be bad for Natalie to have some fun while getting better, but I want her to learn to not stick needles in her arms, not to catch a wave.

Once I decide on the list, I try to choose which doctor I will pick if they ask me, which I am pretty sure they won't. I choose faces that look genuine and names that sound friendly. I open up separate browsers and google them individually and read their reviews and note the number of stars out of five they have on average. Nothing less than four stars is good enough for my baby girl!

I become distracted from my search and google Peter's name. I actually get a little nervous when I am waiting for the browser to open his photo and bio. I have never seen this picture of him and wonder who took it. He's so handsome and comes across as friendly and caring and approachable. His smile is genuine, just like the one that he gives me when I say something sweet to him. I scan the handful of reviews he has and am mostly pleased—except for the one from Elizabeth R. who did give him five stars but indicated that he didn't spend quite enough time with her.

I am trying not to hold a grudge and take this personally and decide to give her a break and be grateful for the mostly glowing review. After all, her gallbladder was misbehaving and that must be stressful. I wish there was a reply button so that I could tell Elizabeth R. that sometimes I complain that he doesn't spend enough time with me either.

I finally choose the facility and stare at the phone number. I become almost paralyzed with fear and deal with it by procrastinating and going to the bathroom, checking for mail, and putting on lip gloss until I realize that this is not helping anything, so I give myself a pep talk. *You can do this,* I tell myself. *This might be the phone call that changes everything.* I dial the number into my phone and whisper, "God be with me," as I press send.

A woman named Angela answers. Her voice is friendly and comforting—an angel, indeed, I hope. I try to guess her age but only decide she is not old and not young. This is good because this has her sitting neutrally between Natalie and me. She is a good listener and patiently allows me to go on and on, only occasionally interrupting me to ask a quick question. I realize then that she is probably filling out a form, and I wonder how I compare to all the other mothers who have desperately called for help.

When I am done with my spiel, feeling quite exhausted but at the same time satisfied, I wait for Angela's magic answer. The thought occurs to me that maybe this has been the problem the whole time and perhaps our entire situation could have been solved long ago if I would have bucked up and confessed just how bad things had become to a stranger over the phone. Maybe Angela has a gigantic box of answers that she will provide me with now that I have finally caved in and asked for help properly.

This theory goes up in smoke when Angela tells me she understands and is sorry. She doesn't specify exactly what she is sorry for, everything in general, I guess. Then, she tells me that Natalie needs to call herself. My heart implodes.

I thank her and hang up without explaining that Natalie spends most of her time too impaired to even begin to dial the phone. I leave the office and there is Natalie, still passed out in a heap on the couch. I try to rouse her and am unsuccessful, but I talk to her closed eyes anyway. I think I have really found a great place, I say, if she could only wake up to help herself for just a few minutes.

You see an addict
And I see me
I see myself
Even when I don't want it to be

I see me at my bottom
Me at my worst
On the days so bad
I think that I'm cursed

And then there are days
When the clouds begin to part
Days when I think
This could be a start

But I'm careful those days
Careful with hope
Because one wrong turn
Leads back to dope

But no matter the day, one thing remains
You see an addict and I see me
I see myself
Even when I don't want to be

—Natalie

It takes me several days to not only talk Natalie into calling the rehab facility I found but to also get her unimpaired enough for the phone call. There was begging, pleading, yelling, screaming, and threatening, but she is finally on her phone being interviewed by an intake nurse. Peter and I had heard good things about a particular psychiatrist there, and we want him to see her.

I am in the other room eavesdropping and pretending to be busy. I can only hear one side of the conversation, only Natalie's responses to the nurse's questions. The pre-paperwork we received in the mail stressed the importance of Natalie answering the questions honestly. And she promised she would.

The interview process involved in getting accepted into a rehab facility is often lengthy and involved. I understand all of the reasons why this is the case and necessary. But this entrance interview some-times reminds me of an *American Idol* or *Gong Show* audition with the prospective patient singing and dancing their way through the questions, hoping not to get ejected by Simon Cowell or sent away with a gong. The difference being, of course, that a person's life is at stake. Hardly entertaining.

Part of the flaw with this process, in my opinion, is that many addicts are too sick to do what needs to be done to get through the application. Not to be critical, but if the person in need could get it together long enough to jump through all of the hoops to get help, they actually don't need help that badly.

"My grandmother's," I hear her say. "Yes…yes…yes," she tells the nurse.

"Twice," she says. "My mother." I am simultaneously logging her answers while trying to figure out the questions they answer.

"Twelve," she answers.

"My uncle's... Definitely my mom."

Somehow, even though I don't know what the actual questions are, I know that just by hearing their answers, I don't like them.

"Thank you," I hear Natalie say, politely ending the call.

I ramp up my pretend cleaning and wait for her to appear in the kitchen. "Hi," I greet her, trying to seem casual when she does, wondering if my voice sounds as fake to her as it does to me. "Go okay?" I ask her.

"Yeah," she tells me, sounding exhausted. Rehashing your life story to a stranger over the phone can wear a person out. Especially a life as complicated as Natalie's. "They said that they would take me," she says, sitting down at the kitchen table.

"I'm glad," I say with my signature false perkiness. "I think this really could be a good thing. A big part of our solution." I need to write a more varied script for myself; I have said these exact words probably a dozen times in the years since we have been struggling.

When she doesn't answer, I look up from my pretend cleaning, which has now turned into real cleaning, and see that she is staring glumly out the patio window into the backyard. As I wipe off the toaster, I am debating the idea of asking her what some of the questions were. I know it's all supposed to be confidential. But I can't help but think that if I just knew more, if I just knew everything, I could help better. "So, the interview went okay?" I ask again.

"It was all right," Natalie tells me, squinting at something in the yard. I stop polishing the toaster and scan the scene out the window, trying to see what she sees.

"What did you answer 'your uncle's' to?" I ask, daring to be a little braver while turning away and wiping down the coffee maker.

"What do you mean?" she asks, her voice a little higher. I might as well go all in now.

"When you were talking to the nurse, I was able to hear some of your answers but not any of the questions," I confess. "And I was just curious."

She nods and has stopped looking out the window and is now focused on her phone. She doesn't respond right away, and I am not sure if she is angry at my intrusiveness or is just distracted by whatever is on the screen.

"She asked me where I drank first," she tells me. I nod in response even though she cannot see me. I take this in.

"At one of the Christmas parties?" I ask, doing the math in my head. We hadn't been to one of my brother's annual Christmas parties in years, so she must have been quite young. (And knowing me, she was dressed in a fussy red holiday dress and white tights. And she was drinking?)

I look up to see Natalie nod affirmatively. I should have watched her more closely.

"You said yes several times in a row," I point out. "What was she asking?" I worry I am pushing my luck. The coffee maker is clean. I run water over a dish rag and douse it with soap, preparing to wipe off the stovetop.

"She wanted to know what all I have done," she tells me. "You know marijuana, coke, heroin, fentanyl."

I sigh while attacking a grimy burner, hoping that this sigh is muffled by my scrubbing. Obviously and unfortunately, the answers to all these questions is yes. I am grateful for her honesty, though.

"What did you answer 'your grandmother's' to?" I ask.

"She wanted to know where I got my first pills," she tells me.

This time, I am not stifling a sigh, but instead I am muffling a gasp. "Oh," I say, trying to keep this godforsaken conversation going. "You got your first pills from Nunnie's?" I'm light-headed now, a mix of the conversation and the physical exertion I have expelled nearly cleaning a hole through the metal of the stovetop.

"Yep," she tells me, still focused on her phone while simultaneously petting the dog. Why did I assume that she got her first pills from some bad influence in a school hallway or bathroom?

"What did you get from Nunnie's?" I have to ask.

"I started with Pap's sleeping pills after he died," she tells me. "Then Vicodin from the bathroom cabinet...you know, Nunnie's knees."

I am getting warm and my face is flushing. I don't think I can blame the stove for this. "Where was I?" I ask.

"What do you mean?"

"Where was I when you were steal... taking the pills?" I ask, hoping that the urgent way this question is spinning in my head tones down a bit when it flops out of my mouth.

"Usually outside in the car," she tells me, matter-of-factly. "With Nunnie."

I don't need to ask for further clarification. I understand completely. Almost every day in the summer months, Natalie and I would pick my mother up for lunch. Natalie and I would pull up to my mother's house and my mother would get in. And I can remember very clearly that almost every single time, Natalie would say she had to run in and go to the bathroom, get a chocolate from the dish, or a squirt of whipped cream that my mother kept in the refrigerator especially for her. I would put the car in park, tell her to hurry, and my mother and I would sit together in the car chatting carelessly away as Natalie trotted into the house.

Heck! I remember times when I would send her in myself to retrieve something or do a quick chore. While I sat oblivious, she was stealing Vicodin and Percocet from my mother's house. From her living grandmother and her dead grandfather.

Feeling exhausted, I rinse out my rag and soap it up again. I begin to clean the inside of the refrigerator. Crouching down behind the door, I ask, "What happened when you were twelve?" She doesn't answer right away, so I peek up from behind the door to make sure that she is still there. She is. "Nat?" I ask.

"What?" she continues to be distracted by her phone and the dog, still staring at the screen while, without looking, tossing one of the dog's toys into the other room over and over as he lopes after it and returns it to her.

"You answered twelve to one of the questions. What was the question?" I press her, ducking back down and wiping out the fruit drawer. We need peaches.

"She asked me when this all started," she tells me.

Glad that she cannot see my face, I don't have to hide my expression that marks me devastated. Then I ask about the response that I have been avoiding. She had clearly answered, "My mother." But who knows, maybe the question was "Who loves you more than anyone else in the world?" Maybe the nurse had asked her, "Who can you always count on, no matter what?" I worry maybe it was, "Who is the cause of all your problems?" But, as it turns out, the question and the answer were far more horrific than that.

"She asked me if I ever tried to kill myself, how old I was, and who was home with me."

"I think this is it," Peter quietly announces, making a left turn off the dirt road we had taken from the highway.

"We're here, honey," I tell Natalie over my shoulder. Sound asleep on the back seat, curled up in a fetal ball, Natalie doesn't move.

"Natalie," I croon a little louder but still soothingly.

"Nat!" Peter says a little sharper than he probably should have as he navigates the car into a parking space. I reach over and gently touch his thigh to indicate this. He nods and sighs in agreement.

"Nat! We are here, babe!" he amends, softening. Natalie groans and begins to uncurl.

As she stretches, I make a typical mom statement: "I'm proud of you!" Peter grimaces, his rolling eyes hidden from Natalie's view. Again, I admonish him with another thigh touch. This time his rolling eyes are for me.

Tensions are high and Peter's feelings understandable. Truth be told, I feel the same way. This was another one of those times that we could have used a manual. What exactly does one talk about during the forty-minute drive to rehab? What are the appropriate topics to be discussed when you are dropping the precious, perfect baby girl you once held in your arms at a building in the middle of nowhere that looks like a cross between a hospital and a prison? What do people chitchat about when you are headed to a place worse than you ever dreamed you would end up, doing something you never dreamed you would be doing?

We stick to our usual roles, me playing the part of the cheerful, supportive mother while Peter remains the more serious, grounded father. I think his part is easier and more real. You try serving up pleasant platitudes when your life is crumbling.

Natalie awakes from her slumber as Peter hoists her suitcase from the trunk of the car and, through squinted, sleepy eyes, surveys the grey building before her. I wait for her reaction.

Considering we have never looked at the same picture of anything and come away with the same opinion, I should not have been surprised when she deems the cold, unfriendly structure, "Nice, huh, mom?"

"Exactly what I was thinking!" I lie again with fabricated joy.

"Let's go!" Peter growls through the open hatch, then slams the trunk. "It's almost six!" Natalie and I both come to life, unloading ourselves from the car. The rehab facility had made it clear that we should be there by six or we would be turned away.

As we walk the short distance toward the entrance, Natalie and I hold hands. Where in the world am I leading her?

Peter dutifully drags the suitcase. To our frustration, Natalie insists on stopping for a couple of puffs from a cigarette before she takes her last steps in. Peter is about to lose it but reads my pleading eyes, sighs loudly, and says nothing. I'm shocked when he reaches for one of the cigarettes from Natalie's pack, but I swat his hand away before he is able to grab one. I reach out and hold the hand that I have just smacked.

When we enter, the automatic gliding doors hum. The lobby is empty except for us and a receptionist. She greets us warmly with just the right tone that somehow conveys that we are welcome, but she understands that we are doing something difficult.

I make a mental note to learn from her and when I figure out how she does it, I will practice it and replace my normal tone with one similar to hers. She asks who we are, and we introduce Natalie, who is now curled up and laying on the bench in the waiting area. When she looks at her sympathetically, I want to hug her.

Peter identifies himself as her father and tells her that I am Natalie's mother.

Yes! I am Natalie's mother. The failure! I am the one who did not do her job properly and the reason we are here. I'm the one who did not protect her. Please blame me by noting this on whatever form you deem appropriate. Actually, please jot this down on all the forms. Everyone should know.

Somehow, I spew this only in my head and a weak, "Hi," is all that I can muster. I try to swallow the giant lump in my throat that seems to be keeping me from breathing properly.

The entire entry into the facility is painlessly quick. I am sure it is designed this way so there is no time for the patient or the panicking parents to back out.

Peter and I are no sooner seated on the bench with Natalie, her head on my lap and her feet on Peter's lap, when three people in scrubs appear to gently whisk her away. They possess the same quiet, kind demeanor as the receptionist and it seems to have the right effect on Natalie because she calmly begins to go with them.

She is leaving me! I scream frantically in my head. *I am leaving my baby with strangers! Somehow trusting people that I don't know to love, care for, and understand her when she is her most vulnerable! This is completely wrong!*

I want to shout instructions to them: *She's afraid of spiders! And is a picky eater! And although she needs to be here, she is also sweet and kindhearted, and you will really like her if you take the time to get to know her! Don't let the overdone eyeliner or all of the black doodles that she has penned in marker on her body fool you!*

Except for the eyeliner, these were the same things I wanted to scream at the preschool teacher the very first time I dropped her off at school. But just like then, I didn't. Because she didn't need to see my fear. And just like before I dropped her off at preschool, I had told her in the car this time again that she was brave and I was proud of her. I want her to know this is true.

"This will be a good thing, honey!" I call after her just like I did all those years ago on the sidewalk of the preschool. I don't want to be a liar. *I need to not be a liar!*

I know Natalie hears my encouragement because she nods slightly without turning around. I am comforted seeing the way that each of her escorts has a hand placed on one of her shoulders. *Was she really not going to turn around? She turned around just before she reached the door at preschool. I need her to turn around now, too.*

Holding my breath and frozen, I watch her petite body walk farther away, toward the last door. And when she is just a step from the door, she turns. She looks for me. When she spots me, she blows me a kiss. And I blow her one back.

Quietly to myself, I say, "See you in bits, Baby Girl."

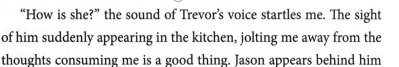

"How is she?" the sound of Trevor's voice startles me. The sight of him suddenly appearing in the kitchen, jolting me away from the thoughts consuming me is a good thing. Jason appears behind him and asks, "Is she okay?"

The two of them stand before me, waiting for my reply; the worried looks clouding their youthful faces make me sad. I try to form my face into a hopeful, confident expression with the intention of comforting them like every good mother would do. But I can feel my mouth sag into a frown.

"She seemed okay when we left," I tell them. Peter and I had just gotten back from dropping Natalie off at rehab and were in the kitchen, heating and reheating a cup of tea over and over again. I would put the mug of water into the microwave to heat, set the timer for three minutes, become so absorbed in my own racing thoughts that I would neglect to hear the beep of the microwave announcing it was done. Every time I would surface from my thinking for a moment, I would open the microwave to discover I had stood there too long, and the water had become cold again.

"She seemed okay," I repeat. "You know your sister. She's a fighter in every way." Jason and Trevor's faces remain grim. "Your sister is tough," I tell them. "And we will help her. We are a good, strong, committed family who won't give up on her. And she is an incredibly strong girl."

As they nod, I launch into a story: "One time, when all three of you were little, we were at Nunnie and Pap's house and we were out in the backyard. It was summer and I bought a toy rocket launcher with three different colored foam rockets. You would take turns putting the rocket on the launcher, then stepping onto the plunger and blasting them off. For some reason, the blue one worked the best so the three of you kept fighting over it. I was trying to sit and visit with Pap, but I kept getting interrupted, having to jump up and break up your fighting to keep the three of you taking turns. I had just collapsed back into my chair when all of you were fighting again and rolling around on the ground. When I went to get up, Pap said, 'Let them go. It's her turn anyway. She'll win.'

"Thinking I needed to defend her from two stronger boys, I said, 'They are boys, I'm afraid they will overpower her, and she won't get her turn.' When I said this, Pap laughed and said, 'You don't have confidence in her because she's a girl and they are boys. And that's exactly why I have confidence in her. She'll win.'

"Sure enough, we watched as Natalie crawled out of the pile, holding the prized blue rocket.

"So, she can do this."

She's my greatest critic
And biggest fan
She believes I can do more
Than I think I can

She's beautiful
Inside and out
I love her soul
And all she's about

She's giving,
And kind
Her happiness
Is always on my mind

She forgives me more
Than she ever should
And loves me more
Than I thought she could

My mom is
My best friend
She's the one who will be with me
In the very end

—Natalie

It is a Sunday afternoon, and we are in the courtyard of the rehab facility. It is a beautiful day, perfect sweatshirt weather. The courtyard is actually pretty beautiful itself with white concrete benches and a colorful brick walkway surrounded by lush, multicolored flowerbeds. For a minute, you forget where you are and that you are locked in. That feeling of entrapment is strange. I can't tell if this bothers Peter or if he even notices. It does not seem to be bothering Natalie, who is chattering happily from the bench across from us. If she could only stay this healthy. If only they could give us a bottle of some medicine or serum or even a pill, a cream, a salve—anything— before we leave to keep her this way on the other side of these walls. No matter what it cost, I would buy it by the crate.

Still nodding supportively at Natalie, I glance around the enclosed area and decide there really is no way out of here except for the one entrance or exit, depending on your viewpoint, that the female counselor is standing at. I look at her and for a moment, we make eye contact. I become uncomfortable and smile weakly, hoping that my expression somehow conveys the fact that I am grateful for what she does here at this facility. Miracle workers and angels. She looks back for only a second, then continues to scan the area with her eyes. I guess she's not allowed to be my friend. Families of addicts sometimes try to sneak in substances to their loved ones in places like these.

Peter gently touches my knee, startling me from my isolating thoughts back to the present. Natalie asked me a question and I have not responded. "Sorry, sweetie," I say. "I was just thinking of how beautiful this place is and how amazing you look."

"She was just saying how great she feels and about some of the things she would like to start accomplishing once she is out of here," Peter says.

"Oh my! That's great!" I say a little too loudly, prompting the guarding counselor to turn and look. I reel it in a bit and say, a little quieter, "Tell me! Tell me!"

"School! A job! Everything!" she proclaims. I smile, enjoying her excitement. Butterflies seem to be dancing in my stomach and I get a little chill on my arms.

"All good things," I agree, a cool breeze washing over the courtyard and me. I feel hope. *We are going to do this,* I think to myself. "You are going to do this, Nat," I tell her.

At my words, she pops us straighter on the bench and smiles. It's her "I am proud of me" smile. It has been forever since I have seen this smile, and the joy it brings to my heart is immeasurable. "You've got this, girl!" I reinforce.

"I just might, Mummy!" she agrees.

Peter touches my knee again and squeezes, silently offering his support and sharing our hope.

"Time," the counselor announces from her post. This announcement threatens to dampen the mood and my spirit, but I push that feeling away and refuse to be any less hopeful.

Natalie hugs Peter and I goodbye and joins a line of girls at the exit while we stay seated on the bench. I try to ignore the sight of each girl being scanned by a detecting wand before she is allowed back into the building. I raise my head upward, hoping for another breeze. I don't feel one and worry that the absence of one is a bad sign. But the sound of Natalie's voice causes this negative thought to evaporate. "Love you, Mummy!" she calls as she makes her way through the doorway.

Once inside the building, the girls parade down the hallway. They are in our view through a row of floor-to-ceiling windows. I watch her. She looks like a happy, carefree little girl with nothing but a beautiful future in front of her. I laugh out loud and nearly trip and fall, rushing to my side of the glass to press my hand on the pane where Natalie has stopped. Holding up the entire line to press her hand on her side of the glass so that I can match it. I laugh out loud, noting that I haven't heard myself laugh in a long time.

On the way home, I ride with the window down, creating my own hopeful breeze.

The phone rings. I check the caller ID and realize it is rehab. Natalie has been there for three weeks. My heart skips a beat. I answer.

"Mommy?" It is Natalie's voice. She sounds like she is ten years old. She sounds eager but not desperate, and because of the number, I at least know where she is. In the milliseconds in between the time when I first hear her voice and I greet her back, my mind races with a thousand horrible scenarios that explain this phone call. She is usually permitted to call only at six o'clock on Tuesday and Thursday. It is a Monday afternoon.

"What's wrong, baby?" I ask, wondering if this is a poor choice of words. I have been told, by my children, that it is slightly insulting that this is always my first question, that I assume something must be wrong.

"Nothing," she tells me. This is always how my kids first respond to my initial question whether this is fact or not.

"It's good to hear your voice," I tell her.

"Thanks," she chirps. "Mommy (I love when she calls me this; she sounds youthful and sweet), I don't have a lot of time. I'm in my therapy. But I wanted you to do me a favor."

I realize then that the counselor is listening in on the line as well. No worries. I really don't mind. "Anything," I tell her and visualize the therapist jotting down the words "supportive mother" on Natalie's chart and adding a few points to my score.

"Could you go up into my room?"

"Sure," I tell her and move from the kitchen toward her bedroom. To fill the time while I am hurrying up the stairs, I ask, "How are you?" even though I'm not sure if small talk is encouraged or permitted during such an obviously purposeful call.

"Good," she tells me, her voice sounding a little weak and thin.

"I'm proud of you!" I tell her (more points), a little out of breath. I am out of shape and shouldn't be. It is only a few steps.

"I'm in your room. What do you need?" I cleaned the room from top to bottom while Natalie was gone and had tried to make it warm and welcoming, adding some "mom" touches: a new heart-shaped pillow, a new bulb for the lava lamp, and a "welcome back" sticky note on the mirror. I am pleased with how it looks.

"There's shit in my room," Natalie tells me through the phone. "Censor yourself; language," I hear the therapist instruct.

"There's stuff in my room," Natalie amends. "And I need you to get it out so that it's not there when I get home."

"Oh, okay," I say, wanting to cooperate but thinking this is unnecessary.

Unfortunately, but not unexpectedly, I had found plenty of "stuff" in Natalie's room. Some in plain sight, other stuff hidden. I found and stepped on syringes on the floor. There were pills strewn all over the bottom of the closet and empty stamp bags, spoons, and lighters everywhere—out in the open as well as hidden behind her bed and in her pillowcase. And then there were more of all of the above secretly stashed in purses, backpacks, books, pillows, stuffed animals, and jewelry boxes.

"I've cleaned pretty well in here, honey," I tell her. "And I did find some things (an understatement). So, we might be okay."

"We're not, and you didn't find it all," she tells me flatly. "Okay," I agree, noting that now she sounds older and worn.

"I need you to go to the air vent," she tells me. "Crouch down and pull the metal part off."

"Daddy..." I am about to tell her that Peter and I had checked in there, but I let my voice trail off and don't finish. Peter had seen on a movie or read somewhere that this was a common place for addicts to hide drugs so we, being "on it" parents, had already looked there. But we hadn't found anything.

Natalie tells me to stretch my arm deeper into the vent, "around the corner and reach," and I pull out a bag full of syringes and pills.

Next, she instructs me to take off Miss Lizzy's head. *Nooo! Not Miss Lizzy!* I whine in my head, devastated that Miss Lizzy is involved in all this horribleness She has always been so innocent. Enough pills to medicate an elephant fall from Miss Lizzy's pretty blond, smiling head.

I need to run back down to the kitchen to retrieve a screwdriver to take off the light switch cover in order to get the stamp bags of heroin out of the crevasses between the wires.

"I am proud of you, honey," I say when Natalie tells me this is all of it.

"Natalie, are you sure that's all of it?" the therapist asks, breaking into the conversation.

"It is," Natalie tells her. The way she says it, I believe her.

The therapist announces that the allotted time for this phone call is up. We exchange quick "I love yous," and the line goes dead.

I am sure I have done a poor job of hiding my devastation and the fact that I have aged ten years since we began this phone call ten minutes earlier. I visualize the therapist deducting all of my previously given bonus points and marking "exhausted" and "running out of steam" in the chart. I'm not sure I care anymore. Not at the moment anyway. I think I couldn't love Natalie more. Which is true and will always continue to be. But I am tired. Exhausted, actually, so I lie down on the bed to rest.

Miss Lizzy is in my arms; she and I go way back. I lie there for a few moments, wondering how in the world we ended up in this horrible, godforsaken place. I realize that no matter how long I lie there, I am not going to get any less tired, so I begin to get up.

But just before I do, still on my back, I catch a glimpse of something above me in the overhead light fixture. I squint to see what it is but cannot tell for sure. I get up and pull the desk chair to the middle of the room beneath the light. I carefully unscrew the center anchor screw and pull down the glass shield covering the bulbs. When I do, a flurry of stamp packets fall on top of my head.

There is a song by country singers Rascal Flatts. I believe it is a perfect recovery song. It's entitled, "I'm Moving On." The song speaks of being a loving, amazing person yet not living as you should.

These words describe Natalie and me perfectly. Our regret is profound, but that regret is also something that we have faced and come to terms with. And I've never met anyone who loves more perfectly yet lives exactly as she shouldn't than my baby girl.

You don't just pour your heart out to everyone. First, because you don't always want to, and second, because not everyone wants to hear it. It's like asking people throughout your day, "How are you?" You ask everyone. But some you care about more than others. Some really tell you, others don't. People arrive at an understanding about this naturally. You figure out who to tell and who not to tell. Who has the time, energy, and interest, and who does not.

And those of us with loved ones who are addicts learn who to trust with our hearts. Sometimes, you just instinctively know who you can trust. And often, this person comes in a rather unexpected form or place. During one of the days that Natalie is at rehab, I decide to mail her a card. I need it to get it there quickly, so I head to FedEx to send it. I stand in line, approach the desk, and hand the card to the clerk.

This is my local FedEx store; I have been here many times before and I know the clerk casually. Whenever I've gone in, she's always been helpful, and we've exchanged pleasantries. I expect this visit to be nothing out of the ordinary. As she types the address into her register, I fish for the crumpled dollar bills in the bottom of my purse. When I look up, she has a complicated expression on her face. There is sympathy, understanding, and compassion in the lines of her face. I smile weakly and hand her the bills. She pauses, and I think now that she is deciding whether to say something.

"Who's here?" she simply asks, pointing to the rehab address.

My mind does that thing people's minds do when it instantly bounces from one thought to its opposite counterpart. She obviously recognizes the address. But is she judging? Looking for gossip? Genuinely interested? Is she as sympathetic as her face appears to be? Next, my mind races with the pros and cons of lies versus honesty. I try to organize and separate them in my mind into two columns, like they tell you to do when you are making a hard decision. But all of the reasons good and bad become jumbled in my head. So, I take the risk and answer her honestly.

"My daughter," I tell her softly, then wait for her response, which will answer all the above questions I have just asked myself.

"My sister was, too," she tells me nonchalantly. So, then I know the answers to the questions were no, no, yes, and for sure yes. Now it is my turn to decide whether I should ask her a question or not.

"How did it work out?" I ask. A short question, only five words, but somehow a question as dangerous as a loaded pistol.

"Twenty-two years later," she grins. "And all's good." Her grin turns into a full smile. I am sure my eyes are wide, and I know my smile is just as big as hers.

It is a Wednesday evening and we have driven out to the rehab facility for a visit. In addition to the Tuesday and Thursday ten-minute phone calls, family is allowed to visit on Wednesday evening and Sunday afternoon.

Peter left work early, which he never does, and is exhausted from a long day. I am tired, as well, from a long day of worrying and waiting for 6:30 to come. We don't talk much during the hour-long drive. Peter concentrates on the road and I study the houses as we pass them, wondering about the lives of the people who call them home. I always imagine their lives simpler, less complicated, and not nearly as messy as mine. Peter always insists that there is mess behind their doors, as well. But if there is, they are doing a good job of hiding this mess and lying to me by putting their innocent playsets in their backyards and cheerful holiday wreaths on their front doors.

Driving to see your daughter at rehab is not like going to visit your daughter in New York City because she just landed a part in a Broadway play or a position as a CEO of a fancy company. All of the conversation you can think to have is pretty dismal anyway. So why bother? I am grateful that Peter and I are a solid enough couple to not have to talk all the time.

An hour later, we and the other parents are seated at separate tables in the cafeteria, waiting for our daughters to arrive. I exchange weak, sympathetic smiles with some of them, a quiet hello with a few, and nothing with a couple of others who refuse to make eye contact. Mostly, we are all quiet.

I wonder if they are all as nervous as I am. I wonder why I am so on edge. I am sitting there waiting to see my own daughter, not some stranger. Maybe I am afraid she will have changed. But that's an odd fear, too. Didn't we bring her here to change? Yes, we did. But we don't want to change all of her. There is so much good to her. So, don't change everything. Maybe I should have sent her with a list of what to change and what not to change. I should have written a note. *This is Natalie. My daughter. The love of my life. She is completely wonderful, and we love everything about her except the part that likes to do drugs. Change that part. Please leave the rest of her, the parts that make her funny and fun, caring, sweet, and smart alone. Sincerely, Natalie's Mother.* I am worried that all of the other parents thought to write a note and I did not.

I am secretly worried that Natalie might be angry when we see her. I am worried that an angry girl will show up and will have replaced my sweet, kind girl. I don't really know what kind of place this is. I don't know where we have left her or what we have committed her to.

We are all sizing up one another. People do this and it is not always in a critical way. Sometimes, I think people are trying to identify with others like themselves. I think we all find comfort when someone like us is close by in unfamiliar circumstances. And it is human nature to also search for someone who you believe is beneath you. If you can find someone who you think is worse off, it might make you feel better about yourself. You can tell yourself that at least you are not the worst one here. In this particular setting, though, I believe we are all in a dead tie. We are all in last place.

I scan the room and decide I am like everyone and no one. I would definitely wear the sweater and shoes that the woman in the corner has on. (In another setting, I would have complimented her and asked her where she bought them. But I am pretty sure this is not rehab appropriate). I think I am unlike the lady seated in the center of the room because I heard her make a joke using the word "junkie" at the entrance when we were waiting to get in. But then I soften and think that people say dumb things when they are nervous. I do this. Maybe she is just nervous. I amend my original assessment. I am like all of them.

Peter and I sit holding hands, outwardly silent but actually speaking a thousand words through the facial expressions we have perfected over the past twenty-five years. I say things like, "This is awful," and "I can't believe we are here and doing this," and "I hope that she is okay," and "I'm sorry," and "This is all my fault."

He answers me with his kind eyes and gentle squeezes to my hands, saying things like, "I know, it is horrible," "Me, too," "I am sure she is fine," "I'm sorry, too," and "No, this is all *my* fault."

I am about to actually speak aloud when a commotion, a combination of tennis-shoed footsteps and female giggles, interrupts my crazy thoughts. All of the families' heads turn collectively toward the entrance to the cafeteria. After a few seconds, the sounds come closer and get louder and the source of the noise appears in the doorway. Seven teenage girls are being led by a female therapist, who acts more like a prison guard, and whom they are now practically running over.

In unison, almost like church, the parents all rise; except, unlike church, the harsh sounds of the metal chairs scraping against the linoleum floor accompany us as we get up. There is a gleeful, collective squeal from the girls as they see their loved ones, a noise that contradicts the unsettling metal scraping sound.

When I see Natalie's face, everyone else in the room disappears. Peter and I sandwich her in a hug and she hugs us back.

She looks wonderful. I mean really good. Clean and fresh-faced and honestly a little happy; finally looking youthful like someone just twenty-one years old should look. Giddy, we settle back into our seats at our assigned table and rapid-fire chat. We ask questions about her time there so far and she answers our questions eagerly, barely able to keep up with her excited, rushing flow of words. She tells us the schedule of her program here. Of the early mornings, the classes and therapies, meals, tiny dabs of free time and the early-to-bed policy. Honestly, it all sounds very nice and I am glad that we chose this particular place.

No matter how carefully you research, you are still choosing with a little bit of a blindfold over your eyes because while one place is perfect and proves successful for one, it ends up being the wrong fit and unsuccessful for another.

As Natalie tells us all the details of her time in rehab so far, I am editing what it all means to me in my mind and the words "strict yet compassionate, understanding and firm" come to my mind. "That's my friend Ellie," she tells us, calling our attention to a tall blonde girl at a table to our left.

The private bubble that we are in pops and the rest of the people in the room reappear. I am grateful that she is able to use the word "friend." I smile my approval. Friendships have always proven difficult for Natalie. I am not sure I can pinpoint exactly why. There were times when I thought she didn't try hard enough in some of her friendships. But now I am embarrassed that I once thought this, realizing that she actually doesn't know how to try and tries too hard. She is far from flawless, but she is truly loyal to a fault to people who don't deserve her dedication. And she is beyond understanding of other people and their flaws. And honestly, she is the first one to forgive other people of their sins, the same sins that everyone else condemns her for.

"That's Cara," she tells me indicating another girl, petite and brunette. "She's the lucky one. She has a baby."

I cringe and stifle the urge to say, "Poor her. Poor baby." I want to break into my well-rehearsed speech about there being nothing better than the blessing of a baby. But that babies are a lot of work and responsibility. So, it is best that they come at the right time, but I don't because I don't want to dampen the mood by recycling this sermon. No one wants to hear it anyway.

Peter, realizing that I am holding back, touches my leg gently, silently commending me.

Encouraged, in place of my speech, I say, "How nice," and ask the baby's name.

"It is!" she gushes and tells me his name is Caleb.

"That's Emily," Natalie tells me, her tone changing. Instead of going into detail, she simply tells me, "Mean girl." My heart sinks, but I should have known there would be one. I am hoping that the niceness of the others can dilute this somehow.

"I'm sorry," I tell her. It is not even necessary to ask what exactly she says or does to make her mean. I imagine that it is the same horrible, standard behavior of most unkind girls, with a few personal touches of her own. Knowing the details wouldn't help anyway.

"How about the rest?" I ask her.

"They are new. So, I don't know yet," she tells me. I eye them warily, trying to remember the interactions I had with their parents and trying to recall whether they had said hello or smiled at least a tiny bit.

"So, you are good?" Peter says, redirecting the conversation back to her.

"Want to see something?" Natalie asks.

"I do!" I say, before realizing that she is looking around at each of the two rehab employees posted in chairs at the exits, who I had not noticed even existed until this moment.

Peter and I are silent as Natalie, deciding that the coast is either clear or clear enough, reaches into her pocket and begins wiggling something out. Nervous, I am now looking over my shoulders. I am not the calmest under pressure and not the person anyone should choose to rob a bank with. Natalie retrieves what she had been fishing for and sets a tangled string on the table between us. On the string, a combination of stickers and beads are hung alternately. The string is tied into a circle. I blink. Is it what I think it is? I know what this is! I smile.

"Do you know what it is?" Natalie asks, grinning. "I do!" I laugh, feeling my face flush with color and my eyes becoming moist with emotion. Hopefulness washes over me.

"Daddy?" Natalie asks and giggles when Peter says, "I have no idea."

"It's a rosary!" Natalie announces. Peter's eyebrows fly up as he says, "Wow! Okay, I see it now!"

Knowing that this falls more under my domain and in line with my area of expertise, he leaves it to me. "So great," I say. "Tell me about it!"

"I don't know…" she begins. "I've just had a lot of time to think. While I am not sure how I feel… I have been thinking… And who knows? Maybe He's here," she partially concedes, waving her hands around the cafeteria. My body remains seated while in my head, I am simultaneously jumping up and down and doing a celebratory happy dance.

Suddenly, the monitor at the door calls out, "Five minutes!" There is a collective chorus of *"awww"* from the girls. I look at Natalie. She makes a disappointed face.

"I'm sorry," I tell her. "But this is the best place for you right now." She nods, then softly confesses, "It's hard."

Under all of the chatty, happy talk, we know there is more to all of this process and this place than we see or know. And behind closed doors, this is a hard place to be. "We are so proud of you," I tell her, putting my hands in the center of the table, palms up.

"Thanks," Natalie says, reaching out and placing her hands in mine. Then Peter rests his hands on top of ours, covering them. Together, they are a tangled pile of heartfelt hope.

"Time," the monitor who has moved from her chair to the door announces. My heart aches.

We say our goodbyes and Natalie turns away from us. As she starts for the door, I notice the rosary on the table. "Nat, you…"

"You keep it," she tells me, somehow knowing what I was about to say without even turning back around.

When Natalie was in third grade, she was an altar server during Mass. The first time she was asked to serve Mass, I was excited and proud but terrifically nervous, as well.

I am sure I felt the same way all parents do when they are getting ready to watch their children do something special for the first time. Whether it be playing a sport, singing in a concert, or performing in a play. Watching your child serve Mass is almost like watching your child in a play. But a silent, serious play: one in which they don't have any lines, yet their part is critically important.

As the music started with the opening hymn, I craned my neck to see my tiny girl lead the priest down the center aisle of the church. She looked so adorable dressed in a white robe, holding the Bible above her head and taking long, deliberate, slow strides down the aisle.

Having been to Mass thousands of times, in addition to witnessing all of the mandatory practices that were required for Natalie to become an altar server, I knew what each of her next moves would be, and she performed each one perfectly.

After the priest finished reading the Gospel, the congregation sat down in anticipation of his Homily. I watched Natalie sit down on one of the cushioned red velvet benches as I settled into my own pew, scolding myself for being so nervous and for not having complete confidence in my child. I shifted my body so I had a perfect view of her between the heads of the couple in front of me. I smiled at how cute she looked with her short legs dangling from her seat, swinging ever so slightly.

I breathed a sigh of relief and turned my focus to the priest's message. He was explaining the parable from the reading and was drawing in the virtue of generosity when I heard a voice from a few pews behind me say in a loud whisper, "Oh my gosh! The altar girl is hysterical. I love her!"

I sat straight up and peered over the other worshippers' heads. I was puzzled as to what they were talking about. I studied Natalie, who was sitting just as she should be. Granted, she was swinging her legs a little more aggressively now, but that couldn't be what they were referring to. It took another second of studying her before I began to understand. I doubted myself at first, questioning my own memory; didn't we put her hair up in a bun before we left the house? Yes, yes, we did. Okay, no worries. Her long brown curly hair was now down and cascading onto her shoulders. Not a crime, I told myself.

"Wait!" whispered the girl who was not good at whispering. "She's doing it again!"

I watched as Natalie removed a hair tie from her wrist (did she sneak that in?), reached up, and quickly reassembled her hair so it was all pulled to her left side.

I felt myself getting warmer and more nervous. I zeroed in on her with laser-sharp focus, hoping to connect with her telepathically and tell her to knock it off or else. But of course, she did not so much as make eye contact with me.

I continued to watch with my temperature rising, my anger heightening, and my embarrassment building as Natalie tried on four more hairstyles while the priest droned on. First the head bun, then straight to her left side, then entirely to the right side of her head. Then, with the assistance of yet another contraband accessory, she divided her hair into two pigtails, one on either side of her head. Finally, she gathered it all up on the top of her head in a Cindy-Lou-Who-from-the-Grinch sort of fashion and bobbed her head a bit so her hair playfully bounced on the top of her head.

The young girls behind me had given up whispering, completely dissolving into fits of laughter. I glanced back for just a split second, hoping to catch sight of them, but they were laughing so hard they were sort of doubled over, hidden behind the pew.

The priest's voice rose in a finale style as he finished up his sermon, and Natalie must have sensed the end was near. She quickly and expertly fashioned her hair back into a proper bun just as the priest uttered his final syllable and directed us to stand for the next prayer.

As we collectively recited the Our Father, Natalie and I made eye contact. She smiled, gave me a thumbs-up with a tilt of her head, and seemed to ask, "I'm doing great, huh, Mom?" I smiled, fanned myself with the prayer book, and gave her a thumbs-up back.

One hit
Two pills
Three shots
Four

How many until I hit the floor

Five bottles
Or was it six?
How much to take
Until I don't exist

Six. Five. Four.
Three. Two. One.
When did this stop
Being for fun

One. Two. Three.
Four. Five. Six.
When I get
The perfect fix

—Natalie

Peter and I are in the classroom of the rehab facility where Natalie has been a patient for a couple of weeks. They offer a group class to the parents the hour before they meet with their child. Peter and I were unsure at first whether we wanted to attend because we don't think of ourselves as "group people." But we reasoned it through and decided that if we went, we would probably be uncomfortable, but if we didn't go, we would feel guilty for not taking advantage of everything offered.

The first half hour is educational, with the therapist doing most of the talking. She schools us on the importance of tough love and eliminating certain people, places, and things. We have all heard this before and collectively get defensive.

We take turns telling her that, yes, that's all good advice, but honestly, you try it. The places start off as new places then turn into the same familiar, newer unhealthy places that they originally were. It is difficult to change things mostly because they are around every corner and, unfortunately, there are always new worse things.

Same with the people, for that matter. They loiter on the corners, providers of all things bad. Their faces and names change, but they are always there. And because there are angels in disguise and bad guys with cherubic faces, we don't need to bother trying to figure out who is who.

We have all attempted to accomplish this task and failed. Some of the scariest and most unsavory characters—dressed in black, adorned with skulls, cross bones, or weed leaves—have delivered our children back to us, impaired, albeit, but home safe. Meanwhile, the ones dressed like valedictorians and honorable lawyers, in plaid sweater vests that look like they had been bought by their grandmothers, left them helpless in alleys or passed out on curbs.

We are in no way suggesting that eliminating the people, places, and things is not appropriate and nothing short of great advice because yes, get rid of all of these things, and underneath all of them is your answer. But arranging for their dismissal is a monstrous, challenging task. A task that none of us has yet to accomplish successfully.

"Be stern with them. Be stronger. No nonsense. Let them know that you mean business." Yes, tough love. It is a good solution to a lot of things. But if we agree that it is not a bad plan and often helps, maybe you can admit that it is not the cure-all, instant fix it is often believed to be.

Yelling people through sickness has never been a suggestion published in any medical journal I've read. And contrary to what critics near and far might believe, we have been strict and stern and shown our children who's boss many times over. It's just that addiction is more formidable than we are.

But stand before the casket of a young girl whose parents instituted the tough love approach that everyone promised would instantly whip her into shape; they kicked her out, only to have her lying dead in a wooden box with the rest of us milling around her among a room full of flowers four days later. Then you might be more inspired to give a hug than slam the door. Stand among flowers that once smelled sweet, fresh, and hopeful but now just smell like funeral flowers, a sour smell that reeks of the end.

It is not lost on us that, because the state of addiction significantly and genuinely changes people into those different than they would like to be, we, the loved ones dealing with them, have had no choice but to become different people, too.

It is still possible to preserve your natural kindness, compassion, and love. I know that some might think this statement is delusional.

But the reality is that we are not curing the epidemic of addiction with the way we are treating it now. Because if we were, it wouldn't be an epidemic.

Finally, before it gets too heated, we all decide we should call it a draw and admit that cuddles and kisses aren't working, and neither is abandonment and cruelty. (I actually feel a little bad for the therapist. I mean, what else is she supposed to say?)

The second part of the meeting is even more painful as we introduce ourselves and share our stories. The brutal honesty in this sharing is excruciating, and the hurt on the people's faces as they tell of their struggles brings tears to my eyes over and over again as each person seems to bleed in front of me.

When things are not so bad, you are guarded, thinking that you might preserve something by not telling the complete truth. But when you are at your rock bottom and have nothing else to lose, tearful confessions that double as cries for help are what you are left with. I can honestly say that I never felt closer to a group of strangers in my entire life.

I learned quickly that all addicts steal and lie. And that all of us loved ones believe them over and over. I learned that none of the addicts ever meant for it to get this far and that every loved one feels guilt and regret. I learned that both the addicts and their loved ones are in pain. I learned that all of us are sorry.

Peter had designated me the talker as we entered the classroom saying, "You say something if we can't get out of it. Not me." I had nodded in agreement as my mind instantly began doing gymnastics, flip-flopping between telling about the time that I found the syringe in the dog's mouth or when I FaceTimed a drug dealer. They are both such spectacularly horrific stories, I cannot decide which of my badges of honor to flash or which one makes me look more heroic.

My heart begins to beat faster as the spotlight gets closer to Peter and me. As the mother with the daughter who has two children with her drug dealer cousin is finishing up her story, I clutch Peter's hand, not exactly sure if I am panicking because it is almost our turn or if this mother's story is so crazy tragic. Either way, this lady wins (unfortunately for her). Even if I discovered syringes in the drug dealer's mouth and FaceTimed the dog, I couldn't compete.

But when it is our turn, Peter surprises me. He introduces us and tells of the guilt he feels from not being able to save his daughter from the horror of addiction. When his voice falters and he calls Natalie his princess, teardrops fall on my shoes.

One thing worse
Than disappointing yourself
Is the thought of disappointing
Someone else

This happens again and again
Every time I relapse
Every time I think
Recovery is in my grasp

I promise
That I am trying
Just need a release
From feeling like dying

I hide myself
Until no one can see
Then I beg that someone
Sees the pain in me

If I can get this dark cloud
To stop its endless hover
Then maybe then
I can start to recover

—Natalie

"Go there!" I challenge in a voice I don't quite recognize. I feel my legs leave the seat, threatening to become airborne in my attempt to leap the table to smack my daughter.

Peter puts his hand on my thigh as some sort of soothing signal. I firmly grab his hand and toss it away so harshly that I have slapped him with his own hand. Natalie has just objected to one of the rules we have proposed, and Lila, our rehab exit meeting referee tells her in a very calm, therapeutic voice that "your parents have a right to approve or disapprove of how you live, considering that you live under their roof." And Natalie responds by saying that she does not always approve of how Peter and I live. So, I am screeching, "Go there!"

The night before you pick your patient up from rehab, you get together for a family conference with a therapist who has been working with your loved one; then you come back the next day to pick them up and take them home. At the time, I thought this arrangement a little inconvenient and strange. Why is it that you don't just have the conference and then take them home with you at the same time?

I now know the reasons for this. And I know now that this procedure is a good one. The reason is because after this very real, honest, and commonly brutal meeting, they are not ready to leave with you and you are not any more ready to take them either. At least, this was the case with us. And I am guessing many others, hence the policy.

Peter and I are sitting side by side at the far end of a table a little more than an hour into Natalie's exit meeting. Natalie sits on the other side of the table and the director, like a referee, is positioned between us. This positioning is correct, especially the positioning of Lila, our director and referee, who is very much earning any extra overtime pay for this added duty, mostly by intercepting me as I continuously try to leap over the table to shake sense into my daughter.

In addition to being furious at Natalie, I am also pretty angry with Peter, who I know deep down inside feels that this is all ridiculous and that Natalie needs a kick in the ass more than anything else, and who is next to me acting like the model prisoner. He is wearing his "thoughtful doctor" expression and listening to Lila like she is actually imparting some precious knowledge. He is even pretending to be entertaining what Lila is calling Natalie's "living suggestions," which I will call her "list of entitled demands."

I go on to say that I would like to know *exactly* what about our lifestyle she doesn't approve of. "Actually, better yet, tell us what you have that disgusts you so much, you would like to do without it?" I spit out. "Would it be the designer clothes on your back? The fancy restaurant meals? The expensive vacations? The college education? How about this hoity-toity rehab?!"

Lila must realize now that she has lost control of the meeting and tells Natalie that it is not necessary to actually answer me; my questions are rhetorical.

My questions are not rhetorical, I tell Lila. And I am puzzled by her suggestion that I calm down, considering she just told the three of us that we should "own our feelings."

"Well, this is me, owning all sorts of feelings!" I yell. "I am owning being very pissed right now!"

Part of the point of the meeting is to clear the air, orchestrate a new start, and set up mutually acceptable rules. There is a lot to go over and they tell you to set aside two hours—which before you begin seems like a long time, and while it is happening seems like an even longer time.

By this time, not only in my head, but outwardly as well, I have pretty much pronounced this meeting "hogwash." I don't even know what hogwash actually is. But I know that it is not good, and it is the only word that I can think of quickly enough. I only chose it in a pinch when I was practically foaming at the mouth over something Natalie just said and I was trying not to say "bullshit."

After I do finally mutter, "Bullshit," loud enough for all of them to hear, I spend the rest of the meeting in the penalty box, staring out the window at the beautiful green trees that are swaying in the summer breeze and wishing to be anywhere but here.

Twenty minutes later, hanging in there just long enough to save face by proving she could wrestle the meeting back from me and continue, Lila, escaping with her life and calling the game over, tells us that she believes this was all *so very productive.* I want to say I believe the entire thing was rubbish, but I don't think I have to. I am quite sure the three of them know how I feel.

We leave without Natalie and ride home in silence so I can get started on a sleepless night.

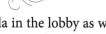

The next day, we meet Lila in the lobby as we wait for Natalie to finish packing up. Lila hands each of us an envelope. Mine is a thick manila envelope stuffed with thirty pages of support meetings that "she believes I might benefit from attending."

Peter receives a thin business-size envelope containing the receipt for the rehab from his American Express card and a tiny sticky note with the name of a book written by a doctor about addiction.

I roll my eyes.

As we wait, Lila tells us it usually takes at least three visits to rehab for the average patient to respond. In my head I think, *Fun fact!* and *Well that's encouraging,* and *Any more good news?* while Peter solemnly says that he understands. Finally, Natalie appears and as I hug her, taking in a breath of her freshly washed hair, all I can think is how being afraid to take your own daughter home with you is a truly horrible feeling.

On the hour-long drive home, I have many of the same feelings I did on the car ride there. How are we supposed to act? How do other people act on their way back from rehab? There is awkward conversation; we are not sure how to behave.

Thirty minutes into the ride, Natalie announces that she is hungry. I give Peter my "There is no way I am cooking" glance, and he pulls into a diner advertising meat loaf and mashed potatoes. Apparently, people who are on their way home from rehab often console themselves with gravy.

Eleven days later, Natalie relapsed.

Hello there darling
My oldest friend
What happened to us?
Why did the fun end?

We were oh so perfect
At least for a bit
Between me and you
It was love at first hit

I was there when you needed me
At least I thought I was
It's not my fault
You need more for the same buzz

I was there in sadness
To make you happy when you're glum
Or in the very least
I was there to make you numb

But I thought we were friends
And now you push me away
No matter how hard you try
Under your skin I will stay

—Natalie

chapter *Seven*

Books Unwritten

I am sitting in a restaurant one day for lunch and there is a TV hanging above us on the wall. The news is on and the lead story, which is about our city's professional sports team that has just been knocked out of the playoffs, has everyone's attention. The announcer rebreaks our collective hearts but half-heartedly encourages us to look forward to next year.

Quickly, before anyone has the chance to look away, he segues into another dismal story, telling us that the opioid crisis in our city is running rampant. On the screen, images of syringes and various drugs flash in front of us. Before the newscaster begins his next sentence, a middle-aged man sitting in a booth in the back of the restaurant says, "Let them all die." He is referring to the addicts the announcer has just estimated are living in our city.

I flinch and can feel my face instantly flush. A mix of anger and hurt overcomes me. I want to disappear. The man's words hang there as I am silently praying that no one will reinforce his opinion, and it will evaporate due to lack of acknowledgment.

"They really should," a woman at a nearby table agrees. "That would take care of the epidemic."

I gulp, trying to swallow the lump in my throat, wishing I had the courage to either stand up on the table and make a monumental, educational speech on the reality of living with addiction or at least the bravery to run out of the restaurant, which for as scared as I am, might as well have been on fire.

Daring to look up from my own white-knuckled, folded hands, I glance around the full restaurant. It is impossible that everyone has not heard him. His voice is kind of booming and he has spoken too loudly for all the other diners not to have received his message. No one else speaks and or otherwise acknowledges him. I am grateful for this and begin to half-heartedly eat when my salad arrives, glad to have made it to the other side of this storm. Grateful that no one else supports him, I look at each of the other patrons, wondering why they don't support the man and his cruel suggestion. I wonder if they feel the same and just don't want to engage with a stranger, if they disagree because they are or have struggled, or if they love an addict. Maybe all of these could be true.

The only thing I know for sure is that I don't know anything for sure.

While I do believe we control much of our journey through life, I also believe we can neither predict nor dictate what life puts before us. For the most part, I believe that the path we travel upon is unique to us and was meant to be. I also feel that the people we meet while walking down this path are all people we are supposed to meet, finding ourselves in the company of these individuals when our roads intersect.

The part that never stops amazing me is that just when I think I have my life and its direction all figured out, I realize that I don't. Because, I have thought things that I never thought I would think, have said things that I never thought I would say, have been places that I never thought I would be, have done things that I never thought I would do, and I have met people that I never thought I would meet. But I guess if there is one thing I know for sure it is that I wouldn't change any of it.

Lately, it feels as if I am having the same party with the same five people over and over again. This is a gathering that no one wants to be invited to. But even with this being the case, there we all are. The people on the guest list are the addict, the dealer, the loved one, and what I like to call a "helper" of some kind, usually a medical professional or a cop.

I glance sideways, just in time to see them join hands and bow their heads. Hoping they don't notice—I'm pretty sure they won't because they have closed their eyes now, too—I fold my hands. I have no one's hand to hold, so I bow my head, close my eyes, and listen.

They are an older man and a younger man who I think might be grandfather and grandson, and they have been sitting in the booth next to me at the diner where I often eat breakfast. The older man, who has a baritone voice like Morgan Freeman, begins by thanking God for everything they have, including the food that they just ate. He asks forgiveness for where he has been less than God would like him to be, then he asks for continued blessings and guidance. I pray with them, my entire heart soaking up every word, and hoping their prayer will seep into me and bless me, as well. At the end, the man says thanks again and then hands it all back to God.

In my mind, I do the same. With my eyes still closed, I draw in my breath, then let out a sigh. I worry that what I am doing is a crime. I wonder if secretly listening in on someone else's prayer is like logging into the neighbor's Wi-Fi. Well, there is no way that they will know anyway.

I open my eyes and realize that they have, indeed, noticed and are staring at me. I can feel my face instantly color. Knowing that I am cringing, I offer a sheepish, "Sorry."

The older man with the booming voice tells me, "No apologies; the more the merrier!" The younger man doesn't speak but nods agreeably.

"What's your name?" the older man asks.

"Christine," I tell him. Then I add, "And my daughter's name is Natalie." He introduces them; his name is Warren and the younger man's name is Thomas.

"And what's Natalie's deal?" Warren asks. For some reason I like the fact that he uses the word "deal."

"Addiction," I tell him.

"A monster!" he bellows. I love him. He definitely understands.

"Let's get on this," he says, as if we are about to do some horribly difficult physical work like push a stalled car to the side of the road and we all need to dig in and work together. He holds out one hand to me and one hand to the younger man and we both take his giant hands into ours with the three of us now making a circle.

"We're back!" he announces, and at first, I look around, not sure who he is talking to. But his eyes are closed; he is talking to God again. Thomas and I steal a glance at one another and share a grin before we close our eyes, too.

"Lord," Warren says, "Enough of this with Natalie. Enough of this monster controlling her. Let her get the care she needs, become well, and be the person and gift to others that you created her to be." I am taken aback. This stranger summed up my most heartfelt prayer in such few words.

"And bless Christine, Natalie's mother, because she is hurting, too, Lord," he continues. "When the babies hurt, the mothers hurt," he adds.

I think my heart actually skips a beat, and it aches for a second. I take a moment, then open my eyes and face him. No one can be wordier than me, but I am at a loss. And can only, with tears in my eyes, manage to say, "Thank you, Warren. Thank you, Thomas."

"He hears us," Warren says, and Thomas nods again. They rise from the booth and tell me goodbye. Warren briefly puts on of his giant hands on the top of my head as he walks by, and I just know that this will be the healing touch that will turn it all around.

I watch the two men walk out of the restaurant, wishing I had found some words and said more. I wish I would have at least thought to pay for their breakfast. When I share this with the waitress, she tells me that they already paid for mine.

I am in the drive-thru lane of the local pharmacy, picking up thyroid medicine for my mother. The clerks and techs are familiar faces. I've always lived here, so I know some of their names, as well.

I have signed and paid for my mother's prescription and am waiting on the other side of the tube when the pharmacist speaks to me from behind the glass window. "Hey," she says, speaking into the microphone with a grimace and a tinge of hesitancy. "We got a bunch of these in, and we were wondering if you might like to have a couple?"

I squint to see a box of Narcan dangling from her fingers. I gulp. I can feel my face flush and know it is coloring. The letters on the box blur through my now moist eyes. I try to answer casually and am tempted to floor it before the tears of embarrassment begin to pathetically dribble down my cheeks. "That would be great!" I tell her perkily, like she has just offered me petunias from her garden.

"Oh great!" she says, matching my joyous manner. (This wasn't her fault. I started it.) She puts two boxes into the bin and presses her "send" button. The swooshing air sound falsely indicates that they will arrive in record time, yet I'm still waiting. The tube must surely be malfunctioning. I never recall anything ever taking so long to deliver. The delay gives us more time to awkwardly smile at each other while I repeat, "Thank you! So nice of you!" and "Really nice!" over and over again as the temperature in the car rises.

As I am yanking the box—of course it sticks and becomes jammed in my end of the bin—free from its trap, I manage to say at least one thing I am genuinely feeling. "It's really nice to be thought of."

I have insisted that Natalie and I do something "normal" together. And going out to eat is normal. Almost instantly, I regret the idea and my insistence. When I first got the idea, Natalie seemed okay. It seemed to be a good day and she wasn't impaired.

We get to the restaurant and she disappears into the bathroom. (Always a bad sign.) She takes too long, and I beg her via text to come back to the table. When she does, her eyes are bloodshot and her speech slurred. By the time we order, she can barely stay awake.

When the food finally arrives, she spills drinks and runs the waitress around unmercifully for everything under the sun: extra napkins, replacements for the spilled drinks, to-go boxes, all erratically and too loudly. I know that we are disturbing the other customers because they are watching her intently and there is no mistaking the judgment in their eyes.

While Natalie is being terrible, I make it a point to be the most grateful diner that ever patronized a restaurant. The waitress seems unfazed and shows nothing. She deserves an Academy Award. I do not. I have broken out into a mortified sweat.

Finally, putting a halt to the disaster of a meal, I suggest to Natalie that she go ahead of me to the car. Wobbling, she does and passes out in the passenger's seat while I stay to pay the bill. I blink through tear-filled eyes at the check and try to do math (my worst subject) in my head. I figure out ten percent, double it, sigh, add ten more dollars, check and recheck the addition, and scribble my signature. I am not exactly sure what percentage of the bill I have tipped the waitress, but hopefully it is a million because that is what she deserves.

She is young, too, I think to myself. *Maybe that's why she understands.* I scan the restaurant but don't see her. Mandy is her name. I had noted it. Respecting her by using her name was the least I could do. Suddenly, Mandy reappears at the table. "All set?" she asks perkily.

"Yes," I sigh with a weak smile, handing her the slip. She smiles back with a smile that is less worn than mine but also says she understands. I should have left her another ten.

"Your daughter will figure it out," she says.

Never wanting any words to be truer, I nod and sigh and grab her hand, giving it just the quickest squeeze. "Thank you," I say and rise from the table.

"Good luck," Mandy tells me, turning toward the kitchen, her arms loaded with our dirty dishes.

I watch her back for just a moment, then suddenly can't resist the urge to call after her. "Hey, Mandy?" I call out. "Why do you think she'll figure it out?"

"Because I did," Mandy tells me, still juggling the plates. "I was her a few years ago."

She turns and heads to the kitchen.

"I bet you miss her," she says. Her words are sympathetic, and they go straight to my heart. I am having a cup of tea with my friend Denise, and we are discussing Natalie. She is a very dear friend and aware of all our struggles and is a great support to me. I am touched she could realize that while Natalie is just a mile down the road, it would not be possible for me to miss her, but I do. Because right now, she is a stranger living in a world different than the one I live in.

I take comfort in my friend's next words—she believes Natalie can beat her illness—that I have to hang on. I am consoled by them because while many people say this, she genuinely wants it for us.

I think to say, *From your lips to God's ears,* but I don't think I can without crying. So, instead, I sit with tears in my eyes, rubbing the gold cross around my neck in between my fingers and staring out the window.

There are puffy white clouds in the sky, and I watch them shift ever so slightly. I am hoping God will form one into the shape of an angel and hang it in the sky, a message from Him to me.

Oh my god, he fucking sold me
It's midnight
My phone is dead
The guy that I came with left
But he has to be coming back right?
I am too nervous to make eye contact with the man on the bed
He doesn't seem to mind
I keep busy with the friendly face next to him
A pretty girl, my age
"You should stay" she coaxes with a smile
"Don't worry. I got you Baby Girl" she assures
My phone is dead
The guy I came with is coming back right?
"Lock the door" the man on the bed says
I do not move
"I have to go home" I say
I glance at the drugs on the bedside table
I hear the door handle click
The friendly face is behind me
She gestures to the table
"We will take good care of you"
The man on the bed looks at me,
I look at him
The guy I came with is not coming back, is he?"
"Oh my god, he fucking sold me"

—Natalie

A FaceTime pops up on my phone. I panic. I am old and technologically stupid. I don't know how to FaceTime. I pull over to the side of the road and put on the flashers. Who would FaceTime me? When you are living the life I am, you don't ignore phone calls or texts from random numbers, though. I envy people who have that luxury.

I, on the other hand, sleep with my phone clutched in my hand. Too many times, it has been Natalie from a random number from a phone from God knows who.

On this day, she has been missing awhile. I have been praying for a text or call from her. So, the ring on the phone is jarring in the first place with that unique mix of hope and dread. I look down at the phone and a face that I do not recognize stares back at me. Apprehensive and actually a little scared, I gulp, gather my courage, and press "accept."

I peer into the phone. I can tell now that the man on the other side of the screen can now see me, too, by the way that he straightens his posture a bit. He smiles at me. This throws me off. I am not sure why, but I wasn't expecting this stranger to smile. This is a good sign, right? Bad people don't smile, do they? I tell myself to stop being stupid. Of course, bad people smile. Who knows, maybe they smile more than good people.

"Hi," he says, warm and friendly. I know that he is a drug dealer.

For a second, I wonder how he got my number, but I figure Natalie's phone was probably dead and she had once used his phone to text or call me and he had saved it. You would think I would be angry that this unsavory individual had my number. And the first time I realized one of them did and I received an unwanted random phone call, I was furious. But when you finally come to terms with the fact that these are the people your child is with and are also her so-called friends, you also realize these are the same people she will be with if she is ever in danger—or worse.

While the possibility of any one of them doing the right thing instead of covering their own tracks and running away is very slim, they do have Natalie's mom's number and maybe they will call me if she needs help. Maybe these people are my only chance at getting a call when Natalie needs me most. And if it is ever worse, maybe they will at least tell me where to find her, so I don't spend the rest of my life wondering.

Strangely, I don't wonder how many of them are out there with my number; instead, I wonder how they have me titled in their phone.

In my head, I skip the greeting and urgently ask him, *Who are you? Where is Natalie? Do you have her? Is she okay? You better not have given her anything or done anything to her or I will track you like a dog and... and... and you will be sorry is all that I am going to say!* What actually comes out of my mouth is a whimpering and weak, "Hi." He smiles again or continues to smile. I am not sure if he ever stopped.

"Don't be scared, Mom," he tells me. I am instantly mad that my face has betrayed me, and I can tell that my face is coloring in fear, embarrassment, and now anger.

"Who are you?" I ask, surprised when this boldly spurts from my mouth. He doesn't answer me but asks instead, "You're Natalie's mom?" It isn't a question but instead an affirmation. I nod.

"Do you have h..." I begin the sentence but decide this phrasing is too accusatory. So, I back up, delete, and start again. "Is she with you?" I am holding my breath just like I do when I ask all of my questions these days.

"Naaah," he tells me. "I'm just looking for her."

"Me, too," I admit, trying to remain calm. "Any ideas?"

"I don't," he tells me.

My face must fall in disappointment. And he appears to feel bad for me. Do drug dealers have sympathy for their addict's mothers?

"Don't worry. She'll surface," he tells me like he really believes this, and I am ashamed for letting myself be consoled by him. "I'm sure she's fine."

"Um…if you see her, could you tell her to come home?" My voice breaks when I say this, but I don't care.

"Will do," he tells me like he means it. Then he smiles again. "And if you see her first, tell her I'm looking for her." This time, his grin looks less genuine and I am unsettled by it. There is a moment when we are just looking at each other, our eyes locked.

FaceTime is clearer than I thought it would be. I don't know what I am looking at. And I wonder what he sees when he looks at me. For a split second, his genuineness reappears. "Take care, Mom," he says.

I nod and because it is what polite people do and also because maybe there is the slightest chance he actually meant it, I say, "You, too."

I hang up. I start to save his number in my phone, but I don't know what to title it.

I'm writing these words
For just in case
Just in case I failed you all
And have lost this race

Just know I loved you dearly,
I loved you all so much
Just know I'm still with you
Even when we cannot touch

Remember my smile,
My laugh and my stare
Remember my nose,
My mouth and my hair

Remember my love most
And my embrace
Even if you can't quite
Remember my face

Remember anything,
Anything that made you smile
And just know I'll see you
In just a little while

—Natalie

The mothers of addicts know each other. We can spot each other a mile off, and if we are put in the same room with a bunch of other mothers who do not have children who are addicts, we will gravitate toward each other.

I am not sure exactly how this works. But I can always tell if another mother has a troubled child. I am drawn to her. Sometimes, I think it is the way that we have learned to be cautious in social situations. We withhold our judgments and our derogatory comments and, most of all, we hold back and dance around what we say and share about our kids. It's a little difficult, after all, to slip into a casual conversation that my daughter does heroin when another mother just answered that her daughter is a lawyer.

I found another mother of an addict at a crowded function once, lingering alone at the dessert table. And I found another in the bathroom. Mothers of addicts often do this, too. We linger around the periphery of things. Usually, we excuse ourselves, trying not to act rudely to others while we check our phones a million times.

Once a man caught me and asked—too loudly—in front of a group of people, "What could be so important on that phone?" I excused myself to the ladies' room to hide my horrible habit in a stall.

I stood with my back against the door, grateful for the solitary space. I thought I was alone but realized I wasn't when I heard a panicked voice coming from three stalls down. "He needs to go to rehab!" she shrieks. "I can't do this anymore with him! Where do you think he is? Well, call somebody else!" I feel instant empathy. I have been exactly where this poor woman is, and I have had pretty much an identical conversation.

I am glad she softens things with whomever she is talking to, apologizing for her tone and telling them that she loves them. She storms out of the stall, banging the door so hard, it shakes the cubicle I am in.

I'm sure she thinks she is alone, so when I creep out of the stall, I make just enough noise to announce myself, wanting to let her know I am there in an effort to save her any embarrassment. I startle her and she flings around from the sink that she is washing her hands in.

"Hi," I say with a weak smile. She looks embarrassed and nods. "Sorry," she offers.

"No need," I say. "I've been there. It is impossibly hard."

There is an instant understanding. Her face softens into an expression where the anger and frustration have disappeared, leaving only pain and exhaustion.

"Your son?" she asks. "Daughter," I tell her.

"I'm a horrible mother," she tells me, pumping the dispenser again and filling her hands with more gel.

"Me, too," I tell her, soaping up my own hands. "I'm pretty sure that I am the worst. I have a good friend and when we get together and talk about our kids and the things that we have done wrong, she always jokes that she wonders if the Mother of the Year award that the National Association of Poor Mothers will be sending us this year will be a plague or a trophy," I say. "We joke that we are running out of space on our walls and mantles for all the awards that they have sent us so far." I am grateful that she laughs out loud at this. "I think of this every time I get my mail," I tell her.

"And now I will, too," she smiles. "But I am pretty sure that I will win this year. I kicked him out and he overdosed in an empty house. I did get him to go to rehab, but now we can't find him." She begins rewashing her hands for the third time. Her hands are getting red.

I dry my own hands and, after using the paper towel, tear off some extra for her, hoping this will encourage her to switch from washing to drying.

"We do what we do," I shrug. "My father says we make mistakes, but at least those mistakes are out of love."

"I was so sick of all those bastards calling him that I shut off his phone. I don't know how I expected him to call me with no phone!" she says, thankfully drying now. "We have been doing this since he was fourteen! I was so naïve! He would come home impaired, and I would tell everyone that he was just overtired."

Knowing that I have her beat on naivety I say, "Twelve. And I dusted stamp bags of heroin when she was only fifteen." The recounting and admission of this event, with me armed with my pink feather duster, usually declares me the winner in any Bad Mommy battle I have ever entered into. It is my secret weapon.

Her eyebrows rise, questioning. "I didn't know what they were!" I say, defending myself with a little laugh. "I thought they were stickers and put them in a ballerina jewelry box."

She grins, clearly stifling a fuller smile that is threatening to come out. But then, unable to help herself, a huge smile appears, and she laughs.

"Let's share the award this year," I suggest, laughing with her.

"Deal," she agrees.

Almost comically, we both turn to the mirror at the same time and fluff our hair very purposefully like women do when they are trying to make it look like they have not fussed with their hair at all and it just grew this way.

"Maybe they will be okay," I tell her, looking at her sideways in the mirror as I put on some lipstick. She joins me and applies lip balm to her lips and looks back.

"Some people do beat this," she points out. "Maybe our kids are them?"

"They just could be," I agree.

We turn and begin to walk out of the bathroom and are almost to the doorway when her phone rings. We both stop dead in our tracks. I don't want to intrude, but I do pause as she looks down quickly to check the number. She looks up and her face is suddenly older and tired again.

"It's him," she says, sighing heavily in a way that tells me that she is relieved, grateful, and terrified all at the same time.

"He's alive," I tell her, pointing the most important fact. She nods.

"Take care," I tell her, offering a sympathetic smile, excusing myself, and turning to exit the bathroom.

She nods at me as she answers her phone. "Josh!" she says as she turns to go back into the bathroom to barricade herself in the stall again. As I leave, I can hear her voice in the distance saying all the things that I have said.

I live in a glass house; therefore, I judge no one.

Specifically, I don't judge other people's parenting or their children. I was a kindergarten teacher for ten years before I became a mother. So, I spent those years genuinely loving other people's children. And if I learned anything from those years, it was that good parenting comes in many styles and good kids come in many varieties. I think my not judging people for all of those years should have counted for something. Counted for exactly what, I am still not sure. Maybe I think I deserve an easier road on this motherly ride. Maybe I think people shouldn't judge me so harshly.

Admittedly, our resumé could look better. But what do we look like to other people? Natalie's eye makeup is sometimes too dark and overdone. And her jeans are sometimes too tight and shirts too low-cut. Would subtle makeup and more modest clothes make her look more acceptable? And me, maybe I wear too many designer clothes and shouldn't drive a Mercedes. Would some less expensive clothes and a more modest car improve how people look at me?

When she was falling into all this, where was I? My blamers may be surprised to know that maybe, just maybe, we were everywhere that you were. We were blowing out birthday candles on a homemade cake, making turkeys out of our handprints on paper with paint, getting our Christmas photos taken, choosing pumpkins at the pumpkin farm. We were at the school play, at the parent-teacher conference, and at church.

Natalie took dance and gymnastic lessons, played the flute in the elementary school band, excelled in the gifted program, and was an altar server. Natalie came from a complete home and lived in an upper-middle-class neighborhood. She was with uncles and aunts, cousins and grandparents who loved her.

In some ways, I don't blame my blamers either. And of the people who judge, some are nicer in their judgment. They may secretly feel that there must be more. There must be something we are hiding. Something was obviously done wrong. (Most days, while still failing to pinpoint what that huge thing was, I think this way, too.) The nicer judgers are polite about their feelings and try to hide them and look at us with sad eyes. But there are cruel judgers, too.

"She's great!" I chirp with enthusiasm. "Natalie is terrific!" I am in the middle of an overly nice, ridiculously fake conversation with the mother of one of Natalie's elementary school classmates. I am lying and this woman knows it. I am actually very glad that she knows this. I am delighted that I am frustrating her. I am enjoying myself. This will probably be the highlight of my entire day. She has obviously heard of Natalie's condition and is digging for information that once she gets, she will joyfully disseminate to all of her friends, who will then become equally joyful.

They will stamp themselves and their daughters as "successes" and me and my daughter as "failures." I am not sure whether, in their private conversations, they bother with the "Oh, that's a shame" or "I feel bad for them" cleansing phrases that make what they are doing less evil, or if they don't bother because they don't really mean this, and no one is actually listening anyway. This is something I have wondered about. I'll never know. I am never there. I decide that when they talk, they more than likely just take pleasure in our misfortune, expressing to one another that "they just knew," "had a feeling," and "saw something in Natalie or me all those years ago" that predicted all of this.

And because the kids all went to a Catholic school, they will invite God to their party and exclaim, "I thank God that isn't us." I am sure this is not exactly the way the Lord prefers to receive His invitations, but they include Him anyway.

"Sooo, sheee's gooood?" the woman prods, stretching out her words in a soothing manner that will give me more time to rethink my previous answer and confess to our horror.

I used to use this tactic with my preschoolers after one hit the other. "Diiid youuu hiiit hiiim?" I would croon, trying to give them a safe space to not only get their misdeed off their chest but also an opportunity to do the right thing. I also employed the tactic of leading my students to the correct answer by giving them two choices and always saying the correct one last. "Did you not hit him, or did you hit him?" I would ask.

Usually, no matter the age, they would choose the last one mostly because I just made it very easy to pick that one. If they were a very young child, they would choose this response because they were just repeating the last thing that I said and that was all that they could remember.

"So, she's all good or not so much?" she asks.

Wow! She's actually very good at this. But I am better. "She's super!" I insist, trying to up Natalie's status while mixing up my adjectives.

So far, I have described her as "good," "really good," "great," and now "super." If she asks again, I am stuck. I search my mental inventory of positive states of being and can only come up with my father's favorite, "stupendous," but I am not sure I can pull that one off without laughing. I decide I will recycle "really good."

Because it is the right thing to do, I ask about her daughter. I only use half of her name, letting the second part trail off because I don't exactly remember her name. She is either Alexa, Alexis, or Alexandra. I listen eagerly about Alexandra's accomplishments with such exuberant false pride that a passerby would think she was my own.

I *oooh* and *aahh* in all the right places and offer an understanding sympathetic, "Oh nooo" over that one B-minus in chemistry class that brought poor Alex and, I imagine, her mother to tears.

I finish off my Academy Award–winning performance, wholeheartedly agreeing that she received this grade because the teacher didn't like her—pure jealousy, for sure—adding, "Who needs chemistry anyway!?"

As I promised myself I would, I express "really good!" at her next attempt to get me to confess and am actually impressed when she touches my hand, leans in, lowers her voice, and asks me if I have heard about Jake, another former classmate, struggling with his life.

The combination of the comforting touch and the attempt to draw her and I closer in hopes of uniting the two of us so that we can together throw another mother and child under the bus is genius. It is an old yet effective tactic. But not this time. I have heard about Jake, but insist that I have not. She has gone too far. I will stand and politely juggle all of the questions and insults that she tosses at me to a point. But I will not take part in the broiling of another mother and child.

There are people who feel that we did wrong, fell down on the job, and, therefore, deserve what we have. Some of them feel the need to very bluntly tell us this. They actually seem to feel very satisfied with our pain. *And if it helps to know,* I would tell them, *the only one who could be questioning me more than you, is me.* I promise, I am suffering. I feel the guilt every moment of every day and in more ways than they will ever imagine. And this guilt is suffocating.

Maybe if I was on the other side, I would judge me, too.

When I am gone
Will I go completely
A casket with a bow
Laid down neatly

Or will I linger
In the air or in the wind
And will it be of the good times
Or only the times I've sinned

Will you remember me breaking
Or when I was tough
Will I go silently
Or will it be rough

Will you cry
Because my life has ceased
Or will you be comforted
That I'm finally at peace

—Natalie

I look around at the pale walls of the emergency room. Yes, we are back here. Not for an overdose, but this time for an abscess so severe from injecting needles into her arms that it will probably need an operation.

I think back to the first time I ever brought Natalie to an emergency room. It was my fault. It was an odd accident. I had lifted her out of her car seat, grabbing my purse and a bag of groceries at the same time while turning and closing the car door and in doing this I also closed Natalie's foot in the door. I didn't know that I had done it until I pulled away and couldn't go any farther because she was caught. I actually had to open the door with the handle to release her foot.

For me, it was horrific. For Natalie, less so, because while she fussed, she wasn't nearly as hysterical as I was. I immediately put her back in the car seat and headed to the hospital. All my arrivals at the emergency room are frantic, and this one was, as well. But I guess that's common. Which is why they have to weed people out according to severity and even have signs explaining that this is not a first-come first-serve establishment.

After I explained the reason we were there and frantically waved Natalie's chubby little foot at anyone who would look or listen, I was escorted to the back fairly quickly.

Natalie was still relatively unfazed, but I was about as fazed as a mother gets. So, I think the reason for the prompt service was more for me than for her. Relocated to an exam room, I was still waving Natalie's extremely cute and chubby foot, which now had a white line across it, for the ER doctor and the nurse with one of the best poker faces I have ever seen. I overexplained the event again and again, adding a confession of how I was the worst mother on the planet. I was on an endless loop of recounting this unfortunate event as well as my admonishment of my poor mothering skills, and was grateful when the doctor stopped me.

Viewing both of us as his patients at this point—and apparently evaluating me as the more critical one—he explained that he knows a bad mother when he sees one, and I was not one. I decided I liked him and that he was handsome.

Then he explained to me that Natalie's bones were not fused yet and her foot was not broken or in need of amputation. (He said this last part as a joke, but wasn't it polite of him to clarify this very real fear of mine?) He said that it wasn't even badly injured or even injured at all. I really, really liked this guy. He explained all this while bouncing a now-happy Natalie on his lap.

Natalie struggled to break free of his grasp, pulled at his glasses and stethoscope, and, for some reason, kissed his right ear. He didn't seem to be fazed by any of this. He explained that a dropper full of baby Tylenol before bed was the most Natalie would need. He winked and smiled at Natalie and me from the doorway, saying, "Carry on, ladies." Okay, now I was full-on in love with this guy.

The previously stoic nurse lightened up and invited Natalie and me to sit at the nurse's station while she prepared the discharge papers, mostly because that is the direction Natalie ran when the doctor stopped struggling with her and put her down.

Corralled in the enclosure, Natalie climbed the desk drawers to get on top of the desk, walked tightrope-style across the counter, and spun on every available swivel chair.

By the time we walked out of the emergency room—or I should I say ran, with me chasing after Natalie through the automatic doors—we were the talk of the ER, and they all waved, laughed, and wished us well.

In the same ER, twenty years later, I perk up when the doctor comes into the room. He looks at both of us sympathetically, greeting Natalie in the bed and me in my usual post in the chair. Then he says something amazing: "Hi Natalie. I am sorry that you are here. But I am happy to care for you."

It is one of the kindest, most telling phrases I have ever heard spoken. Within those two simple sentences, I also hear, "I am not judging you. And I am here for you." His low tone tells me that he is compassionate and sincere.

He gives Natalie the best he has. He examines her finger and confirms it will need a procedure but wants to have another doctor take a look at it. He doesn't run out of the room.

So many people run away from people with Natalie's resumé. Instead, he lingers for a few moments, offers some assurances, and really seems to mean them. He smiles and even reassuringly touches her leg through the blanket before he leaves.

"Nice guy," Natalie says softly after he is out of the room. I nod in agreement.

To prove that many people really have chosen the correct profession for themselves, the second doctor is equally as amazing. Like the first, he greets us both warmly and sits down in the chair on the opposite side of the bed, acting like he is in no hurry. Acting in a rush only makes everyone nervous. Ironically, it doesn't speed things along.

He sympathetically cocks his head sideways, trying to meet Natalie's averted gaze. She is obviously embarrassed as he gently asks her questions. He has told her that he just wants to understand her a bit.

Natalie becomes agitated and emotional, blurting out, "There's really not much to me. I'm just a junkie!" I flinch at the sound of my least favorite word in the world. The doctor seems to cringe, too.

"Naaah…" he says, shaking his head. "Don't call yourself that. And you are more than an addict, Natalie."

His kindness overwhelms me. Unable to speak, I hope that, somehow, he feels my gratefulness.

Natalie answers his questions more easily, feeling his acceptance and compassion. Before he leaves, he gives her hand a squeeze. I know and respect all of the important reasons that medical professionals use gloves, but sometimes it helps to feel that someone isn't afraid to touch you.

Once alone, I pull my seat closer to the bed and lay my hand on Natalie's hand. "Good guys, huh, Mom?" she asks softly.

I agree, then tell her, "And you are a good girl."

I am getting out of bed, which makes me a hero.

Lots of people in my position, wouldn't. If I wasn't so sore, I would attempt to pat myself on the back, but my arms hurt. Even when I sleep, I am so tense that I clench my entire body and I wake up aching everywhere. I switch on the TV. The morning shows are all over the opioid crisis. They announce that it affects millions of people in the United States.

"Present and accounted for," I tell the commentator.

I ready for the day and before heading out, peek into Natalie's room. I try not to look because it is always a tremendous mess. Messiness is part of the illness, I guess. I listen closely and hear the sound of her rhythmic breathing. She's alive.

I go to the local diner. One of my favorite places. It's comfortable and familiar. I have breakfast there almost every morning. The waitresses are friends. They know our situation and sympathize. They politely don't always ask, but when they do, it is not out of gossip but out of genuine caring. Some of them have stuff with their children and know the pain. One lost her son to the same illness and the rest of them loved him, so they get it. They are beautiful, kind women and fuss over Natalie when she shows up to join me for breakfast, so, of course, there is a special place in my heart for all of them. They pour me cups and cups of tea while I write or cry or stare off into space. Most days it is quiet, except for this day. Two women arrive and sit in the booth next to mine.

"Tough love!" the one proclaims. I know what this conversation is about and where it is going even before they continue. "Throw him out!" she instructs boldly. "It's the only way he is going to get off the stuff!"

The other one, obviously the mother of "Him," nods in agreement. She looks a little wilted and worn-out. I can tell that she has been through a lot and wonder if that is how I look to people. Do I wear my plight like a neon sign?

"You are right," she tells the other woman.

Her words are words of agreement, but I don't think she is as sold on her friend's stance as she is acting. When you are in as much pain as mothers of addicts are and are searching so desperately for answers, you really will listen to anyone and everyone, thinking and hoping that they just might have that magic answer. When you realize there is not a golden fix for your child's addiction, you begin to understand just how helpless you are.

My father used to use the expression "Everyone goes home alone." He used to say this when people needed to make important, difficult decisions. While he didn't disagree with listening to other people's advice, he always stressed to me that, in the end, you really needed to make your own decision because, ultimately, you were the one left alone with the outcome. This advice served me well many times while making big and small decisions. It helped me be at peace when it was time to make the choice to discontinue treatment for him and let him pass. And I know that his words are guiding my decisions with Natalie. I do listen to other people's opinions, professionals as well as nonprofessionals, but I keep in mind that in the end, it will be me alone with the consequences of my choices.

I understand the concept of tough love and don't completely disagree with it. Addicted people are quite the paradox. As weak as they are, that is as strong as they are, too. They are ill, but the addiction drives them to be feisty. So, they cannot be underestimated. They are often stronger than their families.

I have a friend, a retired ER doctor, who once told me the one thing to remember was that while all of the advice I was getting was well-meaning, I should remember that the difference between the other people giving me so much advice and myself was that no one who was giving me advice on Natalie loved her. And I should factor that in.

When I am deciding what to do with Natalie, I always imagine myself on the other side of the decision I am about to make. I envision myself first with a good outcome and then with a bad outcome. And in each imagining, I ask myself if I will be able to live with that choice.

"You will see!" the friend tells the worried mother sitting opposite her in the booth. "It will fix him!" She stands up and excuses herself to the restroom.

I wonder if the mom of the troubled boy is offended at the word "fix." I am. I push the feeling away. The friend is a good friend, well-meaning and kind. She's not only trying, but trying hard, to help. And those of us with problem kids are often difficult to help. We need to be grateful for those friends that hang in there with us. The mom is alone now and only a few feet away from me. So, I was privy to the entire conversation. I wrestle with my next move and her dejected posture.

She is slumped in the booth, staring off into space, in a world of her own. I want to tell her that she is not completely alone there and that I have been in that world, too. I am her.

"Um...I'm sorry," I say. "I shouldn't have listened." Her head pops up. "But I did. It's not an easy situation. But I know it, unfortunately, too."

Her eyes are glued to mine with an astonished, frozen expression. She looks as if she is noticing me for the first time. Which she probably is. She is motionless except for a deep swallow that seems to make her flinch.

"I don't have any answers," I say, really wanting to make that point clear. "But I'm sure that no one loves him like you do." She blinks. "So, I think you should just do what you can live with," I say, softly. "Do what you will be able to live with...no matter what."

She nods and her face crumbles into a painful expression. "That's what you do?" she asks. I nod to confirm this. "Your son?" she asks.

Out of the corner of my eye, I can see her friend returning from the restroom. Gratefully, the friend stops at the pie counter to browse, giving us another moment alone.

"Daughter," I correct. "What's your son's name?"

"Steven," she tells me, wincing at the sound of her own child's name, her eyes filling with tears.

"What's your daughter's name?" she asks.

Mothers of troubled children are always sure to do this. We ask one another the names of our kids when no one else does. I don't think the fact that other people often don't ask this is intentional. I just think they are caught up in all of the other horrific details of our stories that they forget to ask. But mothers like us always ask. We tell people our kids' names even when nobody seems to care. Saying their names reminds everyone that, despite their troubles, they are people, too. It makes it all more human.

"My daughter's name is Natalie," I tell her and am surprised that my own voice catches a bit when I do this. Sometimes, the emotions sneak up on you like this. "I'll pray for Steven."

She nods gratefully. "And I'll pray for Natalie." I offer her a smile, but her face looks suddenly a bit more troubled. "We call him Stevie," she tells me, a tear dripping down her face. This is important. Her baby's name is Stevie, not Steven. I am glad she shares this. This is just the sort of detail that bothers us mothers after if we leave it unsaid. I smile.

"Then I'll pray for Stevie," I amend. "God probably knows him best by this."

"We call Natalie 'Matlie-Girl,'" I laugh, wondering but not caring if it sounds silly.

"Then Matlie-Girl," she says with a smile that contradicts the next tear that is falling.

Her friend arrives back at the table. I offer a smile to her, as well, then gather my things to leave. As I do, I can hear Stevie's mother tell her friend that she is grateful for her advice, but she thinks that she just needs to do what her heart tells her and that she needs to do what she will be able to live with.

When I imagine myself on the good side of all of this, with a happy ending, I am sharing my story with others. But then of course, way too often, I think of me with what I fear the most in the world happening, and among the many emotions I visualize myself having, what I fear most is a very specific regret.

I have come to terms with the fact that I will have a lot of regret. Because I have already gotten a head start on this, and the things that I wish I would have done differently haunt me. But I know for me to survive on the other side if left alone, I will need to know that while I may have yelled and screamed and was uglier than I ever dreamed I would be (these things I will surely regret), I must know that, even though there are plenty of wrong things that I did do, what I need to know for sure is that I did not turn my back on my daughter.

I will know that I may have fought poorly, but I always stayed. And while I am knowing this from where I am, I will know that Natalie also knows that from wherever she is—I stayed.

Of all the horrible memories and emotions that Natalie may remember or have, the feeling that I left her will not be among them. One picture she will not have is that of her mother walking away from her.

I set my cell phone on the seat next to me. I am waiting for Natalie to call. I'm a nervous wreck. As difficult as she is to deal with—and as hard as it is to see her impaired—her being with me is still better than when she is out of my sight. We had spoken early that morning and we were supposed to meet for lunch. It is past the time that we had planned; not by much, but I am so anxiety ridden.

Natalie actually seemed really good that morning. But she is so unpredictable and unreliable that things often change quickly and without warning. All it takes is one unsupervised trip to the bathroom with that damn suspicious backpack and its forbidden contents, and she is a completely different person. In ten minutes, she can go from energetic to asleep. Or from sweet to combative.

Natalie said that she would call when she was on her way, and I am desperately waiting for that call. I have been in this position many times before and have been everything from mildly let down to devastated. I will my cell phone to ring. I pick it up to make sure it is on. Check to make sure that the volume is up nice and high. I polish the screen with the bottom of my shirt. Then I set it back down to stare at it.

After a few silent moments, I have an idea and search my purse frantically for something that I just know will work. Finally, by feel alone, I locate my favorite clear plastic hand cross. This cross is made of shiny clear plastic and fits perfectly in the palm of anyone's hand. It is meant to be held while praying, and I believe in its power. I bought it at a gift shop when Peter and I were away on a beautiful weekend trip. And I bring it to church every Sunday and dip it in the holy water. It will help; I know it.

Again, using the bottom of my shirt as a cleaning cloth, I rub the ornament until it is shiny, give it a kiss, then balance it on top of my cell phone. The cross promptly slides off. I frown and replace it carefully. But it falls again. I repeat the process and it falls every time. I believe in signs, and I am becoming upset. I pick the cross up again and give it one more kiss, and with even more care and gentleness, I balance the cross on the cell phone. This time it stays.

I hold my breath, and when I finally must breathe, I make sure to do it by not moving and disturbing the cross. Following the a-watched-pot-never-boils philosophy, I turn to focus on some clouds outside the window. I search desperately for hopeful pictures in the clouds—this is another one of my luck-filled games. But I can't find any. All the clouds just look like clouds.

I am lost in my own mind, having almost convinced myself that one of the clouds kind of, sort of looks like Jesus, when the cell phone erupts and startles me—as it does everyone else in the diner because I had the volume turned up so high.

I am so unnerved that I accidentally knock the phone to the floor without seeing who the caller is. I dive down under the table and finally retrieve it. Natalie's name and the two pink heart emojis that I assigned to her shine brightly from the screen.

It only takes me a split second to answer, but in that micro bit of time I feel a plethora of conflicting emotions. I am elated, hopeful, terrified, worried, and anxious. All at once, simultaneously, I imagine every possible logical and illogical scenario. I have Natalie calling to break my already bruised heart irreparably, this time from jail, the hospital, or a ditch on the side of the road. In this same second, Natalie also calls from her grandmother's, or school, or right around the corner to fill my heart with hope.

Any mother can tell how her child is doing simply by the way they say the word "mom" on the phone. Whether our sons or daughters are four or forty, we know just by how they speak our name if they are well or in distress.

"Hello! Nat! Are you okay?" I answer urgently.

"Mom!" she says. I gulp, breathe, and wipe a single tear that snuck into my eye.

"Hi Honey!" I say, not even needing to completely fake all the cheeriness.

"I'm on my way," she says. "I'm good!"

I don't bother telling her that I already know that.

How much skin
Will the next fix cost
How many coins
Will it take to get lost

How much do I need
To forget my past
How much longer
Will this rush last

It always seems like
It's too little, too late
Why does this hell
Seem to be my fate?

In circles
I run and run
How many days
Since I've seen the sun?

I lose a bit of my soul
With every deal I make
I will never know
How much more they will take

—Natalie

So, if I am understanding the woman facing me on the screen correctly, addiction can be solved by exercise and enrolling all of the addicts in Pilates class. I'm guessing there will not be more Pilates instructors than addicts.

I had a falling out with a famous actor—who I had really liked—a few years back when his wife was suffering from postpartum depression and he sat arrogantly (having not just spent the previous forty weeks being pregnant and giving birth to a baby) telling everyone that all women with depression really needed to do was exercise. I've hated him ever since. He does not get my ten dollars at the theater.

And I am an unwilling participant. I signed no forms, did not give my email, or text back "yes" to confirm my appointment, yet I am still somehow a member of this club. A club that no one wants to be in. The Heartbroken Moms of Addicts. Some days, I believe I know so much about all of it—both heartache and addiction—that I should be president and write the newsletter for it. And other days, I am convinced I don't know the first thing about opioid addiction. But I could fill volumes about the heartache.

We have had a lot of care and most of it, in my opinion, was offered with nothing but good intentions. It's just that so far, none of it has actually worked. It is like chasing a target that keeps on moving just a little bit faster and is a little bit more skilled than you are. Every time you are fooled and think that you are getting close, you realize that you are not and are no better off—and possibly worse off—than when you started.

Some people claim that we are doing okay in dealing with it. To them, I would say that, if we are truly dealing with it successfully, it wouldn't be an epidemic. I respect the honesty that some people display and while it sometimes is not cheerful, it is in some way helpful.

I once was watching a news program documenting different treatment programs in other states dealing with the crisis. I was hanging
on every word of one report and was just about to book plane tickets
for Natalie and myself, when the mayor of the community appeared
on the screen, saying, "Stay at home. No one is getting cured here
either." His admittance that his state or community did not hold the
keys to the kingdom impressed me.

I cannot admit fast enough that I have no idea what our solution
might be; I can only speak of what has provided us with tiny bits of
success. Maybe the fact that everyone's answer is different is one of
the biggest challenges. While I have become more educated regarding
opioids and the problems associated with their overuse, I still main-
tain that I know very little and must trust the professionals in charge.
While we are on the front lines together, with Natalie in between us,
most times, I let them lead and look to them for answers. I listen
closely and absorb all that I can, even taking notes.

But every time I am in the doctor's office or clinics with Natalie,
I find myself studying the same thing... the medical professional's
eyes. I guess I am just a mom in this way. I do listen to and weigh and
measure their words. But I am intrigued by the kindness, compassion,
and tenderness that I see or don't see. I don't believe this is something
you can fake. It is either there or it's not. I never shared this uncon-
ventional assessment tool with Natalie.

But once when we were leaving the office of a doctor we had never
seen before and I was waiting to hear her opinion, she said, "He has
nice eyes huh, Mum?"

"He does," I agreed hopefully. It was a good sign. So, in the end,
we look for the doctor with the kind eyes.

Everything fades to black
I'm used to that part
But what I was not expecting
Was to jolt to a start

Naked in every sense
Strangers surround me
Looks of concern and disgust
Feeling gross and guilty

I died that morning
I know that as a fact
But after seeing that sea of faces
I wish they hadn't brought me back

— Natalie

"I hope so!" I say in response to my friend Denise's proclamation that "Things will get better!"

We are calling goodbye to each other across the parking lot of our favorite breakfast spot. Denise is a great friend. She is very busy but makes time for me. She has a beautiful life with a great marriage and super kids and grandkids. She's a little wiser than I am in some ways and tends to do everything that she tries well. I joke with her that I try not to hold all of this against her and am grateful, always, for her friendship.

We meet for breakfast and we share about ourselves—our families, our kids, and just stuff. I have always been able to out-sad her. One day, I hope to have the privilege of sharing successful kid and happy grandkid stories right back at her. But this is not that day.

Denise tells me that one of her daughters gave birth on my wedding anniversary. And I share that on that same day, Peter and I were too exhausted to celebrate, so I heated up day-old tuna noodle casserole.

Denise shares that for her birthday, her sons and daughters went to Mass with her. I share that for my birthday, Natalie was impaired, fell asleep on top of her plate, and Trevor stormed out of the room, calling her a disgrace.

As I drive out of the parking lot of the diner, I am feeling a little energized and don't feel like going straight home. Denise had pointed out the few small positives I mentioned. I treasure her. She calls it as she sees it and doesn't blow disingenuous happy platitudes at me. Instead, she celebrates the tiny successes with me, and when there aren't any, we just drink more tea and coffee and sit a few minutes longer.

So now, as I pull onto the highway, a flurry of positive possibilities for Natalie flutter through my head. After a mile or two, it dawns on me that what I am feeling is hope and this gives me a destination. I pull into the church parking lot and sit for a while, watching the children from the church's elementary school walking in a line to the playground. Their young teacher leads them, walking backward with her finger pressed to her lips, a signal to them to remain silent until they reach the playground.

The children are relatively quiet except for their giggling. The energy that emanates from them—with the anticipation of being set free onto the patchy grass—is practically palpable. I follow them with my eyes and laugh, especially when they explode in happy hoots and hollers right before the finish line. The teacher shakes her head in surrender and surveys the group like a mother duck. I decide she is a good teacher. I like her; she reminds me of a younger version of myself.

I scan the play yard, trying to find the one little girl who most reminds me of a young Natalie. I find her. She is tinier than all the other children, just like Natalie always was. She has messy brown hair and, although I cannot see her eyes, I bet they are chestnut like my girl's eyes are. When I see this almost-Natalie speed around faster than the others, I know she is the one.

I leave my car and press the lock button, carrying only my keys and three one-dollar bills into the church with me.

The church is dimly lit. In my opinion, it is the best light for prayer. I actually think they should keep it like this on Sundays, too, with the overhead lights turned off. The golden hues from the sunlight stream in through the stained glass. When I kneel and bow my head to pray, ever so faintly, I am able to hear the children playing outside. It makes me smile. It was the feelings of hope that drove me here.

I know that in the Bible, hope is mentioned 130 times. So, I believe that with this being the case, and this being the place where hope was created, church is the best place for me to show up.

He was adorable. I hated him. Okay, hate is a really a strong word. I don't really hate anyone or anything. But I truly didn't like him. I didn't want a dog. It's not that I don't like animals. It's just that I liked them best when they belonged to other people.

The dog was the doctors' idea. That's doctors, plural. Natalie's doctor and her father, the doctor. The idea was she would give unconditional love and she would receive unconditional love. So, why not a dog? Personally, I had a litany of responses to this question. For one, "He will pee on the kitchen floor!"

Even though I didn't realize it at the time, it was apparently a common scenario. We went to the shelter just to look. We were not going to take a dog home that day. I remember peering at him skeptically through the glass as he looked pathetically back at me. The next thing I knew, he was peeing on my kitchen floor—as predicted. It started off grand.

There was a definite honeymoon period, for Natalie at least. She took to Obie—a name I gave him. "If he is staying, then I at least get to name him!" I had insisted. While I didn't like him, I felt some obligation to protect him from a stupid name like Fluffy or Sparkle. I had that much compassion anyway. If I was going to be living with him for the next twelve and a half years (yes, I googled how long on average a cocker spaniel lives), he needed to have a sensible name. It came from a hot dog shop in one of my favorite places on earth, Rehoboth Beach, Delaware.

Once it became clear that he was not going anywhere—he was not a guest but instead a member of the family—I tried to get used to him. I admit to sometimes wishing that he were at least a cat. I understand that this is the ultimate insult to a dog. But from what I know, they are much more independent and less of a nuisance.

I knew for sure he was staying when I noticed that in two weeks, he had amassed twice the number of photos on our family-shared camera roll than my third child had in fifteen years and four times the lifetime photos there are of me. Apparently, the only hope for getting a photo op for me and my son Trevor is to be in a picture with Obie.

In addition to this sign that he was on Newbury Drive to stay was that he began receiving mail. The vet wanted to see him again in three months and the local pet store had a sale on some toys he might be interested in. Begrudgingly, I penciled his appointment into my calendar. No one's health should be neglected. I am not a monster. But I disregarded the toy flyer. He would not be getting any new toys. Who would have guessed that I would soften by Christmas, with his pile under the tree being larger than all the rest of the piles put together.

The love between Natalie and Obie is great and still exists stronger than ever. Their affection for one another is undeniable, including plenty of wet on-the-mouth kisses. Gross to me. But I am practicing not judging.

She is great with him, tending to his every need. Always a bowl full of food and fresh water at the ready. She spent time training him and patiently took him for walks even though he preferred to sit down on the sidewalk and chew on the leash instead of explore the neighborhood.

Much to my chagrin, they sleep in the same bed, which only accomplishes both of them smelling like dog. But they tell you to choose your battles. This one I wouldn't win anyway. She is his mama and me his nunnie. Our goal of mutual, unconditional love is accomplished and exceeds our expectations.

Witnessing this and softening, I decided to give him a break. I studied this beast living in my home, and figured he had to have some redeeming quality, or that there needed be something rewarding about owning a dog because too many people do it. Fast-forward a couple of years, and I am not sure who owns who.

The bond between Obie and me grew naturally in the way you would expect. With everyone else in the family heading out to work and school every day, he spends the majority of his time with me. He doesn't seem to mind housework and loves making dinner. He's not much of a reader, choosing to cuddle up when I do. Preferring to watch television, he, like a toddler, enjoys the commercials the best. So, he is a good companion.

But often, we spend our time waiting. Waiting for Natalie to come home. He stays awake with me during the sleepless nights when Natalie has been gone too long, only dozing when I do, and jumping with a start when we hear the click of the lock on the front door. When I am restless, he paces with me. And I do believe he worries with me, too. He seems to listen thoughtfully when I am pouring my heart out, verbalizing my worst fears.

When he first arrived, I was certain he could offer me nothing. Now I worry he has sacrificed too much. He is the most nervous, scared dog on the planet and is actually greying prematurely.

On one visit to the vet, Obie displayed such a high degree of anxiety, the vet offered us a puppy sedative. I declined on his behalf, assuring the doctor that we would try to work through our issues privately.

When I told Peter of the vet's offer, he scolded me jokingly for not accepting it, saying, "You should have taken them! You and I could have tried them."

The family joke is that the dog that was supposed to be Natalie's emotional support animal became the dog who needed emotional support. And we wouldn't trade him for the world and love him dearly. Even me. Okay, *especially* me.

I was looking at him the other evening when he was sleeping at my feet, keeping me company. It was not quite 3 AM and we were waiting for Natalie. We always wait and worry, but we only go into overdrive worry after midnight. The dog could rest, but I could not. I remember thinking as he snored his soft puppy snore that I can honestly say that I would hurt anyone who tried to hurt him. Funny how love changes everything.

And then I remember thinking that maybe I am not giving him enough credit and that he actually did become the emotional support dog that we needed. He just ended up supporting another member of the family—me.

I am not sure that anyone else has noticed this. But I keep it to myself and just keep on with the original joke. It's funnier that way. I make the kids take turns doing daily affirmations with him. They sit him on their laps and, making eye contact, remind him of his virtues and talents.

"You are a great dog...you are intelligent...you are loyal...you have a wonderful bark...you are brave, everyone is afraid of the cleaning ladies...and we love you." So far, he just sits there shaking a little and looking concerned, waiting for the lecture to be over so he can go sit by the door. But we try.

But there is no denying that Obie came through exactly when he needed to and saved Natalie's life. He forever secured his place in our hearts and in heaven.

When Natalie was in third grade, there was a debate in her classroom as to whether pets went to Heaven. The dog of one of her classmates had died and the little girl was teary and sad, and the other students were consoling her, telling her that she would see her precious pet in Heaven.

Another little girl was having none of this and explained to the rest of the students that this was ridiculous because only beings with souls went to Heaven and everyone knows that dogs don't have souls.

The conversation became quite heated with Natalie explaining to the little girl that she would not be going to Heaven because she apparently didn't have a soul either. The teacher intervened and ended it. They compromised by agreeing to pray for Ella and her broken heart, as well as Sparky's soul or lack thereof, whichever they chose.

I was proud of Natalie. At the time, I didn't give much thought about whether animals went to Heaven. But with Obie's arrival into the family and into my heart, and knowing that Heaven is a place that contains everything and everyone you love, I have decided that Obie will be there with me.

And because it will be my version of Heaven, which is a place better than any of us could ever imagine, I expect he will be better potty-trained there than he is here on Earth. But either way, he will be there.

Like we are a lot of the time, the dog and I are alone. And like we do a lot of the time, we are missing Natalie. I am tortured and wondering where she might be. I wonder if Obie can wonder. He spends a lot of time looking dreamily out the front window, and I can't help but believe that he is thinking about something.

While I do believe Obie to be the greatest dog on the planet, I also admit he's not the smartest. I'm actually glad that he doesn't know or understand everything. I worry, though, if Natalie leaves us, how I will explain it to him. They say the average trained dog knows about 165 words and that genius dogs know over 1,000 words. While I couldn't love him more, I would say it is safe to say that he is not a genius or even average.

They say the average twenty-year-old knows about 42,000 words. Natalie is a genius; her IQ once tested at 150. So, she knows a lot of words. But I would guess her favorite word is "Obie," and I know for sure that Obie's very favorite word is "Natalie." Natalie's face lights up when she talks about Obie, and at the sound of Natalie's name, Obie becomes undone. He reacts as if an electric shock has gone through his body, causing him to bolt up, spin in circles, and even sometimes pee himself.

Natalie reacts just as passionately, becoming gooey and emotional and often saying, "Aww, my baby." I think it amazing and beautiful that two creatures so different in intelligence can be so bonded together by the love that they share.

"Oh Natalie," I sigh now with my head in my hands.

I regret saying this almost instantly because the moment Natalie's name is out of my mouth, the dog jumps from his slumber and bolts to the door.

"Wait! I'm sorry! Come back!" I yell to him. "She's not home yet." I cannot undo what I have just done, and he doesn't believe me. "I'm sorry Obie, Na..." I stop myself from saying it again. "She's not coming right now." I am using my most comforting, soothing voice. He remains on high alert by the front door.

"Obie!" I call from the family room couch. "I'm sorry I said that. She's not coming right now. The news is on. Look, it's David Muir! We like him! Come watch with me."

I leave David and go sit on the steps by the front door. "She's not coming now. But will soon. I'm sure of it," I say, consoling him and myself. We sit together for a while until he figures it out. He watches me questioningly, and it kind of breaks my heart. But Obie starts to adjust. First, he sits, then he lies, until finally he is snoring peacefully, still in front of the door. I give him a pet on his little brown head, walk back to the family room, and plop down on the couch.

David Muir is still on and looking quite handsome in a black blazer. He also looks serious. I grab the remote and turn up the volume. He is talking about how bad the opioid crisis is in America and how it is affecting all of us. "I know, David," I say, looking back at Obie. "I know."

It was a Saturday morning. We all slept in just a bit. I was the first one up and dressed and decided to head out. Peter was still asleep in our bedroom and Natalie was asleep in hers. It is typical for me to just leave and I was just about to when I heard Obie bark from behind Natalie's closed bedroom door. I was tempted to ignore it. But it was a different kind of bark, difficult to describe, maybe a little higher pitched and longer in duration. I actually did ignore him at first, but he made the sound again and then began to paw at the door.

What and why we do things and the consequences of these reasons and actions always amaze me. For the single reason that I did not want him to leave scratch marks on the bottom of the door, I went back upstairs and opened Natalie's door to let him out. Usually, I just open it a small bit, just enough to let Obie wiggle out. And this is what I did this time, too. Happy to be out of the confinement of the bedroom, he always scurries out and darts down the stairs. But this time he did not. Instead, he took a step out of the doorway, then quickly turned and went back in the room. He did this over and over while he kept making this rare sound. Every time I went to close the door, I couldn't because he kept positioning himself in the path of the door.

"Obie," I scolded. "What are you doing?" He took a step out into the hall, then two steps back into the room again and again until I realized he wanted me to go into the room.

That's when I opened the door wider, peered into the bedroom, and saw Natalie overdosed, lying naked on the bed. She was face-down, and when I went to pull her up, I experienced for myself the expression "dead weight." Natalie is not a big person, only about 110 pounds and not quite five feet tall, but I was still unable to move her.

I ran to get Peter and woke him frantically. He broke into action, running first to the bedroom, flipping her, and assessing her condition. Then racing to the kitchen to retrieve the Narcan that we keep in the kitchen cabinet.

I was useless. I panicked and stood by frozen, unable to help, my eyes glued to the sight of my daughter dead on her bed. Peter administered the medicine twice before it miraculously brought her back to life. She popped up and did what is common for overdosed people to do—she asked, "What happened?"

You would think there would be so much to say, even a lot of screaming and yelling in response to this question, but for us, there were no words. Only relief that bordered on collapse and a mix of emotions that included gratefulness and anger.

"You were dead," I told her, walking over the syringes scattered on the floor with a gentle supportive hand on Peter's shoulder.

My husband and I hugged in the hallway. Making another addition to the list of experiences that we never thought we would live through together. We apologized to each other, each of us accepting the blame in an attempt to lighten the burden of the other, then spent a couple of quiet minutes emphasizing that things have to change and pledging to figure this monster out and quickly.

Together, we knelt and petted and hugged Obie, who also appeared relieved by the way he wagged his tail.

When Peter and I walked away, instead of following us, Obie dutifully went back into Natalie's room and curled up on the foot of the bed. He really is a spectacular dog. That night, I made him a filet for dinner to try to prove this to him. As he ate, his tail wagged in overdrive.

I am silent as I settle into the maroon, leather armchair, which I was relieved to find in his office instead of a couch.

He is quiet as well, as he closes the door and settles into his black desk chair. At first, I miss the fact that he is looking at me because I am busy looking around the room. It is a nice office, decorated well enough in a manly sort of way. Which is okay because he is a man, after all. I probably look silly with my eyes gawking and my head turning in every direction. But I am nervous, and I can't help but want to take in my surroundings.

I notice him looking at me and without meaning to, I say, "Hi." I regret this because I already said hi when he greeted me from the waiting area. I thought it was really nice that he himself retrieved me. It is kind of a warm touch instead of an informal, clinical shout-out of my name or initials from a receptionist or nurse. I think maybe I should tell him this but decide against it.

I take one more scan of the room and note that he likes guns and motorcycles. Then I force myself to focus on him, noticing that he is nicely dressed in black slacks, a grey-and-black plaid sport coat and white shirt. He is not wearing a tie. I kind of like that, semi-casual.

I am tempted to tell him that I don't know why I am there. I did know a month ago when I googled and chose him. And I knew why I made the appointment during the previous three weeks that I walked around with the appointment reminder card in my pocket. I even knew why I was going there during the drive over. It's just when I got into the waiting room that my mind went blank and I completely forgot what I was doing there. I face him and give him my attention.

"Thanks for having me," I say, instantly wondering if this is an odd thing to say.

"Thanks for coming," he replies.

I continue to feel stupid, thinking that "Thanks for having me," is what drop-in company says, and I am definitely not drop-in company. If I was, I would have brought pastry or something. But instead, all this was very planned, and nicely scheduled.

When I lay in bed in the wee hours of the morning, worrying and wondering and contemplating canceling this appointment, I decided that since it was 2:00 AM, he was also probably lying in his bed—but he was not worrying or wondering what I was like, contemplating canceling what he was going to do at 2:40 PM.

But I did make the appointment, wait three weeks for the date to come, and then give the young lady out front my thirty-dollar co-pay in exchange for a complete stranger to listen to me. When I think of it this way, I feel a little bit embarrassed and panic a bit that this whole thing might be a mistake. Maybe I should have just invited my friend

Denise out for lunch. She would have listened to me. And I would have insisted on paying for lunch, and that would have cost me the same thirty dollars.

There is an uncomfortable silence, during which I can't help but look at him directly and notice that he has kind eyes. I worry about what he has noticed about me so far. Probably much more. After all, he is the trained professional. I am just a snoop, and I already know ten things about him, none of which he told me himself.

I can't think of anything to say. So, I don't say anything. I scan the desk and notice that there is no chart or even a pad or pen. I guess this means that he is not going to take notes. I am grateful for this. I think that watching him scribble as I am talking and then scribbling even faster at some points would bother me. And I probably would have tried to figure out what I was saying that was triggering the most writing. When he wrote slowly, I would know that I was losing him. If I actually told him the truth, I bet the paper would catch on fire.

I am tempted to ask him what kind of motorcycle he rides and what kind of gun he owns, but I don't. I am thinking that I am the one who is supposed to do most of the talking. I bought these minutes with my money, after all. So, I say, "I have never held a gun or ridden a motorcycle." That is what's on my mind after all, and even though he has yet to ask me this directly, I do believe this is where we are headed.

He nods and takes in my confession. It is a pretty perfect nod as far as nods go. It is a neutral nod. Not too far up or too far down. Not too animated and definitely not with wide eyes or raised eyebrows. That would be a mistake. Just kind of an acknowledgment-without-judgment nod. I wonder if there was a class for this somewhere in his training. Were there notes, a quiz, and a practice session on nodding?

If there was, I decide he did well and probably earned an A.

There is silence after this that I feel obligated to fill but have no idea with what. I frown and look at him. I sigh and, with compassion, he frowns just slightly back at me.

"My daughter is an addict," I say.

"Medical school?" I ask.

"Of course," he answers.

We are playing a game we sometimes play while in the car on longer rides. We visualize our children's futures. Believing, like most parents do, that we know what is best for our children, we speculate about which paths in life they will choose.

We always begin with the cleansing disclaimer that we are reasonable and grounded and understand that good parents allow their children to live their own lives. And we are good parents. But it is fun to imagine successful lives designed by us. After securing bright, beautiful futures for our sons, we have saved Natalie for last and are now visualizing hers.

"She could help people like herself," I point out.

"Let them all go to medical school!" Peter tells me happily. "Like I did."

"Not realistic," I say, ignoring the fact that nothing about this game is realistic in the first place.

"Why not?" he asks.

"What's good for the goose is not always good for the gander," I say, dating myself by using this expression.

"Jason cannot stand the sight of blood," I remind him, as Peter googles the origin of my goose-and-gander expression.

"Don't google and drive," I remind him. "And Trevor, *maybe*. But they all certainly have the God-given ability." Peter clicks his phone off and grins at me, and I grin back, knowing that he is going to make a boastful comment about father-given ability. "They do get their smarts from you," I say.

He compliments me back, assuring me that our children get plenty of their positive qualities from me.

"I really thought one of the boys would become a priest," I lament, wistfully.

"I know," he says, sympathetically. I would have loved the way "My son, the priest" would have rolled off my tongue. But then I think: *Why be stuck on that when the great possibilities are endless?*

I am just about to suggest that chief executive officers of just about anything would be great when Peter shouts joyfully, "Let them all be doctors!"

"Let them all be writers!" I cheer.

"Books unwritten," Peter bellows. "Books with happy endings!"

Yes, yes, yes, I whisper quietly to myself. *Please.*

Epilogue

As this book goes to press, Natalie has made great progress in fighting her addiction. While she still has a long way to go in her recovery journey, I continue to love and support her, no matter what. I could not be more proud of her and how far she has come.

If you are a parent with a child who is an addict, please know that I have walked in your shoes. Do not give up hope. Every day offers an opportunity for progress and change.

About the Author

*C*hristine Naman was born on a wintery February day in 1964 to father Frank and mother Angie. They were great parents, always, and because of them, she had the privilege of being able to witness what a good marriage should look like. She was the youngest of three children, so she fell into a pretty good spot from the start being the only girl and the doted on baby of the family. She had two exceptionally super brothers whom she spent her childhood chasing after, idolizing them while begging to be included in their adventures.

Her strong, well-read father led by good example. But just like a lot of children, Christine never realized until she was older that her mother was the rock and the rock star of the family. As a child, she always knew that her mother was hardworking, kind, and caring. But it wasn't until she grew that she realized the intelligence and wisdom that her mother had blessed her family with.

Growing up in Pittsburgh, Pennsylvania, she had a traditional childhood with the average amount of bumps. Brought up in an Italian, Catholic home full of traditions, there was Mass on Sundays, Christmas Eve fish feasts, and trips to the Dairy Queen on special occasions.

Shy, sensitive, and hesitant to express her feelings outwardly, Christine took to writing, with her first story telling the tale of a chipmunk that lived under the porch of the family's home. Her father said that he liked it, and that was all she needed.

Christine has the absolute blessing of being married to the one true love of her life: her husband, Peter, whom she met on a blind date. Saying instantly, "I think I am going to marry this guy." Peter's understanding, kindness, and love keep her grounded and sane. He is a steady partner and a balance to Christine, who lives life with her heart on her sleeve.

Together, Peter and Christine enjoy movies, dinners out, traveling when time and money permit, and long car rides. Christine's favorite hour of every week is Saturday morning breakfast with Peter, where she talks and talks and talks so much that she is surprised that Peter's ears haven't fallen off yet. She worries that Peter's favorite hour of the week is the hour after Saturday morning breakfast when Christine leaves him alone to be in peace. Christine also wonders what it feels like to be Peter, knowing that he is someone's favorite thing in the entire world. So much so, that someone else's heart beats a little faster and they get butterflies in their stomach when he shows up. Peter dutifully reads every word that Christine writes, which makes him pretty much a martyr. He corrects all the misplaced and mis-used periods, commas, colons, and semicolons. And there are many because Christine seldom knows how to use these helpers. Especially the colons and semicolons, which she still finds mysterious.

Christine has been blessed with three amazing children: Jason, her oldest, the guy who made her a mother and is a smart, hardwork-ing, caring son. Natalie, her girl in the middle, is a brilliant, funny, quirky, part daughter part girlfriend. And Trevor, forever her baby, is intelligent and mature beyond his years. He is solid, kind, and always there for his mother. Even with all the stumbles that her children have encountered, and there have been many, Christine considers her children the best things that ever happened to her and her greatest accomplishments.

In addition to her husband and children, Christine also has a chocolate cocker spaniel. Obie is a remarkably dysfunctional, poorly trained dog that Christine never wanted but now cannot live without.

Christine earned a bachelor's degree in early childhood education and a master's degree in health education. She taught preschool and kindergarten for ten years, where she had the privilege of watching precious children grow and learn. She still remembers their names and thinks of them fondly.

In addition to her writing, which she does early mornings in her favorite coffee shops while eating eggs sunny-side up and drinking gallons of tea with cream and sweetener, she passes her time crochet-ing, painting, and volunteering at her local hospital. The crochet-ing and painting she does very poorly, having discovered that she is excruciatingly talentless. But the volunteering she hopes she does pretty well. She would like to say that she eats well and exercises often because that always looks good in a bio. But the Catholic girl in her doesn't like to lie.

Christine's first book, *Caterpillar Kisses,* was a collection of short stories about her adventures teaching young children. Her next works were a series of books: *Faces of Hope, Faces of Hope: Ten Years Later,* and *Faces of Hope at Eighteen.* These were chronicles of fifty children, one from each of the fifty states, who were born on September 11, 2001. The idea for these inspirational gift books were born along with her son Trevor, with Christine having given birth to him on the morning of 9/11. The *Faces of Hope* series has been donated to the archives of the 9/11 Memorial Museum in New York City. Her other writings include: *The Novena,* a work of fiction about a young woman's journey to feel closer to and understand her deceased mother; *The Believers,* a story about the unlikely friendship between a young boy and his elderly neighbor; and *Christmas Lights,* a heartwarming holiday story.

Christine prays that *About Natalie* will be her make-a-difference book, her important story to tell, and the book that will help others heal and know that they are not alone.

Christine is grateful to all her readers, especially thanking those who don't actually have to read her writing because they are married to her, or born to her. Strangers who quickly become friends. It is her dream to hear from all of them.

Christine would love to hear from you. You can reach her at:

cpnhope@aol.com

Facebook: Christine Naman

Facebook: About Natalie

Christinenaman.com

Aboutnataliebook.com